9·25·79

Syndicated Columnists

Syndicated Columnists

Third Edition

Richard Weiner

Other books by Richard Weiner:

Professional's Guide to Public Relations Services
News Bureaus In the U.S.
Professional's Guide to Publicity
Military Publications

Library of Congress Catalog Card Number: 78-64585
ISBN-0-913046-108

Printed in the United States of America

Published by Richard Weiner, Inc.
888 Seventh Avenue
New York, N.Y. 10019

CONTENTS

INTRODUCTION

Since the first edition of this book was published in 1975, many significant changes have taken place in the newspaper business. The Long Island Press folded in 1977, the Chicago Daily News was terminated in 1978, and several major newspapers continued to lose circulation.

A few syndicates also folded, while others, notably United and NEA, merged. The newspaper syndicate field now is stronger than in recent years. This third edition of Syndicated Columnists reports on changes in 1978 in the syndicate business, and includes information about new columns and hundreds of data revisions.

Several completely new chapters have been added, including discussions of past and current columnists in two major categories, health and advice. As a result, the book is considerably longer than the second edition.

It is a pleasure to note that newspaper syndicates have vastly improved their technology, particularly the delivery of scannable and computer-compatible materials, and introduced a greater variety of feature columns.

Columns which appeal to older readers have suffered or been dropped, while dozens of new columns report about music, fashion, decorating and life-styles. Gossip columns have made a resurgence, though none are as big as in the heyday of Walter Winchell, Hedda Hopper, Louella Parsons and Dorothy Kilgallen.

Reasons for the disbanding of a column include ill health, dwindling number of subscribers and, occasionally, strife between the columnist and the syndicate.

Several new syndicates were started in 1978. Most are small

operations. One which has considerable potential is the Miami Herald Syndicate, which started with a weekly financial column by Carter Randall, a banker who is a panelist on the public television program, Wall Street Week.

The biggest business news among syndicates in 1978 was the consolidation of United Feature Syndicate and Newspaper Enterprise Association into a new company, United Media Enterprises. Both have been owned since their foundings by The E.W. Scripps Co., but they previously had operated independently at different locations. William C. Payette, president of United Feature Syndicate since 1969, now is chairman of the board of United Media, and Robert Roy Metz, president of NEA since 1972, now is president and chief executive officer of United Media.

The new company, located in the Pan Am Building in New York, now is a close rival to King Features, the country's largest syndicate.

NEA, which sells its columns to newspapers as a unit or package, also publishes The World Almanac, the largest-selling single volume book of this type. United, which sells individual columns (including Jack Anderson), also produces a TV listings service.

The New York Times Syndicate Sales Corporation has been expanded considerably during the last few years and now is markedly different from The Times itself. Many columns which do not appear in The Times are sold by the Syndicate to several hundred subscribers. The supreme example was indicated in 1978 when the syndicate introduced SuperScene, a weekly feature for 8- to 16-year-old readers.

A major development in 1978 was an acceleration of the trend to electronic editing, with video display terminals and other sophisticated equipment and high-speed (1,200 words a minute) transmission.

Over a dozen syndicates now transmit their columns on DataFeature, the 1,200-word-per-minute circuit of The Associated Press. Subscribers include The Chicago Tribune-New York News, Field, Gannett, King, Knight-Ridder, Los Angeles Times, McNaught, Newhouse, The New York Times, NEA, Register and Tribune, United, Washington Post and Washington Star.

Syndicate proprietors almost always are crying the blues. A few years ago, it was the newsprint shortage which squeezed out lots of columns. Another problem was the merger or termination of major newspapers, such as the Newark Evening News.

In 1978, more newspapers than ever before changed or enlarged their formats, with the accent on features. The search by imaginative editors for fresh material to recapture readers is both a problem and an opportunity for the syndicates.

The intense competition of newspapers, particularly in major urban markets, to attract and retain fickle customers, especially younger readers, has resulted in a greater freneticism among syndicates than

2

ever before. In 1978, it appeared that newspapers introduced and dropped columns with greater alacrity and less apprehension ubout upsetting the habits of older readers.

This problem, combined with the failure of column prices to keep pace with spiraling costs, has forced syndicates to look for other sources of income. King Features, the long-time leader in spin-offs, is extremely active in television versions of comic strips, and a variety of licensing and merchandising projects. Special Features, a New York Times Company, only has one cartoon strip, but it does a big job in syndicating books, including a few which are linked to films. Recent Special Features book serializations included the Nixon and Haldeman memoirs, Roots, Schlesinger's biography of Robert Kennedy and James Fixx's book about running.

Books also are big business at NEA and Universal, and are being developed at Copley, The Register and Tribune and other syndicates.

Liberals still outnumber conservatives among political columnists but the trend in 1978 was to the right. George F. Will is the hot shot among the new crop of conservative columnists. He's young, has a sense of humor, and is irreverant and iconoclastic to the point of winning praise from liberal readers of The Washington Post and other subscribers.

For 62 days in early 1978, New Yorkers were able to read David Broder and lots of other columnists in The Trib, but the newspaper folded. One of the reasons that the "real" Trib, the New York Herald Tribune, folded was that it had great columnists (such as Jimmy Breslin) but spotty news coverage.

In August 1978, the three major dailies in New York, The News, Times and Post, suspended publication due to a strike. A new newspaper, City News, printed Jim Bishop, Marianne Means and other Hearst columnists who were familiar to some readers, but it wasn't really satisfying because most newspaper readers are accustomed to reading the same newspaper at specific times and places. However, column buffs were introduced to such relatively unfamiliar columnists as Dr. Willard Abraham (Copley) and Joey Sasso (McNaught).

North American Precis Syndicate, which is the most enterprising of any of the sponsored publicity mat services, was quick to fill quite a bit of space in City News with features about insurance, health and other subjects which looked like columns. It made Precis clients and Precis proprietor Ron Levy very happy, but it was not a satisfactory substitute for readers who yearned for their regular columnists.

One alert radio station, WMCA, broadcast several hours a day of commentaries by Daily News writers, and listeners were able to hear Jimmy Breslin, Dick Young, Kay Gardella, Bess Myerson and other columnists.

Liz Smith, Breslin and other News columnists also appeared every evening on WOR-TV, so that in some ways, they were more visible than ever before. Ironically, the News owns WPIX-TV, and the columnists might have boosted their ratings, but the station is located in the News building, which was surrounded by a picket line.

The New York Daily Metro published the columns of Art Buchwald, Jeane Dixon, Cecil Smith, Roscoe Drummond and other byliners of the Los Angeles Times Syndicate, and another ersatz newspaper, the New York Daily Press, published the columns of Joan O'Sullivan, Emily Wilkens, Nicholas von Hoffman, Kevin Phillips, Robin Adams Sloane and other byliners of King Features.

Perhaps the final indignity was the New York Graphic, a thin tabloid which resembled its famous namesake of the 1920's in name only. The newspaper published the columns of John Chamberlain, Bert Bacharach and other King Features byliners and the Broadway column of Joey Sasso. For a few weeks, Sasso was riding high, with a column in two of the interim New York newspapers and in several in north Jersey.

The strike was a bonanza for The News World, the daily newspaper supported by Rev. Moon's Unification Church. Circulation zoomed over tenfold, from under 30,000 to over 300,000, and readers were introduced to the music, philatelic and other feature columnists of the recently formed News World Syndicate.

The News World Syndicate has picked up several subscribers, but its energetic sales people have found that newspaper publishers are very tough buyers, at any price.

Many marginal syndicates and self-syndicators have fallen by the wayside. A syndicate to watch is American Syndicate Inc. of Dayton, Ohio, headed by James H. Dygert, who was city editor of the Dayton Daily News from 1973 to 1977. Columnists include movie reviewer Vince Staten, author of "The Real Elvis: Good Old Boy," a hardcover book published in 1978 by the parent company of American Syndicate.

One of the most successful of the new operations is the Washington Post Writers Group, which sells individual columns as differentiated from the "packages" of auxiliary news services such as the Los Angeles Times/Washington Post News Service. The quest for bargains has led many publishers to the Times/Post and other news-oriented supplementary wire services, such as Knight-Ridder, Newhouse and Copley.

In 1974, an editorial in Public Relations Journal stated, "These days, it seems, everyone wants a by-line, and everyone strives to be a columnist. The news columns are the worse for it . . . Back in Arthur Krock's early days, the in-thing was to be as objective as possible, as a contrast to the yellow-dog journalism which had prevailed prior to that time. Perhaps the nadir of advocacy journalism has been reached, and we are now beginning to see a swing back to greater objectivity."

That has not been the trend. There now are more advocacy columns, interpretive reporting and news analyses than in the early 1970's. However, the effect has not been to dilute confidence in the media, as some journalism purists had feared.

Many newspapers are desperately fighting declining circulation curves with the introduction of teen-age columns and other features to attract new readers. Publishers are trying to shed the image that newspapers are read mostly by middle-aged and older people, whereas television reaches large numbers of people of all ages. In New York, for example, the two morning newspapers, the News and Times, both have suffered from circulation losses in recent years.

The new features are lively and even attract a few male readers, but popular columns such as Heloise and Erma Bombeck still are relegated to the women's section, where they are read mostly by middle-aged and older women, and the quest for youth appeal continues to frustrate most publishers.

One of the new columns introduced in 1978 was written by Stephen Valentine Patrick William Allen, the multi-media star better known simply as Steve Allen. Charter subscribers included the Philadelphia Inquirer, Detroit News, Seattle Times, Rocky Mountain News and Salt Lake City Tribune. The distributor, Inter-Continental Press Syndicate, therefore hoped that the prognosis for the column was described by one of Steve Allen's songs, "This Could Be The Start of Something Big." However, another of his songs is titled "Impossible." A discussion of columns by celebrities appears in the Survey chapter.

In late 1978, Sheed, Andrews and McMeel published "At Button's," the first novel by columnist Garry Wills. The choice of the publisher was appropriate as S.A.&M. is a subsidiary of Universal Press Syndicate, which syndicates the Wills column. S.A.&M. also publishes the books of several of its columnists and cartoonists, including Garry Trudeau (Doonesbury), Charlie Shedd, Niki Scott, Dr. Walt Menninger, James Unger (Herman) and Tom Wilson (Ziggy).

A list of recent books by columnists also appears in the Survey chapter. In 1978, Holt, Rinehart and Winston published "The World of Jimmy Cannon," a book of columns by Jimmy Cannon collected by his brothers, Jack and Tom. Jimmy Cannon died in 1973 and countless fans still recall his "Nobody asked me, but" one-liners and other tough-tender observations which went beyond the sports arena.

Relatively few sports columns are syndicated, as newspapers concentrate on local sports news, supplemented by wire service news. Jim Murray, the Los Angeles Times Syndicate columnists, was honored in 1978 by being inducted into the National Sportscasters and

Sportswriters Hall of Fame in Salisbury, N.C.

The greatest recognition a journalist can achieve is the Pulitzer Prize. Red Smith received it in 1976, the first sportswriter to win the accolade. In 1978, The New York Times received three Pulitzer Prizes—the first such triple honor to any newspaper in the 60 years of the awards. One of the coveted prizes went to William Safire for his 1977 columns which started Bert Lance on the road to resignation as Budget Director. Esquire's national editor, Richard Reeves, called Bill Safire "the most influential columnist in the country."

In 1978, on the occasion of his fifth anniversary as a columnist, Safire stated his credo, "These essays are not intended to be even-handed analyses, sage soul-searchings or detached observations. On the contrary, I am in the business of writing informed polemics, investigative commentaries that seek to make their points with a satisfying zap, so as to affect people in power and their policy in formation.

"In 1973, I was hopelessly defensive; now, I am happily aggressive."

Bill Safire, a former public relations counselor, indeed has reason to be happy about his move from the Nixon White House to The New York Times.

Columnists generally move from a single newspaper to the independence of a syndicate position or contract. In 1978, Saul Kohler went in the opposite direction, from the Washington bureau of Newhouse News Service to the editorship of the Harrisburg Evening News. In the process, he dropped his column, The Presidency.

In 1978, Sam Shulsky, who had written Investor's Guide six times a week for 22 years, retired. The popular King Features question-and-answer column (it's in about 150 newspapers) has been continued. Shulsky, who had been a business writer at the New York Journal American, was succeeded by William Doyle, former business editor at The New York News and The Star-Ledger of Newark, N.J.

Columnists change syndicates, though not as often as employees change jobs. In 1978, Patrick J. Buchanan switched his column, "The Dividing Line," from The New York Times Syndication Sales Corporation to the Chicago Tribune-New York News Syndicate. The column, which never appeared in The Times, now is in The News, so Buchanan has a coveted outlet in New York.

January 1, 1978, was the last appearance of Foreign Affairs, The New York Times column written since 1954 by C.L. Sulzberger. The Times editorialized, "Probably no American journalist has been better acquainted with the stony mountain roads of Montenegro, the heated politics of Greece or the complex character of Josip Broz Tito. Perhaps Cy's most enduring journalistic achievement was his careful and intimate reporting of Charles de Gaulle, the statesman whom he knew best and who gave him an extraordinary measure of trust."

A few days later, a reader wrote, "Maybe Cy Sulzberger's commentary was not everybody's cup of tea. He was never as philosophic as Reston, or as hard-hitting as Anthony Lewis or Tom Wicker, and certainly not as staunchly conservative as William Safire. Cy is a remarkably acute observer of the contemporary political scene, and that is precisely why those of us who like him at all like him so much. In his dispassionate accounts of innumerable political crises abroad he has not been out to prove a point as much as to record his impression of what has occurred. At the same time he has never been an armchair historian. There is ink in his blood, and wherever there was a story he was out to get it. He has made mistakes but he has always done his best to uncover the truth, and he has never catered to anybody."

Though well known among Times readers, C.L. Sulzberger never achieved the fame of James Reston and other Washington columnists. One reason was that he was not on the lecture or talk show circuit.

In 1978, the International Platform Association released a survey of its members about the speakers most in demand. Here are the top lecturers, in alphabetical order: Jack Anderson, Joyce Brothers, Art Buchwald, Gerald Ford, David Frost, Dick Gregory, Paul Harvey, James J. Kilpatrick, Henry A. Kissinger, Ralph Nader, William Simon and Abigail Van Buren. Of these 12 star lecturers, seven are columnists!

Paul Harvey is better known as a radio commentator, but his column has been widely syndicated for many years. Ralph Nader also has been columning for several years, though he's better known for other activities. That still leaves five lecturers whose primary work is as columnists—Anderson, Brothers, Buchwald, Kilpatrick and Abby.

The listings in this book include these superstars and stars, and also many new and relatively unknown columnists.

One of the bright new columnists is humorist Gerald Nachman. In his perpetual quest for subject material and ideas for columns, Nachman says "I tend to think in long rectangles."

This book is about those short and long rectangles which are known as columns.

The net major recent change is that there are more columnists than ever before, and the syndicate business has come alive with a resurging variety of all types of columns.

For many years, the trend has been to reduced frequency of text columns. Political commentators and other essayists who formerly wrote daily columns now write one, two, three or four columns a week. Bridge columns and other features still are issued five, six or seven times a week, as are many of the advisors, such as Ann Landers and Abby. Ann Landers has an edge in this department, with seven columns, as compared to Abby, who rests on Sunday.

The champs in terms of frequency are Jack Anderson and Marilyn

7

Beck, who write weekend features in addition to daily and Sunday columns—a total of eight columns a week. Both are syndicated by United.

The two major aspects of this book are a history and commentary about syndicates, and a list of current columnists. With regard to the lists, the last weekly issue in July of Editor & Publisher features an annual Syndicate Directory. It is indispensable to publishers, publicists and anyone interested in newspaper syndicates. However, the only addresses in the pull-out section are those of the syndicates. The addresses of columnists are not listed.

Therefore, a principal feature of this book is to provide the addresses of major syndicated columnists.

Most columnists are receptive to material from publicity sources, and yet, most publicists virtually ignore columnists. Once reason for this is ignorance of where to find the columnists.

Mail sent to a local newspaper which carries a syndicated column, or a news release sent to the syndicate headquarters, often is not sent to the columnist, or is forwarded after a considerable delay.

The alert professional publicist can obtain a large quantity of well-read clippings from a single placement with a syndicated columnist by following three rules.

1. Know the column. Publicists often are familiar only with the columns which appear in their own cities. It's a good idea to study major newspapers anyway, but especially to become familiar with the style and type of material used by columnnists. In the business field, for example, Sylvia Porter is in the New York News, but outside of New York, there are over a dozen *major* business columnists, including Joseph Livingston, Hobart Rowan, Eliot Janeway, and David Sargeant.

2. Know where to find the columnist. Many columnists work at their flagship or base newspapers, particularly in New York, Chicago, Washington, Los Angeles and San Francisco. For example, Herb Caen, Art Hoppe, Stan Delaplane, Charles McCabe and Terrence O'Flaherty *all* are at the San Francisco Chronicle. However, not all Chronicle Features syndicated columnists are at the home newspaper.

A few columnists work at the main or branch offices of their syndicates. John Chamberlain and Phyllis Battelle, for example, are at the King Features headquarters.

Other columnists, including dozens in Washington, have their own private offices or work from their homes. This generally is the case with the large number of self-syndicators, the columnists who operate their own syndicates.

3. Know how to communicate with the columnist. The entertainment columnists, and others, rely on the telephone. Many columnists are interested in interviews or attend news conferences and press events, and can be reached by mail or phone. News releases and other mass mailings generally are wasted with columnists, as most insist on exclusives. However, many columnists welcome news releases, in order to be informed and to look for special "angles" and slants.

This book is not a primer on how publicists can work with columnists, but it is written by a publicist to assist other publicists, as well as journalists. The unique feature of this book is its compilation of addresses of columnists.

As with all directories, especially adress listings, there surely are errors. In a few cases, columnists do not want their private addresses published and insist that mail be sent to their syndicate offices. In other cases, the private offices or home addresses are "revealed" here with the hope that publicists will not abuse this information. Do not mass mail to most columnists! This type of mail rarely is utilized and simply hinders the professional publicist who operates on a one-to-one basis.

All syndicates strongly recommend:

1. Don't flood columnists with news releases.

2. Don't send trivia or material unrelated to the columnist's interests. Know the columns.

3. Send mail to the office of the syndicate and not to the home or private office of the columnists. Columnists travel a great deal and the syndicate knows where to forward mail.

The home and private office addresses are listed here with some trepidation. A flood of mail from overly aggressive or unprofessional publicists can cause considerable annoyance among many columnists. The author certainly does not want to incur ill will among columnists, for himself and other publicists. So, again, use this information intelligently and with great care and respect.

Phone numbers are omitted where the columnist has requested only mail contact or in cases in which the address is that of the syndicate or other mail office.

This book includes a few wire service byliners, such as Andy Lang of The Associated Press, but the focus is on "standing," regularly published, syndicated columnists. Also omitted are comics and other non-text features, as well as local columnists.

In 1977, local columnists at the Louisville Times, New Orleans States-Item and other newspapers formed the National Society of Columnists and, in 1978, published a collection of their columns.

Perhaps the greatest value of the book is to identify "off-beat" columnists, many of whom are widely syndicated but relatively unknown to almost all publicists, particularly those in big cities.

New columns are introduced continually. Some make the grade and others are dropped. New columns, terminations, retirements and deaths all produce a constantly changing roster of columnists. For example, the demise of the Chicago Daily News, in early 1978, resulted in the dropping of several columnists and the switching of others. Mike Royko and Sydney J. Harris moved to the Sun-Times.

The directory can be extremely useful to public relations practitioners, and it has been prepared in a spirit of mutual service to publicists and columnists, as well as to journalism students and others interested in newspapers.

The sections about anti-trust problems of major syndicates and income of columnists touch on seldom discussed issues. For example, Dr. Frederick Stare, chairman of the department of nutrition of Harvard University, has written a popular column (Los Angeles Times Syndicate) for about 25 years. Dr. Stare has been frequently criticized for conflict of interest since he is or was a director or consultant to several food companies and associations and his department has received sizable grants from many companies.

In 1977, Dr. Stare stated that "every penny (of income from the column) has gone into a fund which helps support the department."

Obviously, whether Dr. Stare or his department received the money is not the issue. Dr. Stare replied that he did not trade his independence for food industry favors. "Breakfast cereals *are* good for you," he added.

In August 1978, The Saturday Review listed over 50 companies and associations which have contributed to Dr. Stare's department. In fairness, it should be noted that one of Stare's angels was The Council for Tobacco Research, and Dr. Stare has repeatedly taken an anti-cigarette view in his column.

A similar flap took place in 1978 when business columnist Eliot Janeway appeared in print ads for Phoenix Mutual Life Insurance Company and TV commercials for Mazda cars. Two of the 45 newspapers which carried the column dropped it. Janeway, who operates a very successful financial research and newsletter service, shrugged it off by quipping, "Our columns are not our livelihood . . . I think every writer has the right to be paid for his statements."

The survey chapter includes information about income of columnists, notably from books, lectures and activities other than their work for syndicates.

Finally, a few columnists are omitted in this edition, because of retirement or death.

Vivian Brown, longtime author of Associated Press beauty and fashion columns, died in 1978.

Dr. Walter C. Alvarez, one of the pioneer medical columnists, died in 1978, at the age of 93.

Heloise Bowles, author of Hints from Heloise, died December 28, 1977, at the age of 58. Started in the Honolulu Advertiser in 1959, the column became one of the most popular syndicate features and appeared in over 500 newspapers. It has been continued by her daughter, Ponce Cruse, who writes as Heloise 2nd. (Heloise was married several times and Cruse was the name of her second husband.)

The New Yorker quoted a letter from a young man in its Talk of the Town in which he said that "Heloise was probably the most affectionate columnist who has ever written. She was always praising her readers, thanking them profusely for their suggestions, and telling them she loved them, and her readers returned her love. Her daughter, Heloise II . . . is doing a fine job, and I hope there will be a Heloise III and a Heloise IV, and that the column will go on for a long time."

May all columnists live as long as Dr. Alvarez, and may their columns, like Heloise, go on forever.

PROLOGUE

Friday afternoon, April 7, 1972, was dark, bitterly cold, and intermittently sleeting. If there is such a thing as ideal mourning weather, this was it and thus the scene was set for a sentimental memorial service which, though clumsily staged, had more than its quota of laughs, tears, and nostalgia.

The site was the Lambs Club, a half-century landmark on 44th Street near Sixth Avenue, just a few epitaphs away from Broadway. The day would have been the 75th birthday of Walter Winchell, and an odd collection of about 200 people had come to pay tribute to the newspaperman who had died in Los Angeles on February 20th.

Walda Winchell had barred visitors from the funeral services which had been held for her father in Phoenix, and no members of the Winchell family were at the Lambs Club. Those in charge were a volunteer committee from the Damon Runyon Memorial Fund for Cancer Research. Winchell had founded the organization and almost singlehandedly raised more than $30 million for more than 25 years prior to his death—of cancer.

One of the first to arrive was former Postmaster General James Aloysius Farley, still an imposing figure at 85. The other mourners were not quite that old, but many were in their 60's and 70's, and their famous faces almost looked like shadow images of the way one remembered them. Indeed, it was a gathering of the old crowd, columnists, press agents, performers and others who had known Winchell, plus a sprinkling of old ladies who had heard John Gambling and the McCanns talking about the services on the radio.

Winchell's Girl Friday, Rose Bigman, who had never been to the Lambs Club, was stationed in the little lobby, next to the checkroom, greeting old friends and being introduced to others whom she had known only by telephone. A charming hostess, she talked gaily and fondly of the Boss, until someone mentioned Bob Thomas' recent biography of Winchell and then she stiffened. "The book was filled with lies and errors," she said. "For example, Winchell didn't lose subscribers, lots of the newspapers simply went out of business or merged with others. What can you expect from a reporter who lost half his notes!"

Jack O'Brian greeted Rose with a kiss and bear hug, and she relaxed, because suddenly all around her were a fraternity of current and past columnists. O'Brian, who looks like a cross between James Cagney and Jackie Gleason, danced through the lobby, with his glamorous, mink-clad wife, Vonnie, animatedly greeting some of the columnists and studiously avoiding others.

Those who were retired got the preferential treatment, such as Louis Sobol, who covered the Broadway beat for the Journal. Sobol, a short, mild-looking man, solemnly combed his few remaining hairs and wiped his glasses until O'Brian effusively embraced him. Frank Farrell of the World-Telegram chatted with James Kilgallen, the Hearstman whose daughter, Dorothy, established the column that O'Brian inherited.

One of the few performers at the tribute was Hildegarde, whose nightclub career had been boosted by Winchell's orchids.

And then there was Postman Leonard Lyons, casually dressed in slacks and a turtleneck sweater, but looking more haggard than in the days when he resembled a bantam-weight fighter buzzing from table to table in his search for items. Lyons, who started in the business by providing items to Winchell, dropped a peripatetic item—he was leaving within minutes after the services, for Europe.

Quiet and respectful was the demeanor of some of the others, especially Ed Sullivan, looking more solemn than ever, and accompanied by his smiling wife, Sylvia.

In 1951, News columnist Sullivan had written, "I despise Walter Winchell," and referred to him as a "small-time Hitler." Now, the hatchets were being buried as the columnists, like old bees who had lost their sting, gathered for a self-indulgent lament to the queen bee.

Clustered together were theatrical press agents Mike Hall, Paul Benson, Bernie Green and Jack Tirman, a pitifully small number, compared to the army of publicists who used to thrive on their relationship with Winchell. Selma Gore, wife of former publicist Larry Gore, ushered a few late arrivals to seats in the third-floor auditorium. Irv Mandel, a publicist who is a director of the Runyon Foundation, escorted 11 speakers to the stage. Mandel had been at the Roney Plaza in Miami Beach when Winchell got the call about the death of Runyon.

The loudspeaker had been playing Winchell's favorite music, including "Star Dust," one of whose writers, Mitch Parrish, was in the audience. At 20 minutes after two, the music was replaced with a recording of Winchell's immortal Sunday night greeting, "Good evening, Mr. and Mrs. North America and all the ships at sea."

Ben Grauer stepped to a lectern bearing a color photograph of Winchell, wearing his fedora trademark.

Grauer, like so many of the other men, wore his hair long and swept back over his shirt collar, but like almost everyone on the platform and in the audience, it was hard to affect the youthful vigor with which they once had been associated. Grauer, who had been Winchell's announcer for about 15 years, still had the melodious timbre, and served as Master of Ceremonies for what turned out to be a two-hour show. The Lambs Club was the proper theater, because Winchell had started out as a vaudeville performer.

The show started with Rabbi Arthur T. Buch, Chaplain of the News Reporters Association of New York and once a columnist. The Rabbi's column was called "The Bible on Broadway," and he read from a few frayed, yellowed newspaper pages which had printed his column and also *The* column, as Winchell referred to the column which for more than 20 years appeared in over 600 newspapers.

Archbishop Fulton J. Sheen, also a columnist, was supposed to have appeared but he was ill. Rabbi Buch said that Winchell loved the sun—he was a Miami Beach devotee and spent his last few years in Arizona—and expressed the hope that Winchell will always enjoy the sun.

The lighter part of the program commenced with the internationally respected columnist Bob Considine, a ruddy-faced, burly raconteur who resembled W.C. Fields. Considine said that he found it difficult to be solemn since Walter had never been solemn. Winchell didn't enter a room, said Considine, he burst into it.

Considine, a newspaperman since 1929, reminisced about President Eisenhower's trip to the Orient. The press contingent had included Considine, Elaine Shepard, and other headliners, but the top attraction was Winchell. The Secret Service insisted that WW remove his pistol, which he always carried, though never once in his entire life did he fire it. The incident caused Considine to quip that Winchell was "the first major power to accept total disarmament."

Miss Shepard, in the audience at the Lambs Club services, corroborated Considine's anecdotes, though noting that his recollection of the dates and other details was not wholly accurate.

Considine recalled that when he was 70, Winchell had said, "I am not 70, I am just two 35s."

Next up at the lectern was Alfred Clark, a night rewrite-man at The New York Times and a former president of the News Reporters

Association, who, as a police reporter, had prowled with Winchell and, as a public relations director of the Damon Runyon Fund, had worked closely with him. Clark noted that one of Winchell's contributions was to bring out into the open a discussion of cancer, the very mention of which had been taboo.

Police reporter Pat Doyle of the New York News revealed that he and Winchell once had rushed to Tenth Avenue where two men had just been murdered. A Hell's Kitchen urchin provided a tidbit of information to Winchell and asked for a buck. Winchell took out a roll of bills and peeled off a C-note. In characteristic fashion, Winchell made Doyle promise never to tell of his soft-heartedness, but the flabbergasted recipient of the $100 never forgot it. He became a policeman and often called Winchell with tips. Today, the man is a detective in lower Manhattan and still calls Doyle, identifying himself only as "Winchell's kid."

Jack O'Brian told about Winchell's love of dancing and the numerous occasions on which he squired chorus girls. Winchell was not a gourmet but he loved eating at all-night restaurants and at the homes of friends, such as the O'Brians, where Winchell spent his 70th birthday.

All of the speakers were laudatory, of course, but O'Brian was the only one who interspersed a few criticisms, only they weren't about Winchell. "I don't like Arthur Godfrey," said O'Brian in an aside, but Winchell did, and made Godfrey famous with Winchell's dictum "repetition makes reputation."

O'Brian also expressed his ire at John Crosby, one of the few columnists who wrote a post-mortem panning of Winchell. O'Brian noted that Winchell had been one of the few writers to praise Crosby when his TV show was being pummelled by almost everyone else. "I will never forget your kindness," Crosby told Winchell one night at the Stork Club.

The only female speaker was glamorous singer Lisa Kirk, who Winchell had called "my fair Liza." Miss Kirk, in New York to appear on the Tony Awards telecast, emotionally told about speaking to Winchell on the telephone three days before his death, and making a date to see her old friend and mentor on Monday, February 21, so that they could rumba in Winchell's room at the U.C.L.A. Medical Center.

The eldest statesman among the eulogists was Harry Hershfield, who had known Winchell almost from the beginning and used to provide him with jokes. Hershfield, who was born in 1885, said that he had been offered the nightclub column at the New York Mirror, but elected to stay at the Journal because he wasn't enamoured of night life, and instead recommended Winchell.

Hershfield's memory of old jokes probably is a lot better, because most biographers omit credit to Hershfield for having started

Winchell, and also state that Winchell's starting salary was $500 a week and not the $125 which Hershfield recalls. Afterwards, O'Brian bitterly remarked to a friend that Winchell had disliked Hershfield for several reasons, one of which was that Hershfield once had playfully written that Winchell's name really was Lipshitz.

The longest speech was read by Ernest Cuneo, a rotund, dignified attorney, who presented a brief, in an eloquent attempt to put Winchell in a significant historical perspective. Ernie Cuneo, who had been Winchell's personal lawyer, emotionally compared WW to Herman Melville and said that Winchell was an utter genius, "Possessed of the full force of the careening flight of the 20th century."

Winchell invented Broadway, said Cuneo, and Broadway belongs to Winchell, "as the Prairies belong to Carl Sandburg and the Mississippi to Mark Twain."

There were other historical analogies, but by now the afternoon was wearing on and the audience started to filter out. Cuneo proclaimed that it was Winchell who promoted FDR's third term, that FDR privately credited Winchell for his election in 1940, that Winchell was much more than a peephole gossip columnist, and that George Jean Nathan was right when he called Winchell the first great American Elizabethan.

The last speaker was Navy Chaplain Don L. Robinson, who hadn't known Winchell but reviewed Winchell's naval career, which started as an apprentice seaman during the first world war and ended with a second world war tour of duty as a Lt. Commander.

Tom Dillon, the handsome Shepherd of the Lambs Club, and a former stage singer, concluded the program by singing, to a piano accompaniment, "God Bless America."

No one had mentioned the epitaph which Winchell himself had once written, "Here is Walter Winchell—with his ear to the ground—as usual."

The stragglers filed out, past a bulletin board which announced that next week the Lambs would honor singer Lanny Ross, and on to 44th Street. Across from the club, the marquee of Avon-at-the-Hudson announced "Naked Encounter" and other "movies for mature adults," down the street the Belasco Theatre was getting ready for its nightly showing of "Oh! Calcutta!," and at the corner, on Broadway, several hundred movie goers were lined up, like mourners, to see the head of another syndicate, "The Godfather."

SURVEY

Harold Ickes called them calumnists, though he acknowledged that there were "good and bad, decent and discreditable." In a particular burst of churlishness, Ickes, who himself was a columnist, wrote, "The columnist's stock in trade is falsification and vilification. He is journalism's Public Enemy No. 1, and if the American press is to improve itself, it must get rid of him."

Westbrook Pegler put it this way:

"Of all the fantastic fog-shapes that have risen off the bay of confusion since the big war, the most futile and, at the same time, the most pretentious, is the deep-thinking, hair-trigger columnist or commentator who knows all the answers just offhand and can settle great affairs with absolute finality three days, or even six days a week."

New York Times managing editor Turner Catledge agreed with Pegler that columnists often had little to add to the news, wasted valuable space, and were the "malignancy" of the newspaper business.

It wasn't a new complaint. In 1931, in his first column in the New York Graphic, Ed Sullivan stated, "The Broadway columnists have lifted themselves to distinction by borrowed gags, gossip that is not always kindly, and keyholes that too often reveal what better be hidden."

During more than sixty years as a newspaperman, Arthur Krock observed hundreds of political columnists and noted that their proliferation replaced the personal journalism previously practiced by Horace Greeley, William Randolph Hearst, Joseph Pulitzer, Henry Watterson, James Gordon Bennett, and other publishers and editors. Many syndicated columnists were talented, but the major reasons for their acceptance by publishers, according to Mr. Krock, were their low

19

rates, and the opportunity for a newspaper to present differing viewpoints, thus alienating readers and advertisers less than if the same controversial views were presented in the editorial columns.

Do op-ed page columnists fulfill a function beyond that of providing a low cost, convenient source of diversity of opinion? Are James Reston, Joe Kraft, Bill Buckley and other contemporary political commentators less influential than Arthur Krock, Walter Lippmann and the bygone columnists who literally advised presidents?

If political columnists have waned—and the supposition may not be true—what about other syndicated columnists? Can Jack Anderson be compared to Drew Pearson, Ann Landers to Dorothy Dix, Suzy to Winchell, Marilyn Beck to Hedda Hoppper?

In 1937, Leo Rosten asked 77 capital reporters which columnists they thought were most fair and reliable. Raymond Clapper topped the list, followed by Paul Mallon, Walter Lippmann, Arthur Krock, Drew Pearson and Robert Allen, and Heywood Broun. In 1965, William L. Rivers of Stanford University asked the same question of 242 Washington correspondents, and this time Walter Lippmann was the overwhelming favorite, followed by Marquis Childs, William S. White, James Reston, Roscoe Drummond, Joseph Alsop, Peter Edson, David Lawrence and James Marlow.

Rosten is best known as an author ("The Education of Hyman Kaplan," among others) and magazine writer (for many years he was editorial advisor to Look) but it was as a political scientist that he surveyed the press. His 1937 study, published as "The Washington Correspondents," also asked 110 reporters which newspapers they read regularly. The top three were The New York Times, Washington Post and Washington Star, which retained their positions in the Rivers survey 28 years later. One change was The Wall Street Journal, which moved from ninth to fourth position.

Critics of newspapers often cite the phenomenal success of The Wall Street Journal as an exception which proves the diminished interest in *general* newspapers. Television has hurt many newspapers, but not as much as one might think, and certainly not in the sphere of columnists.

Despite the assertions of the broadcast media and its proponents, newspapers still are the dominant news source. Television's power, with regard to news, is its ability to attract enormous numbers of people to watch the coverage of special events, such as space voyages, elections, and championship games. It is the action medium, a powerful dramatic means of involving audiences of all ages. However, on a day-in-day-out basis, more adults read local newspapers than watch TV news broadcasts. Furthermore, even one-hour TV news programs present only brief sketchy versions of the news as compared to the quantity and variety in most daily newspapers. News buffs often watch network and local newscasts, and then avidly read about the same events in newspapers, for fuller details, and sometimes for corroboration, as well as interpretation.

To some older adults, an event is fascinating when seen on television, but somehow isn't confirmed until the newsprint is "felt." Many newspapers, and not just The New York Times, are looked to with a respect ("The newspaper of record," "newspapers are for history, and not just for now" are typical comments) not accorded television.

In their attempt to present highlights of the news quickly, televison programs rarely are able to provide analysis and commentary. Many stations now present editorials, but they are brief, and often bland, and only a few programs include political commentaries.

A long-time feature of the CBS-TV network program, "60 Minutes," has been the mini-debate between a liberal and a conservative. The conservative end has been held by James Kilpatrick, a syndicated newspaper columnist. The liberal end formerly also was a syndicated columnist, Nicholas Von Hoffman, and, in recent years, has been Shana Alexander, a magazine columnist.

Contrast this with the number and diversity of news analysts available in almost every daily newspaper. Furthermore, even a relatively short column of 250 words is longer than the typical TV commentary. And it generally is more incisive and better written.

An exception among TV stations is WDVM-TV (formerly WTOP-TV) in Washington, D.C. Commentators include James J. Kilpatrick, Carl Rowan, George F. Will, Hugh Sidey and Elizabeth Drew. All are Washington journalists and the first three are syndicated columnists.

Television not only has added to the importance of newspaper political columnists, but it also has stimulated interest in other types of columnists. In their attempt to compete with television, newspaper publishers have added columns which deal with sex, business, hobbies and dozens of other subjects which television doesn't have the time to handle, or treats irregularly or superficially.

Of course, all of this is reflective of a bias in favor of newspaper syndicates, and columns do have some shortcomings. For example, the Washington correspondents have been called Brahmins, but the pressure of deadlines often produces a sameness among many of the daily columnists.

David S. Broder of the Washington Post modestly wrote on April 11, 1972, in the heat of the presidential primary campaign, "The hardest thing for any newspaper to learn, if my own case is any example, is how to wait for the story to end before leaping into print to tell its meaning."

In recent years, the pressure to be first, and also sagacious and unique, has been considerably reduced for most columnists. The seven-times-a-week column is rare (Jack Anderson still does it, but he has a large staff and a relatively short column) and most political analysts now write three times a week.

The reduction in number of newspapers also has drastically reduced the competitive pressures among columnists. In New York, for example, it wasn't too many years ago when the Times, Herald Tribune, News and Mirror published in the morning and the Post, World-Telegram and Journal-American followed in the evening. Most people used to read a morning and also an evening newspaper, and many scanned more than two papers a day. This encouraged columnists to try harder to be better, or, at the least, to be different.

Today, the majority of newspaper readers in New York, and all over the country, read only one newspaper, and the number who do not regularly read any newspaper is alarmingly increasing.

"My monumental ignorance of American politics impels me to read the other columnists," says Jim Bishop. "All across the spectrum I am a bewildered, confused rotten capitalist who doesn't know his Lerner from his Kilpatrick. I not only read the political columnists—I study them.

The news coverage by the Associated Press and United Press sometimes is perfunctory. In their attempt to be objective and unbiased—which is almost impossible—newspaper and wire service reporters often miss the significance of an event.

Columnists, particularly the political analysts and other "armchair correspondents," are expected to be less superficial and more analytic and probing. A good newspaper thus is a blend of "straight" and interpretive reports. Political columnists recognize their function as critics and often become nags of the government. A constant diet of carping and criticisms can become boring and predictable, as evidenced by the diminished interest, during their last years, of perennial snarlers Westbrook Pegler and George Sokolsky. But even in his eclipse, an important event could provoke a Pegler to rise to the occasion with the full capacity of his enormous literary power.

The death of a president often has inspired columnists to produce writing of a caliber equal to the most brilliant literature.

On April 14, 1945, Walter Lippmann wrote of Franklin D. Roosevelt, "The final test of a leader is that he leaves behind him in other men the conviction and the will to carry on . . . The genius of a good leader is to leave behind him a situation which common sense, without the grace of genius, can deal with successfully."

After the death of John F. Kennedy, James Reston wrote, "It is clear now that he captured the imagination of a whole generation of young people in many parts of the world, particularly in the university communities. Even those who vilified him now canonize him . . . "

Even without the impetus of historic news events, and allowing for the inevitable repetition found on any given day among various columns, the quality of writing by various newspaper columnists is a lot better than generally thought.

Take the following verse from a column called "Fair Enough."

"The thing we all love most about the glorious old United States of A.

"Is that everybody, irregardless of creed or color, is entitled to have their say."

The author, surprisingly, was curmudgeon Westbrook Pegler.

A political commentary is a journalistic art form quite different from news stories and even other types of columns. Compared to straight reportage, the pace of the column generally is more leisurely, the sentences longer; there usually are more adjectives, descriptive phrases and historical references, as well as opinions.

Conventional journalism calls for the pyramid structure in which the story is summarized at the top—the first sentence or few paragraphs—and then elaborated on in such a way that an editor could cut from the bottom without losing significant details.

In the political column, as well as in other columns, an essay format is followed in which the summary often appears in the first paragraph, and again in the last paragraph. For this reason, and also because the best writing often is crammed into the lead and closing paragraphs, column scanners sometimes just read the beginning and end of political columns, on the assumption that the middle includes the historical and background references, which sometimes are ponderous and repetitive.

One of the best foreign affairs columnists, C.L. Sulzberger of The New York Times, frequently followed this format. The 600-word middle section was far more than padding or background, and indeed was excellent writing, but the best sections often were the first and last paragraphs, as indicated by the Sulzberger column of February 25, 1972, written from Saigon:

"There is a widespread habit of blaming almost every symptom of instability in the United States upon the Vietnam war and notable among such symptoms have been rising race tensions, violence among university students and an alarming rise in the use of drugs. But whether this diagnosis is accurate, whether the sick American chicken hatched the rotten Vietnamese egg or vice versa, is questionable."

Sulzberger went on to quote from his interview of General Abrams, which included comments about drug addiction among American soldiers, then discussed drug and alcohol problems in France, Britain, Russia and other countries, and concluded:

"Vietnam, this forlorn, distant war, is neither the cause of U.S. social disorders and moral disintegration nor the origin of its frequent mood of despair. It is only a sordid catalyst that heightens a process already begun. As a label for everything that ails us it is incorrect, as an excuse it does not truly apply."

Stewart Alsop, who collaborated with his brother, Joseph, for over a decade, once said, "The best way to become a columnist is to have a brother who is one already."

A less genetic and more common path to syndication is to start a column in a single newspaper. Another popular route is to work as a reporter in a bureau, particularly Washington. One of the least common ways to start is as an assistant to an existing columnist, though Jack Anderson did it with Drew Pearson.

A successful syndicated columnist ranks on the same level and perhaps higher than bureau chiefs and newspaper editors in terms of journalistic prestige. The primary motivations among newspaper writers to become columnists generally are the prestige, including what often is celebrity status, and the security. The income may be big in comparison to reporters, but it's not by big business standards, and it's modest when put against the fees paid actors and other celebrities.

The all-time top money earners among columnists were O.O. McIntyre, Will Rogers and Walter Winchell, each of whom received well over $100,000 annually for many years just from their syndicate work. Today, income of this magnitude is earned by Abigail Van Buren and her sister, Ann Landers, but by few others.

Syndicates refuse to divulge the number of subscribers for each column, and the payment from each subscriber. The columnist generally receives half of the gross income, but the price paid by each newspaper is not set by any rate card and varies in accordance with its circulation, size of the market or territory, and the bargain made for that particular column.

Columnists often quibble with syndicate managers about whether their share should come from the total gross income or from *net,* or adjusted, gross income. Financial matters are simpler for James Reston, the highest *salaried* columnist (close to $100,000). Another exception was Joseph Alsop, who was not on the salaried staff of the Los Angeles Times Syndicate but was paid a flat fee—over $70,000 plus expenses.

A typical once-a-week column might have a minimum price schedule ranging from $2 for a newspaper under 5000 circulation to $35 for one with a circulation above 200,000. In between, the breakdown might include a half dozen or more circulation categories, but, in the final analysis, the price usually is determined by bargaining and other factors. The "flagship" newspaper often provides an office. Prices in the Northern markets often are higher than in the South, even among newspapers with the same circulation.

In terms of income, one value of a column is that it provides the author with a degree of fame and prestige, so that book, magazine, radio and other opportunities proliferate from the column. Such is the case with Joseph Kraft, Evans and Novak and others. Columns also provide a tremendous boost on the lecture circuit, and Art Buchwald, for example, makes a thousand dollars or more for each of several dozen lectures given each year.

Buchwald and other columnists also work free for charities and favorite causes. For example, Buchwald is the master of ceremonies at the annual Robert Kennedy Tennis Tournament in New York. He usually also is one of the players, but he was sidelined in 1978, due to an injury incurred playing tennis.

Harry Golden stored his columns in a desk drawer and when it was crammed full, it was time for another book. In late 1972, in time for the Christmas (and Chanukah) book buying season, Doubleday published Golden's "The Greatest Jewish City in the World." The same publisher also issued "Bare Ruined Choirs" by columnist Garry Wills, and, at the same time, book buyers could choose among dozens of new titles by such assorted columnists as Barbara Bradford, Elizabeth Post, Amy Vanderbilt and Judith Viorst.

Collections of columns by Art Buchwald, William Buckley and other columnists are regularly published as books. "Stained Glass," a novel by William Buckley, was a 1978 best-seller. In late 1978, Doubleday published "The Ann Landers Encyclopedia" and a new version of "The Amy Vanderbilt Complete Book of Etiquette," as revised by columnist Letitia Baldrige. Other recent popular books by columnists include Dr. Solomon's "Proven Master Plan for Total Body Fitness and Maintenance," Sylvia Porter's "Money Book," "If Life Is a Bowl of Cherries—What Am I Doing in the Pits" (by Erma Bombeck), Liz Smith's "The Mother Book," and—here's a switch— "Diabetes" (Grosset & Dunlap) by Milton J. Brothers, M.D., husband of columnist Joyce Brothers.

Popular books in 1978 by columnists included "Maxine Cheshire Reporter" (Houghton Mifflin), Tom Wicker's "On Press" (Viking), George F. Will's "The Pursuit of Happiness and Other Sobering Thoughts" (Harper & Row), William Safire's novel, "Full Disclosure" (Doubleday), Garry Will's "Inventing America" (Doubleday), "The Buchwald Stops Here" (Putnam's), and two books by John T. Molloy, "Dress for Success" (Wyden) and "The Woman's Dress for Success Book" (Follett).

Ballantine's payment of $1 million for the paperback rights to "Full Disclosure" set a record for a first novel.

Not as successful as anticipated was ".44" (Viking), the book by Jimmy Breslin and Dick Schaap about the Son of Sam murders.

"The People's Pharmacy," a best seller in 1977 and 1978, prompted King Features to launch in December 1978 a column by pharmacologist Joe Graedon. At the same time, Universal Press Syndicate introduced an advice column by author Ruth Carter Stapleton, and

The Chicago Tribune-New York News Syndicate started a semi-weekly travel column by Stephen Birnbaum, travel editor of Esquire, editor of Diversion magazine and editor of several books.

Doubleday publishes more books by columnists than any other publisher, including, in recent years, several collections of columns by Harry Golden, "Bare Ruined Choirs," by Garry Wills, and, in 1978, "Crystal Clear," a novel by Eugenia Sheppard and Earl Blackwell, and "Inventing America," a discussion of Thomas Jefferson and the Declaration of Independence by Garry Wills. Fawcett probably is the leading paperback publisher of columnists, including recent books by Erma Bombeck and Ann Landers.

Pulling together a collection of recent columns, a delightful chore performed every few years by Art Buchwald, obviously is a lot easier than writing an original book or the original columns. In "On Press," Tom Wicker refers to the "columnist's relentless routine—for me, three articles a week, at the fixed length of 750 words each . . . the three pieces due on certain days of the week, rain or shine, ideas or no ideas, hangover or no hangover."

The biggest-selling 1978 book by a columnist was "If Life Is a Bowl of Cherries—What Am I Doing in the Pits" (McGraw-Hill), a collection of columns by Erma Bombeck, the 51-year-old self-deprecating housewife who describes herself as "too old for a paper route, too young for Social Security, too clumsy to steal and too tired for an affair." Book royalties (her previous book was "The Grass Is Always Greener Over the Septic Tank"), and income from a three-times-a-week column which appears in over 600 newspapers, add up to about a half million dollars a year.

Celebrities don't always click as columnists. Dr. David Reuben found out in 1973 when he tried an abortive question-and-answer column on sex. Joan Rivers sustained a humor column in 1973 and 1974 for Publishers-Hall, and found she could make a lot more in a few minutes in a nite club. Columbia Features was not able to sell an ecology column by Arthur Godfrey.

Business columnist Roger Babson once asked "What is Success" and answered, "Success is not land, money, popularity, attention, or even influence. Success is that 'something' much more enjoyable than any of these things. Success is a spiritual quality, an inward satisfaction."

Spiritual qualities notwithstanding, a successful column is considered to be one with more than 100 subscribers. The few published reports on number of subscribers often are grossly exaggerated by the syndicates for competitive purposes. For example, at the time of his retirement in 1974, Leonard Lyons was in only one major newspaper, The New York Post, and for many years, his column was in only about a dozen newspapers, though one would never know it by talking to

26

Publishers-Hall or by reading publicity about "The Lyons Den."

The annual income of a successful columnist probably is about $50,000, a long way from the astronomical figures which one sometimes associates with celebrities. But successful columnists are celebrities, and, by newspaper standards, they are well paid. For example, the top salary for reporters of United Press is about $20,000.

Perhaps the greatest remuneration of successful syndicated columnists may not be monetary, but rather in the independence and security of writing for a large number of newspapers rather than a single paper. This is especially important for the political columnists, where they can be truer to themselves with a syndicate than with a single paper. If one subscriber drops the column, another is likely to pick it up, and these become matters of concern for the syndicate, rather than the author.

Charles A. Perlik, Jr., president of the Newspaper Guild, said in 1972 that the Guild's first president, Heywood Broun, had been America's highest paid columnist. Broun was well paid in proportion to the relatively few newspapers which carried his column in the thirties, but he came nowhere near Walter Winchell, Will Rogers, O.O. McIntyre and other columnists of his time.

Syndicate managers not only get lockjaw when asked about the number of their customers and prices paid but they also are tight mouthed about their role in editing columns. Theoretically, only public affairs columns are scrutinized for accuracy and other concerns relevant to political charges of libel, but, in actuality, most syndicates do a certain amount of editing, particularly with regard to headlines, length and illustrations. Columnists often are guided about subjects to write and editorial slant, and the over-riding consideration usually is "Will it sell." This guidance sometimes is subtle, but it is not limited to political columns, nor is it always minor.

The author of a major horoscope column was directed by his syndicate to provide uplifting, non-materialistic forecasts with no references to television or other competing media.

Syndicate salesmen aggressively woo newspaper publishers and managing editors but their successes often resemble a treadmill. For a newspaper to accept a new column generally means the cancellation of an old one, and if both columns are distributed by the same syndicate, the net gain can be zero.

The amount paid per column is so small that a major syndicate can only support its overhead with very large volume. Many three-times-a-week columns sell for close to a dollar a column to a newspaper of 20,000 circulation. The price is about two dollars for a medium circulation newspaper (50,000) and about three dollars for larger subscribers.

A.J. Liebling, an ex-newspaperman (he worked for the Philadelphia

Bulletin after being fired by The New York Times) who wrote "The Wayward Press" for 18 years in the New Yorker magazine, discussed columnists in a February 23, 1946, article which included, "Many of them work for bubkis (beans), as the boys say, either because they want the publicity for use in another profession (the stage or radio) or in the hope of catching on and getting a profitable syndication."

Don Marquis, a New York humor columnist known best for his archy and mehitabel stories, wrote:

"I pray thee make my column read
And give me thus my daily bread."

The political essay is only one type of column. Another major category is the advisors, an almost endless group of doctors, do-it-yourselfers, chefs and family counselors. Abby, Heloise, Dr. Van Dellen and more than a hundred assorted experts every day confidently tell millions of readers what to do.

A third major category is the gossip chatterers. Earl Wilson in New York, Betty Beale in Washington, Irv Kupcinet in Chicago, Herb Caen in San Francisco, Marilyn Beck in Hollywood, Suzy wherever she may be, breathlessly tell their readers who's doing what.

The amazing feature about almost all of the writers is that their columns have a certain style which is reflective of their personalities. Fred Sheinwald on bridge reads different from Charles Goren. You don't have to check the byline to recognize Art Buchwald. You get to know Russell Baker like a friend. You can't go to sleep without at least a glance at Abby. The day begins with Scotty Reston expressing new hope.

Bob Considine started his autobiography, "It's All News To Me," with this deposition:

"It takes a roaring amount of conceit to practice daily journalism, particularly if it assumes the form of a column. The deep-domed cosmic thinker who either rattles or soothes the President of the United States is of the same species as the gassy advice columnist who counsels 'Puzzled' to stop sprinkling her corn flakes with powdered LSD.

"Each plays God."

Considine was corroborated by Charles Fisher in his 1944 book, "The Columnists," who stated:

"The columnist is the autocrat of the most prodigious breakfast table ever known. He is the voice beside the cracker barrel amplified to trans-continental dimensions. He is the only non-political figure of record who can clear his throat each day and say, 'Now, here's what I think . . . ' with the assurance that millions will listen."

Television has diminished the pontifical importance of the Washington armchair journalists, but several hundred syndicated columnists remain a major component of American newspapers. They add a

28

spice, personality, diversity of opinion, and style to a local newspaper. They are an exciting, invaluable supplement to the blandness of some wire service reportage and the trivia of much local data.

Art Buchwald lunches daily at the San Souci in downtown Washington. Joe Alsop dines at Rive Gauche in Georgetown. Jack Anderson is a part owner of the Empress, a Chinese restaurant.

What unites these journalists is not their culinary habits, but rather their membership in the syndicated column fraternity. Even with the recent retirement of Joe Alsop, it's a big fraternity, and surprising to some, syndicates today are big business, larger, more diversified and more widely used than ever before.

The death of Walter Winchell on February 20, 1972, was hailed by some as signifying the final demise of gossip columnists. Dorothy Kilgallen and Hedda Hopper had died, Louella Parsons died later in 1972, and names like Louis Sobol and Frank Farrell seemed to be from another era. Ed Sullivan died in 1974. Is anyone still writing this kind of column?

Earl Wilson still is, and so are Dorothy Manners, James Bacon, Marilyn Beck and Dick Kleiner in Hollywood, and then there's Irv Kupcinet in Chicago and Hy Gardner, a New Yorker transplanted to Miami, and more.

But do today's gossipmongers have the clout once wielded by Winchell, Hedda, and Louella? Jack O'Brian succeeded Kilgallen but without a New York outlet how much influence does he have?

All valid questions, but then how about Suzy, the bright gorgeous gossip of the New York News. And have you read Robin Adams Sloan, a King Features columnist who reveals details which would have made Kilgallen blush.

In 1977, the King Features management did a bit of blushing when a dispute was revealed between two Cosmopolitan staffers, Liz Smith and Roberta Ashley, both of whom had contributed to the Sloan column.

Gossip certainly is not confined to the Hearst media.

In fact, have you read The New York Times lately? Albin Krebs and other Timesmen write a daily column, labeled "Notes on People," which is a combination of Time magazine's "People in the News" and Winchell and all of the other gossip columnists.

On March 7, 1972, the Times reported that Tiny Tim's marriage to Miss Vicky was "on the rocks" but that Stalin's daughter Svetlana Alliyueva definitely was not planning to be divorced from architect William Wesley Peters, and Mr. Peters agreed.

In the Times, yes, the Times.

Another new column in The New York Times is Metropolitan Diary by Lawrence Van Gelder. It's a collection of anecdotes and poems submitted by readers and is reminiscent of Franklin P. Adams'

Conning Tower, which appeared in The New York Post in the thirties.

Tattlers still abound, and their prose currently provides several dozen syndicated columns, some of which, notably Earl Wilson and Suzy, appear in several hundred newspapers.

Critics of newspapers and journalism historians sometimes point to the 1930's as the golden age of columnists and claim that the importance of syndicates has declined since then, particularly with the advent of television.

The first golden age of syndicates was in the 1870's. More than 5000 newspapers were started in that decade, mostly in the South or West. Syndicates helped to drastically reduce the production costs of the majority of the fledgling weeklies. Syndicates helped to develop country journalism and bring news from the capitals of the world, as well as magnificent authors of fiction and other literary luminaries, to farmers, immigrants, and other avid readers of small town weeklies.

The following decade, 1880 to 1890, produced the greatest increase in number of newspapers in the history of the country. Circulation soared from 11 million to 37 million, as big city dailies became established. Syndicates now filled a different role, in their second golden age, by providing the variety and exclusivities required by competitive dailies.

Each succeeding decade has been a new golden age of syndicates. Today, it is extremely difficult to distinguish among local columnists, wire services, and syndicates. The successful newspaper uses syndicates to help provide its readers with a balanced collection of news and entertainment in proper proportion to its other editorial sources.

Henry Wheeler Shaw, who lived from 1818 to 1885, was one of the first syndicated columnists. Like other humorists of the 19th century, he used a folksy pseudonym and as "Josh Billings" wrote such immortal one-liners as: "Poverty is the step-mother of genius."

"It is better to know nothing than to know what ain't so."

"The wheel that squeaks the loudest
Is the one that gets the grease."

Finley Peter Dunne (1867 to 1936) bastardized the language and entertained the nation for decades with truisms which were witty and, oddly enough, timeless. Dunne, who wrote as "Mr. Dooley," once said, "Th' dimmycratic party ain't on speakin' terms with itself."

"Ye know a lot about marriage, but ye niver married," said Mr. Hennessy.

"No," said Mr. Dooley. "No, says I, givin' three cheers. I know about marriage th' way an astronomer knows about th' stars."

For years, the nation's number one columnist was a folk humorist in the tradition of Henry Shaw and Finley Dunne—Will Rogers. Among all his aphorisms, the most apt was, "All I know is just what I read in the papers."

30

For decades, all that most Americans knew about New York was through the columns of O.O. McIntyre and Walter Winchell. David Lawrence was the first syndicated capital correspondent and Drew Pearson showed the capital in a new glaring light.

Does this listing of columnar stars of a bygone era mean that today's byliners are less luminous? Absolutely not. Jack Anderson has more subscribers than Drew Pearson. James Reston appears in more newspapers than Arthur Krock. Ann Landers and Abigail Van Buren not only have topped Dorothy Dix and Beatrice Fairfax, but rank with Anderson as America's top three columnists.

In spite of the closing and merging of many well known newspapers, the number of daily newspapers in the United States has not diminished appreciably. The peak was in 1910, when there were about 2200 dailies, and currently there are more than 1700 dailies, with a combined circulation of more than 60 million. More than 200 syndicates offer these publishers more than 2000 separate regular columns, ranging from 30-word fillers to 2000-word interviews and articles. Many of the nation's 10,000 weekly newspapers also subscribe to syndicate services.

The demise of several major morning newspapers has hurt some columnists. It is quite possible that columnists read in the morning are more influential than those read at the end of the day, particularly among businessmen and legislators. When the Los Angeles Examiner, a morning paper, was absorbed by the afternoon Herald, to form the Herald-Examiner, Louella Parsons shifted from the morning to the afternoon, and, more than coincidentally, she lost a great deal of her authority and clout. Hollywood agents and producers simply didn't talk about her gossip during the business day, as they once did. The same was true when the New York Mirror folded and Walter Winchell was stranded. Of course, there were other factors, but it was more than just coincidence that Walter Lippmann, for example, appeared in morning newspapers in New York and Washington.

At the United Nations, and in Congress, the most quoted newspapers are The New York Times, Christian Science Monitor and the Washington Post—all A.M.'ers. Commenting on the Times as the universal breakfast diet among all of the U.N. delegates, a foreign minister quipped that some of the delegates may confuse later in the day what they read in their own cables with what they earlier read in the Times, with the result that the newspaper grossly influences policy.

Syndicates are found in Germany, Italy, and other countries, but nowhere in the profusion as in the United States. One of the reasons for this American phenomenon is that the U.S. does not have a tradition of national newspapers. In England, Japan, the Soviet Union, and France, for example, several of the leading newspapers are distributed throughout the country and have a domination which is far greater than even the largest and most influential American papers.

Izvestia and Pravda in the U.S.S.R. each have circulations well in excess of seven million; Japan's Mainichi Shimbun, Yomiuri Shimbun and Asahi Shimbun all top 4,500,000; the London Daily Express and London Daily Mirror are almost in the same league, whereas America's top dailies are four morning papers—the New York News, with a circulation which has decreased to under two million and the Los Angeles Times, The New York Times and Chicago Tribune, all of which are close to a million.

Newspaper syndicates in America also are a reflection of our free press. We do not have government-owned newspapers or news services, as are found in many countries, and syndicates add to the diversity of opinion, to styles and sources available to independent newspaper publishers.

Finally, American newspapers are filled with a far greater amount of editorial matter, as well as advertising, than newspapers elsewhere in the world. The Sunday edition of The Washington Post, for example, runs well over 200 pages and contains several dozen syndicated columns, in addition to thousands of words from several news services and its own enormous staff.

Many newspapers devote about a quarter of their editorial space to syndicates. Journalists sometimes are critical of newspapers which are top heavy with columnists, pointing out that the publisher's motivation in using syndicated material oten is to reduce costs. The other side of this argument is that syndicates enable local newspapers to publish high-priced talent which they otherwise could not afford.

The fees paid by newspapers vary in accordance with the circulation, size of territory, and other factors, all of which are kept highly secretive in this intensely competitive business. Several syndicates, such as the Los Angeles Times-Washington Post, New York Times, Copley and Newsweek sell their columns as part of a total package, whereas the so-called independent syndicates, such as United, Universal, Field and King sell columns separately. The cost of a single daily column, such as Jack Anderson's "Washington-Merry-Go-Round," is astoundingly low, often only about five dollars or less. On the other extreme, a few major newspapers pay as much as $500 a week for top columnists.

Add up all the columns, and their revenue is sufficiently sizable to make newspaper syndicates a big business. Most syndicates are privately owned or are divisions of publicly owned companies which do not release the separate income from their syndicates. The combined sales of all U.S. syndicates is considerably in excess of 100 million dollars. The largest syndicate probably is King Features, a Hearst company, with estimated annual sales of over 15 million dollars.

A large part of the income of some syndicates is from comics.

Leading comics purveyors are King, Chicago Tribune-New York News, United and Field. These syndicates also are giants in the distribution of text columns, as is United Feature, a Scripps-Howard subsidiary which acquired Bell-McClure, one of the nation's oldest syndicates, and merged with NEA.

The press entourage on former President Nixon's trip to the Soviet Union in May, 1972, included more columnists than were permitted on the earlier visit to China. Readers of The Washington Post, for example, were treated to an insight into the perennial problem of a columnist—how to turn up exclusive inside peeks, significant analysis and reportage which does not duplicate and rehash the wire service and other news articles. Three of the Post's columns, Joseph Kraft, Marquis Childs, and Rowland Evans of Evans and Novak, emanated from the Soviet Union during the summit meetings.

Kraft also had been on the voyage to Peking and compared the two trips in color and significance, giving the Moscow meeting top place in the latter category. Evans seemed to be hard pressed for new angles and delved into the technical details of the sale of American feed grain to the Russians. Childs proved that he is far from jaded, even after several decades of reporting, and possibly was overwhelmed when he wrote, "It is a great adventure, a remarkable beginning, and no matter what the end, nothing can ever be the same again."

There is a constant temptation for all journalists, but especially political columnists, to use superlatives, such as *unique, first, most,* and *historic,* to denote the significance of their writings. Even those columnists who generally are classified as "sober, restrained and objective" get carried away at times by the emotional drama of colorful incidents, and syndicate managers usually encourage this.

During the last 20 years, William F. Buckley Jr. has commented on just about everything, and most pungently, about other columnists. Following is a sampler, arranged alphabetically.

Joseph Alsop "simply cannot forgive the rebirth of conservatism in America, having himself taken the pain on more than one occasion to pronounce it quite dead." (Written in 1963, Buckley's admiration of Alsop probably has increased, as Alsop's own conservatism has.)

". . . Harry Golden, high priest of left-wing yahooism."

"Concerning Goldwater, finally, there is not a breath of personal scandal. Even Drew Pearson, who can find scandal in Snow White's relations with the Seven Dwarfs, tried it and failed."

Murray Kempton, "although in some respects he is innocent beyond the imagination of Walt Disney, is as a columnist the noblest of us all."

"Walter Lippmann, whose consistent misreckonings on the subject of the Soviet Union have contributed much to the strategic impoverishment of our leaders."

Westbrook Pegler "is easily the greatest satirist in American journalism, and probably in American letters; that he is the most vigorous, and sometimes the most amusing polemical journeyman in the country."

Eleanor Roosevelt "treated all the world as her personal slum project; and all the papers, of course, remarked on that fabulous energy—surely she was the very first example of the peacetime use of atomic energy."

Finally, of himself, Time quoted Buckley in 1967, "I feel I qualify spiritually and philosophically as a conservative, but temperamentally I am not of the breed."

Another column smorgasbord was dished up in 1974 when Bill Safire wrote a Lincoln's Birthday column in which he speculated how other columnists might have commented had they been writing in 1863, on President Lincoln's Emancipation Proclamation.

Mary McGrory "revealed" that the real authors were Wendell Phillips and William Lloyd Garrison. Evans and Novak predicted a backlash in the next election by anti-Lincoln forces who will sweep New York, Pennsylvania, Ohio, Indiana and Illinois.

William Buckley concluded that "conservatives can support the restoration of certain muniments, if not the aureate rhetoric;" C.L. Sulzberger looked for reaction abroad, particularly pro-Lincoln sentiment among England's workingmen.

"Now that emancipation is here," wrote Art Buchwald, "everyone wants to be a slave."

Finally, James Reston complained that Mr. Lincoln's Proclamation "deals with the politics of the problem and not the problem itself."

When big city daily newspapers were extremely competitive, delivery trucks and newsstand posters were used to advertise important columns. Winchell sustained the New York Mirror, the Journal trumpeted Westbrook Pegler and the Post promoted Franklin P. Adams.

Most newspapers now are home delivered and impulse purchases of newspapers are a relatively small factor.

A few more big city dailies may fold, but the number of daily newspapers seems to have leveled off at about 1700. When The Morning Telegraph expired in 1972, the 139-year-old newspaper had become a horse racing guide. Engraved on its tombstone were the names of such columnists as Whitney Bolton, Heywood Broun, Ben Hecht, Ring Lardner, H.L. Mencken, George Jean Nathan, Tom O'Reilly, Louella Parsons and Walter Winchell, who, as "Beau Broadway," anonymously wrote a Sunday piece for the Telegraph while turning out a daily column in the Graphic. In 1938, the 2084 U.S. daily newspapers had a combined circulation of about 41 million copies. In 1976, the number of dailies had declined to slightly over 1700, with a total circulation of about 61 million.

Excitement still abounds in the newspaper business. Today, the suburban weeklies are prospering and are switching to bi- and tri-weekly, and even to daily publication. Many of these newspapers started as shoppers, "penny savers," and throwaways, with little or no editorial content. Their prosperity and improved quality presents an opportunity for syndicates.

The trend to automated typesetting and offset reproduction also is a boon to syndicates as they are able to provide an abundance of low-cost ready-to-use features. This mechanization favors the larger operations, and the smaller syndicates, which often handle only one or two columnists, are likely to dwindle. 2060684

Another major development is the multi-media diversification of syndicates, enabling them to parlay a successful column into radio and TV programs, books, movie short subjects, lectures and other sources of revenue and exposure. Walter Winchell made more money from radio than newspapers; Will Rogers' fame and income were from lectures, vaudeville and movies. With the column as a base, and newspaper serialization of books, which goes back to the earliest days of the syndicate, it is possible to diversify in a lucrative manner. The new twist is that syndicates, such as King Features, are getting into these businesses themselves, which obviously gives them greater control as well as profit.

In 1972, the Publishers-Hall Syndicate introduced "compatible scanner-ready copy" for use by newspapers equipped with Optical Character Recognition systems. OCR still has a long way to go to replace conventional typing and printing, but the trend is obvious, and with a conversion from the syndicate column to printing tape at the rate of 700 words a minute, it is obvious that this will favor the big syndicates, as well as the big newspapers. The big breakthrough took place in 1974, with the introduction of automated typesetting at the New York News.

Most syndicates have not raised their prices to subscribing news-papers in many years. Cost-conscious publishers are likely to continue to tap this bargain source with its almost unlimited variety. Astrology, automotive, beauty, books, bridge, business, education, entertain-ment family, fashion, food, health, hobbies, household, movies, nature, patterns, pets, political, religion, science, sports, surveys, television, travel, youth—the categories barely describe the bounty of text columns.

The major lecture bureaus feature dozens of columnists.

The topics aren't very original, and audiences generally pay to hear the same views these speakers espouse regularly in their columns. In fact, the more familiar readers are with their columns, the greater the celebrity value and lecture appeal of the columnists. The same is true for columnists as guests on television programs.

Writing about the New Journalism in New York magazine of February 14, 1972, Tom Wolfe criticized the old journalism, and commented, "Newspaper columns had become a classic illustration of the theory that organizations tend to promote people up to their levels of incompetence. The usual practice was to give a man a column as a reward for outstanding service as a reporter. That way they could lose a good reporter and gain a bad writer.

The statement may apply to some local columnists, but is absolutely inaccurate with regard to syndicates, which operate in a highly competitive manner in which weak columnists constantly are dropped and replaced by fresh, bright new writers.

During the summer, some newspapers try out new columnists while the regulars are vacationing.

William Randolph Hearst once suggested to columnist Arthur Brisbane that he take a vacation. "No, I'll never take a vacation, said Brisbane, "the readers might not miss me."

HISTORY

The origins of syndicated newspaper columns go back to the Revolutionary War, and were related to the war. The first continuing syndicate operation started during the Civil War, and, oddly enough, also resulted from a wartime problem.

The first syndicated column in the United States was distributed by the Boston Patriots for about ten months, starting in September, 1768. The column was a propagandic attempt to cover the impact of the Revolutionary War on the Boston area. This weekly news packet appeared under the title, "Journal of Occurrences" in the New York Journal and the Pennsylvania Chronicle, as "Journal of the Times" in the Boston Evening-Post and, in varying forms and times, in other colonial newspapers.

In December, 1841, Moses Yale Beach, publisher of the New York Sun, printed extra copies of President John Tyler's annual message to Congress, and distributed them to other newspapers, thus cutting the time and production costs of the publishers. In 1847, Andrew J. Aikens did the same thing with the annual message of President James Polk, but these were isolated experiments, and the product, which had space for the purchaser to imprint the name of the newspaper, really was a newspaper supplement rather than a syndicated service. Incidentally, buyers of Beach's supplement included the Albany (N.Y.) Advertiser, Troy (N.Y.) Whig, Salem (Mass.) Gazette and Boston Times.

The Civil War prompted the development of the feature syndicate. Wartime enlistments had severely depleted the editorial and printing staffs of many newspapers. In 1863, Ansel N. Kellogg, publisher of the Baraboo Republic, a four-page weekly in a small town a few miles west of Madison, Wisconsin, solved his production problem by making an imaginative arrangement with David Atwood and Horace E. Rublee, co-publishers of the Wisconsin State Journal in Madison. The Wisconsin State Journal supplied Kellogg with a four-page paper. Pages one and four were left blank, for Kellogg to fill with local news and advertising, and the two inside pages were filled with national news, mostly that of the war. Other Wisconsin country weeklies soon provided the Journal with a flourishing business for its ready-print. Thus, Wisconsin could be considered the birthplace of the American newspaper syndicate.

Syndicate pages had been used occasionally in the United States and by English provincial newspapers in the 1850's, but it was A.N. Kellogg who developed the concept into a major business.

While the Wisconsin State Journal in Madison provided its syndicate service to about 30 weeklies, a major competitor developed in Milwaukee. Andrew J. Aikens, who had experimented with printed sheets in Woodstock, Vermont, moved to Wisconsin and joined William E. Cramer and his nephew, John F. Cramer. The firm of Cramer, Aikens and Cramer published the Evening Wisconsin in Milwaukee, which offered ready-prints faster and at a lower price than the Wisconsin State Journal. Cramer, Aikens and Cramer soon had close to 300 customers and moved to Chicago in order to expand faster.

Wisconsin was the birthplace of the newspaper syndicate, but in the 1870's, Chicago became the capital of the new industry, a position which it held for many years. The two pioneers were the A.N. Kellogg Newspaper Company at 110 West Madison Street and the Chicago Newspaper Union at 13 North Jefferson Street, formed by Cramer, Aikens and Cramer.

Kellogg hired J.M. Edson as America's first syndicate editor and the company soon out-distanced its rival, in spite of having been almost wiped out by the Chicago fire of 1871.

By 1872, more than 1000 newspapers were supplied with "patent insides" or "patent outsides," as the two types of ready-prints were called. By 1880, Kellogg had branch offices in St. Paul, Cincinnati, and Cleveland, and its total number of clients was more than 800.

1882 was the year of Kellogg's greatest triumph. First, he acquired the syndicate business of the Kansas City Times, which had 55 newspaper clients, and then he acquired the Aikens' Newspaper Union, which then was located in Cincinnati and was selling to 115 newspapers.

Ansel Nash Kellogg—the father of the newspaper syndicate—died in 1886. His company sold printed sheets to 1400 newspapers and supplied stereotyped plates to several thousand other newspapers, from which they printed his editorial and advertising matter. In 1903,

Kellogg grossed close to $1,000,000. He was an astute businessman and a fine journalist whose greatest contribution was to revolutionize the rural press in America. His editorial credo included the following mottoes:

"Spare no pains nor expense to get the best and freshest of news and literary matter."

"It is as much the mark of a good editor to know what not to print as to be able to select good and appropriate matter."

"When in doubt about the propriety of printing an article, leave it out; there is plenty of that which is unquestionably good and desirable."

"In the news columns avoid, as far as possible, the giving of details of scandals and crimes—confining the accounts to mere statements of facts of general interest or importance."

"There is always room for improvement and betterment. The best is none too good for the Kellogg service."

A major component of the Kellogg and Aiken syndicates was advertising, and the ready-prints thus were the predecessors of This Week, Parade, Family Weekly and other newspaper supplements. The first syndicate advertising manager was W.W. Hallock of the Kellogg Company. Aikens introduced the term, newspaper union, to describe the cooperative arrangement whereby newspapers received the editorial ready-prints at extremely low cost, because of the advertising and the centralized production.

By 1875, Aikens' Newspaper Union, in New York, served more than 1000 newspapers throughout the country, and various other "newspaper unions" thrived in the midwest, south and west.

On June 11, 1880, W.E. Andrews, W.H. Welch and W.A. Bunker formed the Western Newspaper Union (WNU) in Des Moines. The new syndicate quickly acquired several of the regional unions and became the country's largest syndicate. George A. Joslyn, president of WNU from 1890 to 1916, became the principal stockholder and the person primarily responsible for its enormous success. One of its innovations was the concept of providing all or portions of its service on an exclusive territory basis, a controversial method of business which became a major difference between syndicates and the news associations.

WNU's most famous editor was Wright A. Patterson, who was editor-in-chief from 1906 to 1935. In 1906, WNU acquired the Kellogg company and, in 1910, it acquired the Aikens and Cramer companies. WNU now served more than 4000 newspapers, and had a virtual monopoly in the field, with only one major rival, the American Press Association.

Founded in 1882 by Orlando Jay Smith, publisher of the Chicago Express, the American Press Association was located in the same building as a sheet iron factory and Chicago printers dubbed the noisy American Press offices as a boiler plate factory. The term "boiler plate" was used derogatorily to describe the mechanical stereotype plates generally provided as single columns by syndicates. Editors often were criticized for filling their papers with plate matter which they cut into "fillers" and "shorts" to satisfy their needs, often on the basis of space rather than content, a process known as "editing with a saw."

The criticism was valid, though the American Newspaper Union introduced the writing of Jack London, Booth Tarkington and other quality authors, including C.B. Lewis, a humorist who wrote as "M. Quad."

George Joslyn and John H. Perry, president of the American Press Association, were bitter rivals. The conflict included a price war and extensive legal battles. In 1917, WNU acquired American Press for $500,000, and modernized the operation, including replacing the cumbersome plates with cardboard matrices or "mats."

The late 19th century was the heyday of weekly newspapers and country journalism. Publishers' Auxiliary, started in 1865 in Chicago as the trade paper of the weeklies, preceded Editor & Publisher, which started in 1901 primarily to report news of interest to daily newspapers.

In 1877, for example, there were 749 daily newspapers in the U.S. Among the 28 dailies published in New York City were the Bulletin, Commercial Advertiser, Evening Express, Evening Mail, Evening Post, Graphic, Herald, News, Star, Sun, Telegram, Times, Tribune, Witness and World.

WNU soon took over Publishers' Auxiliary and the conglomerate became a major factor in the publicity field. At its peak, WNU provided mats to about 7000 newspapers. A large part of its operation consisted of household hints, dress patterns, and other anonymous features, but the "budget service" also included mat versions of the columns of other syndicates, including, in later years, such top stars as Drew Pearson and Walter Winchell. Subscribers were able to buy the entire service, rather than individual columns, and the total annual cost was relatively small, hence the term "budget service."

In 1938, John H. Perry acquired full control of WNU and the business further diversified to include newspaper printing equipment, with total annual sales of $20 million. The ready-print service was dropped in 1952.

The original purpose of syndicates then was to fill a production need. The greatest boost to syndicates was their literary contribution. This late 19th century development affected not only the small town weeklies but also the big city daily newspapers, as well as all newspapers, and even books and magazines.

In 1883, Irving Bacheller founded the New York Press Syndicate, the first general feature syndicate which provided subscribers with literary articles, household departments, news and gossip letters. Clients included the Louisville Courier-Journal, New Orleans Times-Picayune, Dallas News, Salt Lake Tribune, St. Louis Globe-Democrat, Boston Herald, Chicago News, Chicago Herald, Washington Post, and scores of others, and Bacheller thus was responsible for extending the syndicate concept to the big cities.

A year later, Bacheller was faced with a major competitor, Samuel Sidney McClure, and, in 1886, Edward W. Bok entered the field, and these two men overshadowed him.

Bacheller teamed up with Kellogg in order to obtain wider distribution for such writers as A. Conan Doyle, Rudyard Kipling and Stephen Crane (whose 40,000 word "Red Badge of Courage" was syndicated).

Stories by Bret Harte and Henry James were syndicated by Charles A. Dana.

During the next 20 years, the syndicate business experienced its greatest growth. The giants who entered the field during this period, particularly Samuel McClure and William Randolph Hearst, had major, lasting effects on America's newspapers and magazines.

The Wisconsin ready-prints were sold to newspapers as a means of saving production costs. Syndicates then became the principal source of features and columns and provided a diversity of opinions and ideas to provincial newspapers and an excitement and flavor to major dailies.

Syndicates originated in the midwest and for many years Cleveland (home of NEA) and Chicago were the headquarters of major newspaper syndicates, including the Field Newspaper Syndicate (formerly Publishers-Hall). For many years, Chicago also was the location of a lively, independent company, National Newspaper Syndicate, which folded in 1975.

National was best known for its former medical columnist, Dr. William Brady. When Dr. Brady died in Beverly Hills in February, 1972, just a few weeks short of his 92nd birthday, he had established several journalistic records, as author of one of the longest, continually syndicated columns and the country's pioneering medical columnist. But perhaps the oddest record of all took place during the months after his death. Most readers were unaware of his passing and the syndicate had rather an extensive backlog of columns which were not outdated, so they continued the column, and readers continued to write to Dr. Brady for medical advice.

In 1916, when John Dille left the George Matthew Adams Syndicate to start the National Newspaper Syndicate, he lured Dr. Brady from Adams and the "Personal Health Service" was his first column. In late 1972, National finally phased out the Brady column, though the syndicate retained another medical column called "For Women Only," by Dr. Lindsay Curtis of the University of Utah (later syndicated by United).

National specialized in sports instruction, with the largest lineup of any syndicate in this category. The 1975 team was golfers Arnold Palmer and Billy Casper, skier Jean-Claude Killy, tennis player Dave Kornreich, bowlers Don Carter and Marion Ladewig, and Stan Davies, who wrote about boating in the summer and snowmobiling in the winter.

The tradition among sports columns bylined by celebrities is that they are ghostwritten by professional writers. In the case of the National roster, a great deal of the writing was done by Dick Aultman and John May of Golf Digest, Doug Pfeiffer of Skiing, and others, who changed them from season to season. Some of the golf pros write year-round and a few even do some of their own writing, but generally their attorneys or business managers retain ghosts on a seasonal basis.

There is a stylistic difference among sports columns. Killy, for example, preaches the good form but often abandons it for the sake of breaking out of the gate a few fractions of a second faster. Palmer has historically psyched himself up in much the same manner as Killy, and writes as a "go for broke" golfer, while Casper tends to be dedicated to the traditional methodology, with perhaps a greater attention to accuracy. Killy, Palmer and Casper all are syndicated by United, which also syndicates Rod Laver's Tennis Tips.

When John Dille died, National was inherited by his two sons, John F. Jr. and Robert. John moved to the Elkhart Truth and radio and TV stations in Indiana, and Bob operated the syndicate. In 1973, J. Willard Colston sold his syndicate to the Trib-News and returned to National (he previously worked for National) as president. When National closed, Colston resumed his own business, with his wife, in Harvard, Illinois, near Chicago. In 1976, United acquired National, and in 1977, Colston became executive vice president and editorial director of The New York Times Syndication Sales Corporation.

In 1978, Colston went west and became president of the Los Angeles Times Syndicate.

As for Dr. Brady, he is survived by two daughters and several grandchildren, including actor Robert Redford.

Today, more than 200 syndicates offer publishers a choice of over a thousand columns. In an era of cost-cutting, syndicates now sell their columns in formats designed to eliminate typesetting. Whether it's a mat, or camera-ready offset proof, or magnetic tape, or computer-to-computer operation, syndicates are back to fulfilling the production function conceived in the Civil War. But syndicates are much more than a production service. They have become an indispensable part of the editorial operations of almost all newspapers.

Rupert Murdoch, the press baron of Australia, England and the United States, discussed his opinions about columns in an interview by Alexander Cockburn in the Village Voice in late 1976.

"There really are too many columns in the bloody paper" (the New York Post), said Murdoch.

"They seem to be there because they're available, rather than for any quality—a cheap way of filling the paper.

"I'm growing irritated by Evans and Novak. It doesn't represent my political point of view, but I like Buckley. I tend to read him. I get cross about it, but his column is articulate. Evans and Novak tend to be sucking up to the political establishment in Washington, because Kissinger is leaking to them, or someone is. But I shouldn't knock them too much. They often break a story. Carl Rowan I can't read. Sylvia Porter—everyone tells me she's wonderful, but I'd put her back in the finance or the women's pages or some service area. You should have a page or two of first-class political columns and leading articles and cartoons."

In 1977, the shakeup at the Post included the addition of syndicated columnists David Broder and George Will. A few local and syndicated columnists were dropped, but the best news of all was the return of Murray Kempton, an old favorite. As for Sylvia Porter, she joined former Postmen Jimmy Breslin and Pete Hamill at The New York News.

MAJOR USERS

In television and newspaper syndication, a New York City outlet is not essential, but it certainly is extremely important. The influence of New York media with others around the country, is one of the obvious reasons. New York City has seven major TV channels and three major general daily newspapers. It thus often is easier to place a syndicated TV program than a newspaper column. The New York Times uses only its own columns, so the competition among syndicates zeroes in on the News and the Post.

The New York News has the largest circulation of any American newspaper and publishes many columns. The majority of these are from the Chicago Tribune-New York News Syndicate, though in recent years, the News has been more receptive to outsiders and has launched such newcomers as Canadian humorist Nancy Stahl. In 1976, the News lured Jack Anderson from the Post, where he, and his predecessor, Drew Pearson, had been a fixture for many years. For the politically conservative News to publish Jack Anderson indeed is extraordinary, but it is indicative of the trend to balanced views on op-ed pages, and, more important, it reflects the battle for circulation being fought by all big city newspapers, including the News.

In early 1978, Sylvia Porter also switched from the Post to the News. The current all-star lineup at the News features Jimmy Breslin on page four, Liz Smith on page six, Suzy on page 12, and Patrick Buchanan on the op-ed page along with Jack Anderson. Other luminaries at the News are Rex Reed, Ann Landers and Eliot Janeway.

The overall orientation, particularly on Sundays, is to use service and leisure interest columns, rather than columns on political subjects. The lineup includes Saul Kapel, M.D., G. Timothy Johnson, M.D.,

Frank Miller, D.V.M., Harvey Gardner (social security), Al DeCicco, Andrew Greeley, Charles Goren and Omar Sharif, and Jon-Michael Reed, Charles and Vivian Jayne (astrology) and Katy (dreams).

Jack O'Brian appears only in the Queens edition, one of the few instances in which a syndicated columnist is not published full-run. The explanation is that O'Brian's column previously appeared in the Queens-based Long Island Press. When the Press folded in 1977, the News picked up several columns.

The third New York newspaper, The New York Post, has undergone more changes than just about any other American newspaper since Rupert Murdoch purchased it in early 1977. In pre-Murdoch days, the Post was loaded with a variety of columns, local and syndicated. The largest number was from the Field Newspaper Syndicate, which reflected the Post's former ownership of a syndicate which was merged into what now is Field.

Murdoch has drastically changed the newspaper. Page one and the first few pages are designed to attract mass readership. The Post out-zaps the News in sensationalism; the newspaper has a resemblance to The Star, which also is Murdoch-owned. Bureaus have been opened throughout the metropolitan area, suburban editions have been started, and potholes in Queens now get as much or more news coverage as major international events. In terms of circulation, it's worked—from a long-time plateau of about 500,000, circulation has zoomed to about 700,000.

The drastic overhaul has meant the dropping of quite a few features, including several local columns. Advisor Rose Franzblau retired and Pete Hamill moved to the News. Diane Judge, who formerly assisted Liz Smith at the News, started a gossip column. Joey Adams, whose column appeared in the Long Island Press, was recruited.

Among the columns from the Dorothy Schiff era which remain in the Post are Mary McGrory, William Buckley, Art Buchwald, Eugenia Sheppard, Abby, Jeane Dixon, Earl Wilson, Alfred Shein-wald and Harriet Van Horne.

Thus, the Post still satisfies column loyalists.

Critics often pointed to the pre-Murdoch Post as being overly loaded with columns, to the detriment of news, but the fact is that the current Post stacked up favorably with other tabloid-size papers in news lineage, and even when it was full-size, the Post was noted for its features. The newspaper was founded by Alexander Hamilton in 1801 and it has published many of the great names in American journalism, including Franklin P. Adams, Samuel Grafton, Leland Stowe (of the Chicago Daily News), Christopher Morley (whose column in the twenties was called "The Bowling Green"), Dorothy Thompson, and labor expert Victor Riesel.

Oliver Pilat, who wrote with Victor Riesel in the forties, produced two of the best books about columnists, biographies of Westbrook Pegler and Drew Pearson.

The ageless party-goer Elsa Maxwell wrote for the Hearst newspapers for many years, but for a while she appeared in the Post, and in her column of September 21, 1942, she reminisced about the first time she met Bernard Baruch—at the Versailles Peace Conference in 1919. Today, readers of the Post receive continuing nostalgic reminders of the past from Earl Wilson.

Harriet Van Horne writes a very personal kind of column in the Post which has among its fans Nora Ephron, Esquire's media commentator, who calls her "the last lady in America."

Van Horne's ladylike manners evoke her outrage and concern about an enormous variety of abuses, including pornography, rudeness, drugs, sexual promiscuity and other mores. A long-time TV reviewer at the New York World-Telegram, she still writes an occasional comment about television, sprinkled with quotations from the Bible and classic literature.

Nora Ephron visited with Harriet Van Horne in her Manhattan town house, and transcribed this evaluation.

"When I took the Post column, I thought I would travel. Well, you don't travel to Yonkers on a New York Post expense account. I had planned on going places, but I could not even go out in the daytime. I was the veiled lady of East Sixty-eighth Street. I decided the only way I could write this column was to be a commentator, which limited me quite severely. But I do have this devoted band of readers—school teachers, and elderly Jewish ladies, and sweet dear well-bred gentlemen who value manners, and lots of young mothers, and it all comes as the loveliest surprise."

The Harriet Van Horne column appears in only a few newspapers outside of New York.

Though only tabloid size, the Post generally runs columns in their entirety, whereas many subscribers scissor Wilson and other "item columns," generally from the bottom, in order to cram them into smaller spaces.

In tallying the number of syndicated columns, the New York Post emerges far behind the national champs, which, in the New York area, undoubtedly was the Long Island Press.

The Press was a prime example of a newspaper which subscribes to syndicates which sell feature packages, rather than individual columns. As a result, the Press published lots of family entertainment and enlightenment, at very low cost. A Newhouse newspaper, they used material from the Newhouse News Service. Since Newhouse was distributed as part of the Chicago Daily News/Sun-Times Service, the Press used Arthur Snider, Patricia Shelton and other Chicago byliners and also columns from the parent company, Field Newspaper

Syndicate. The Press subscribed to both The Associated Press and United Press and used wire service byliners who are the equivalent of syndicated columnists, such as George W. Cornell (religion), Andy Lang (do-it-yourself), Irving Desfor (photography), Vivian Brown (beauty) and Cecily Brownstone (food) of the AP and Patricia McCormack (family), Gay Pauley (women's) and Joan Hanouer (TV) of UPI.

The breathtaking lineup of 1976 columns in the Long Island Press ranged from the Aces on Bridge and other daily features to Betty Yarmon and others which are plucked from Women's News Service and other packages and published irregularly. Here's a partial 1976 listing, in alphabetical order: Joey Adams, Olive E. Allen, Jack Anderson, Phyllis Battelle, James Beard, Dr. Joyce Brothers, Art Buchwald, William F. Buckley Jr., Ira G. Corn Jr., Norman Cousins, Dr. W.G. Crook, Ernest Cuneo, Frances Deitrich, Steve Ellingson, Larry Evans, Dr. Michael Fox, Marilyn and Hy Gardner, Louis Harris, Heloise, David Hendin, Margaret Herbst, Paul Hightower, Joyce Lain Kennedy, James J. Kilpatrick, Saul Kohler, Joseph Kraft, Arkady Leokum, Peter Lisagor, Jack O'Brian, Joan O'Sullivan, Carroll Righter, John Roche, Carl Rowan, Mike Royko, Louis Rukeyser, William A. Rusher, Mark Russell, Dr. Lee Salk, David R. Sargent, Charles B. Seib, Arthur J. Snider, Dr. Frederick J. Stare, Jason Thomas, Dr. G.C. Thosteson, Pat Trexler, Gus Tyler, Sander Vanocur, Carlton Varney, Katherine B. Walker and Emily Wilkins.

Most of these columns still are published, though not in New York City, and several are in major, prestigious newspapers.

One of the major newspapers in the New York area is Newsday, the Long Island tabloid. The readership is heavily skewed to housewives, and there are lots of service columns. However, the total number of columns is not as many as one might expect, and Newsday relies on its large staff for extensive local reports and features. Political columnists include David Broder, James Kilpatrick and Mary McGrory, and other columnists are Dr. Lawrence Lamb, Ira Corn, Jeane Dixon, George Gallup, Barbara Gibbons, and, here's an extraordinary treat, both Abby and Ann Landers.

Outside of New York, take a look at the Milwaukee Journal, which appears on almost every list of the top-rated dailies.

The Journal carries Russell Baker and other New York Times columnists, and also subscribes to the news services of the Los Angeles Times, Washington Star, Washington Post and other syndicates, as well as the two major wire services, the AP and UPI. Columnists include Marilyn Beck, Oswald and Jim Jacoby, Senator Soaper, Ask Andy, and an assortment of features such as Anecdotes of the Famous and Words, Wit and Wisdom.

The Milwaukee Journal, founded in 1882 and long one of America's most important newspapers, for many years refused to use any syndicated columns on the theory that it achieved a unique cohesive identity with its Green Sheet, a four-page collection of local features, and its local columnists.

The Chicago Tribune also has abandoned its policy of using only columns of its own syndicate.

The leading examples of the no-outside-columnists policy are the Christian Science Monitor and The New York Times, both of which syndicate their material to other newspapers. The Monitor and Times have another distinction—they are among the few daily newspapers which do not publish comics.

The Washington Post is unusual in that it carries lots of comics plus lots of outside columns plus lots of columns from its own syndicate plus lots of local columns. In short, the Post is a thick newspaper. Its daily comics section of four cartoons and 25 strips is spread on three or four pages, which also include two local columns and the columns of Jack Anderson and Dr. Frank Miller. Art Buchwald appears in the coveted first page of the Style section. Among the other Post columns are those by Joseph Kraft, Clayton Fritchey, Dr. Frank Falkner, Peter Weaver, Hobart Rowan, Rowland Evans and Robert Novak, Garry Wills, Ann Landers, Fred Karpin, Louis Harris and others. The Saturday real estate section, for example, includes the columns of Andy Lang (Associated Press), Robert J. Bruss, Earl Snyder, Samuel Fishlyn and Bernard Gladstone.

The Post used to honor the tradition of running a photo of the author along with most of the political columns. On Sunday's op-ed page, for example, the Evans-Novak column was bridged on the left by a balding Rowland Evans, whose left eye appeared to be winking, and on the right, by his younger, albeit more sober, associate. Joe Kraft was always grinning whereas Jack Anderson had only a trace of a smile, which perhaps changed to a smirk, depending on the column.

The columnist's views vary considerably, not just in political orientation, but in terms of where they are looking. A few peer directly at the reader, but most, like Clayton Fritchey, look to the side. Stanley Karnow peers down at the reader, perhaps to balance one of his peers looking up from the bottom of the page.

Another popular style of identifying columnists is with sketches. This often solves the ticklish problem of not having to show the double chins or other signs of aging, but newspaper reproduction is not always ideal, and sometimes those drawings which are thinly inked appear faded, while heavier drawings, often called poster art, appear blurred.

Be that as it may, the Los Angeles Herald-Examiner belongs to the art school, and its op-ed page often resembles a drawing catalogue, what with its miniature sketches of Bert Bacharach, Ann Landers, Earl Wilson, Dr. George C. Thosteson and others. One conceivable advantage of the art, as compared to photos, is the use of profiles instead of full faces. Steady readers, however, sometimes wonder why Earl Wilson is always staring off to the side of the page, and in an opposite direction from the editorial page. Bob Considine said that he preferred the sketch to his less flattering photo.

One final advantage of drawings over photos pertains to The Wall Street Journal. The Journal has a policy of not using photos in news columns so a columnist with a sketch is all set to be profiled by the Journal. This front page honor has been given to Leonard Lyons, Sylvia Porter, Bernard Meltzer and, in 1978, Merle Ellis, the nation's best-known butcher. Ellis' offbeat column, The Corner Butcher, started in 1973 in the San Francisco Chronicle and now appears in about 65 newspapers, including The New York News.

One would think that a photo provides a more accurate depiction of the columnist, but most syndicates rarely update photos, and, as a result, readers generally see a younger, better looking version of the columnist. The promotion pieces used by the syndicate to sell to publishers often use especially flattering photos. General Features, which was absorbed into the Los Angeles Times Syndicate, was particularly adept at using 20-year-old photos to promote aging columnists.

The toughest looking of all columnists probably was Harold L. Ickes, who was Secretary of the Interior and a powerful New Dealer in the thirties. He had been a reporter on the Chicago Record and, after resigning from Truman's cabinet, he became a Scripps-Howard columnist. His acid comments included "I am against government by crony" and his sourpuss photo indeed was frightening to cronies and others.

The Miami Herald publishes a staggering array of columns, some with sketches, some with photos and other unadorned.

The Herald has a daily circulation of 406,000 and Sunday circulation of over 500,000. Unlike many other newspapers, these figures are higher than the circulation of a decade ago, and they make the Herald the biggest newspaper in Florida and one of the biggest in the country. Its enormous advertising lineage has ranked it among the top five in the country for many years. As a result, the columns, particularly the features, often are bland fillers, tossed in among the advertising, and the newspaper lacks the editorial quality of The Washington Post and other large users of columns. This is especially noticeable on Sundays.

Among the syndicated regulars in the Miami Herald are Jack Anderson, Jenifer Anderson, Herman Baum, Barbara Taylor Bradford, William Buckley Jr., Ernest Cuneo, Margaret Dana, Steve Ellingson, Dr. Frank Falkner, Barbara Gibbons, Sydney J. Harris, James Kilpatrick, Dr. Michael Fox, Joan Beck, David Broder, Alan

Truscott, Mark Russell, Sydney Omarr, Ann Landers, Garry Wills, Don Campbell, Jim Bishop, Suzy, Liz Smith, Jon-Michael Reed, Sylvia Porter, Carleton Varney, Judith Randal, Dr. Neil Solomon and Arthur Hoppe.

As with other lists of syndicate subscribers, columns continually are being added and dropped, and undoubtedly the preceding roster has been changed by the Miami Herald. The corps of syndicate columnists undoubtedly remains extensive, supplemented by a cadre of local byliners.

In the coveted position on the comics page, local columnist Jack Kofoed appears Tuesday, Thursday and Saturday, Jim Bishop appears Monday and Wednesday and Arthur Hoppe appears Friday.

In addition to these regularly scheduled columnists, the Herald subscribes to several package services, such as Women's News Service, where it obtains a flock of columns, all for a flat fee, which are being used almost on a space-available basis. On a Sunday, the Herald may use two consumer advice columns by Betty Yarmon, and other days the Yarmon byline does not appear at all. The amazing thing about these low-cost fillers of space between the ads is that several of them, such as the Yarmon column, are extremely well written.

Among the new columns at the Miami Herald is Doctor Jock, who is David Bachman, M.D.

Though the Miami Herald is one of the nation's top publishers of syndicated columns, the Herald uses fewer columns today than a decade ago. One of the reasons for this is the increased use of the Knight-Ridder News Service. This operation has expanded considerably and the corporate headquarters is in the Miami Herald building.

Miami is the home of several major columnists, including Hy Gardner and John Keasler, and quite a few writers who handle their own syndication.

ANTI-TRUST

The New York Post, Washington Post and Miami Herald are prime examples of the importance and diversity of columns.

A more serious examination of the power of newspaper syndicates is obtained by a visit to the fifth floor file room of the United States Court House at Foley Square in Manhattan. In November, 1967, the Justice Department initiated litigation against three syndicates. The legal documents of the numerous pre-trial hearings held in the succeeding years provide some insights into the syndicate business. The government complaints, numbered 67-4596, 67-4597, and 67-4598 and signed by Attorney General Ramsay Clark, alleged that the selling of exclusive territories for individual columns is a violation of the Sherman anti-trust act since the "inability to supply popular features significantly limits a newspaper's capacity to provide a well-rounded service to its reading public."

The defendants were the Chicago Tribune-New York News Syndicate, Field Enterprises (Publishers-Hall Syndicate) and the Hearst Corporation (King Features Syndicate), and their reply basically was that copyright law provides a monopoly by which a licensor has the unrestricted right to grant exclusive licenses, and there is no shortage of features since there are over 300 feature syndicates.

The government research included a few errors, such as that feature syndicates were formed around 1910, when it was much earlier, but the principal contention came from the government's successful prosecution involving a "pervasive conspiracy" among Paramount Pictures and other movie producers to distribute their films. Most newspaper syndicates claim that they either do not sell exclusive territories or that the practice is not harmful. At stake in the case was the remote possibility that the government not only could change sales practices but separate producers from distributors, so that companies cannot be in both businesses. This separation of the movie studios from operating their own theaters radically changed Hollywood and benefited the independent producers and exhibitors.

For this reason, the syndicates marshalled a battery of law firms. Paull Weiss Rifkind Wharton and Garrison represented Field; Simpson Ratcher and Bartlett was counsel to Hearst; and the Trib-News retained Kirkland, Ellis, Hodson, Chaffetz and Misters in Chicago and Townley Updike Carter and Rodgers, conveniently located in the New York News building.

It was a legal bonanza, with numerous interrogatories, oral examinations, requests for delays, motions to strike and other strategems, and on May 27, 1970, the Tribune acknowledged many formal and informal territory agreements, such as granting Suzy exclusively to the Boston Globe and Omaha World-Herald in their areas and selling Abby areas to the Detroit News, Minneapolis Star and Tribune, Omaha World-Herald, Philadelphia Bulletin, San Francisco Chronicle and Deseret News.

Donald F. Melchior and other Justice Department attorneys interviewed many editors and publishers. Kenneth McDonald of the Des Moines Register provided an affidavit in November, 1971, attesting to the validity of territorial rights. Joe Seacrest of the Lincoln Star Journal stated that his newspaper had been excluded from purchasing features preempted by the Omaha World-Herald, but Lewis G. Gerdes of the World-Herald agreed with the Des Moines Register.

And so on, back and forth, among the memos, affidavits, and transcripts. In a personal conversation in 1973, Melchior said that he hoped to conclude the case soon.

In 1973, the Boston Globe was added to the defendants, and the case finally was scheduled for trial on February 3, 1975, in the U.S. District Court in Boston. However, three days before the scheduled trial, on January 31, the defendants reached an agreement and the trial never took place. The consent statement agreed to limit Globe exclusivity over small circulation dailies and also weekly newspapers.

In late 1975, the Justice Department withdrew its suit. Though action may be taken against individual newspapers, the net effect of the years of litigation, aside from the income to dozens of lawyers, was to permit additional distribution of major columns to minor subscribers. As a result, Jack Anderson, Abby and Ann Landers now appear in more newspapers than ever before.

Syndicates continue to be extremely competitive, and universally secretive about the fees paid by subscribers and the number of subscribers.

A reason which the syndicates give for not disclosing names of column outlets is to deter boycotts and protest letters to newspapers, which often occur when associations or other large organizations are attacked by columnists.

At least two Washington groups, Accuracy in Media (AIM) and Ralph Nader's office, have compiled lists, by laboriously going through copies of daily newspapers. The lists can be obtained for a fee, but they are somewhat inaccurate, because newspapers change columns, occasionally do not run a particular column or run a column in part.

As to the ranking of syndicates, the three largest in 1967, when the anti-trust litigation was initiated, probably were the defendants, the Trib-News, Publishers-Hall and King. Today, these three (Publishers-Hall now is called Field) still are big, but United Features and the Los Angeles Times Syndicate probably outsell the Trib-News and Field. The reason has nothing to do with the Justice Department; however, and the growth of United and the L.A. Times primarily has been via acquisitions.

· An indication that the litigation produced hardly any changes is a King Features advertisement on August 14, 1976, in Editor & Publisher. The ad promoted the Nicholas von Hoffman column to potential subscribers, and the tag line was, "To learn if Nicholas von Hoffman is still available in your territory, write or phone . . ."

ANALYSIS

The personal recommendations of a columnist often are more influential than the more formal, impersonal opinions expressed on the editorial page. Readers feel a kinship with their favorite columnists, whether they are pundits or serious essayists, which they rarely feel with the editors and publishers who appear to operate from a loftier position.

Column reading can be habit forming, which is what syndicators and publishers hope for, and, in the process, readers feel comfortable with their favorite columnists.

Among the journalistic benefits of Watergate has been an encouragement of investigative reporting, and this has produced livelier writing by several old-time Washington columnists who had become somewhat flaccid. Another recent influence has been consumerism, which has produced several new advice columns and also affected many of the Washington byliners.

Political columnists seem to become most active in their coverage of Presidential elections. Since the primary campaigns take place over a longer period of time and involve more candidates than the November elections, every fourth Spring is the best season to study the columnists.

Walter Winchell was uniquely influential in developing popular sentiment for two of his heroes, Franklin D. Roosevelt, particularly during the third-term campaign in 1940, and Dwight Eisenhower. Winchell's hate of Harry Truman, and his strong feeling that Adlai Stevenson would be soft on communism, made the 1952 campaign extremely emotional and helped to elect Ike.

In the 1960 campaign, Walter Lippmann led the wave of adulation for John F. Kennedy. As David Halberstam noted in The Best and the Brightest, "Lippmann influenced Reston, and Reston influenced the writing press and the television commentators, who influenced the television reporters."

The 1972 Presidential primary campaign produced many surprises, among the politicians, and also the columnists. Early in the year, most Washington columnists were predicting a Muskie landslide for the Democratic nomination. By June, the columnists were so shaken up as a result of the McGovern victories that it was hard to decipher their views and prognostications. On June 2, for example, conservative John Chamberlain opened with, "I never thought I'd be rooting for Hubert Humphrey." Of course, he went on to explain that he was pro-Humphrey only "to head off the calamity of George McGovern." Still, it was confusing, particularly to readers of the editorial page of the Ft. Lauderdale News, where, on the same day, Robert S. Allen, who generally does not agree with John Chamberlain, used the adjacent space to viciously attack Senator McGovern.

One might think that Allen, at age 72, wouldn't get so riled, but, here's his June 2, 1972, lead:

"Sen. George McGovern's extremist scheme to hack some $32 billion from the defense budget is either sheer demagogic claptrap or the most dangerous kind of ignorance and self-delusion.

"On its very face this far-left proposal is ridiculous or suicidal—or both."

Andrew Tully, whose Capital Fare is syndicated by McNaught in more than 100 newspapers, was a McGovern admirer during the primary campaign. Tully, who classifies himself as a "middle-of-the-road Jeffersonian liberal," was "sickened by the way the media gleefully interred Muskie."

My favorite columnist, says Tully, is Scotty Reston, "because he does what I try to do, write right down the middle. I read the Washington columnists and respect most of them because of their hard work."

In an attempt to produce lively writing, particularly lead sentences designed to attract readers, columnists often go further than they would like in their generalizations. This is particularly noticeable when they attempt to develop new insights into Presidential candidates. The columnist tries not to repeat yesterday's news, and constantly is searching for trends. In the process, the columnist often goes overboard in rhapsody or attack. The reasoning is the pro-and-con middle ground may appear too dull or pedantic to most readers.   In the early stages of the 1972 campaign, for example, Joe Kraft predicted that the sleeper candidate would be Congressman Wilbur Mills with his "mix of talent, outlook and power." McGeorge Bundy and John Connally were other Kraft heroes.

In 1976, most of the Washington columnists tried to be aloof during the New Hampshire and other early primaries, and not get trapped into premature predictions and allegiances. The lure of the Democratic Party to columnists is the greater number of candidates, as compared to the Republican contenders. In early 1976, many columnists tried to avoid making premature predictions particularly with regard to Senators Jackson, Humphrey and Kennedy. In addition to these front runners, a few columnists decided to follow Governor George Wallace, Congressman Morris Udall and others who they deemed colorful, including a few—very few in early 1976—who were intrigued by Jimmy Carter.

It seemed like such an open contest rather than a Carter runaway, and most columnists were confused or amused. Conservative James J. Kilpatrick wrote a column in the style of Art Buchwald or Russell Baker, headlined "179 hopefuls running for president."

As for Buchwald, he columned about his Uncle Phil in Brooklyn, who decided to run for President on the Democratic ticket on the basis of such qualifications as a great smile.

Presidential primaries are a good excuse for Washington columnists to travel around the country, to get closer to the people, in the "pivotal," "critical," "crucial," "representative," "turnaround" and "grass roots" states, ranging from New Hampshire to California.

Most of the columnists, including the Democrats, had trouble accepting Carter. At the Times, Tom Wicker and Tony Lewis were surprises, as early supporters of Carter. In March, 1976, Mary McGrory impetuously said that Carter reminded her of Nixon, and continued to praise Senator Frank Church and Governor Jerry Brown. Evans and Novak, who are more conservative than Miss McGrory, preferred Senator Henry Jackson and consistently attacked Carter.

As late as April 29, Joe Kraft preferred Gerald Ford to Jimmy Carter. "The slow and steady man (Ford), however bumbling, may be better than the Knight who seeks the Holy Grail," wrote Kraft.

In early June, 1976, the columnists' brigade was still covering the primaries as if they were a serious contest. Joseph Kraft was in Cleveland to interview labor leaders, blacks, Udall supporters and others in the "Stop Carter Movement."

Evans and Novak also covered the Ohio primary as if it were a serious battle. Though signs of concession began to appear on June 3 when they described Carter as "the man most likely to be the next President."

George McGovern and/or his aides compared Carter to Nixon, which provided lively copy for lots of columnists, including former White House staffer Patrick J. Buchanan, who approved on the basis that Nixon's attributes were desirable.

Except for these minor episodes, press coverage, particularly by the syndicated columnists, fizzled out many weeks before the Democratic Convention in mid-July. TV, the news magazines, and newspapers all contributed to media overkill.

Fortunately, Elizabeth Ray arrived to divert attention and add a titillating new issue, Congressional morality. While Richard Reeves chronicled the "Old Faces of 1976," Jack Anderson and others turned to the "Old Bodies."

The July convention harmony was so dull that most of the columnists were driven to chatter and gossip about the vice presidential nominees and speculation based on a minimum of information, a type of writing called polichat.

In 1976, several Senate contests attracted national attention. In California, Professor Hayakawa (a former Register syndicated columnist) drew mixed reviews from the political columnists. The New York election was more confusing. For example, Rowland Evans supported Professor Moynihan, while Robert Novak stuck with Senator Buckley (brother of columnist William Buckley).

Columnists often reevaluate their views on political candidates and controversial issues, but rarely note these shifts, and it is even rarer for a columnist to admit that he erred in an opinion. In early June, 1972, New York Times-man Tom Wicker wrote a laudatory column about the grandiose plan of George McGovern to change the welfare system and re-distribute income. A few days later, Wicker realized that the arithmetic was faulty and that he had swallowed material from McGovern's aides, without fully digesting it. Wicker not only wrote a correction, but blamed himself for the carelessness. "This was a journalistic sin for which responsibility is hereby accepted; it was also reaffirmation of the cardinal lesson that every political reporter learns and re-learns—that everything said and done by politicians seeking or holding power has to be constantly challenged," stated Wicker, thus retaining the affection of his millions of loyal readers.

Wicker's columns, particularly those about the Attica prison riots, have produced the most emotional reaction, pro and con, among the Times commentators. Anthony Lewis also often is criticized, and his 1972 reports from North Vietnam evoked censure from the White House and violent editorial disagreement among other columnists.

James Reston is far from bland, but he is the least controversial and most influential among The Times columnists. Reston's reports from China almost single-handedly kindled the American interest in acupuncture, a thrilling example of the impact of a newspaper columnist. Indeed, a primary role of a serious columnist is to spin out new ideas, rather than merely report on events or attempt to spot trends. This is a difficult assignment, and the proffering of new ideas may be grasped by only a tiny minority of readers, but it remains a primary, stimulating motivation of such writers as Reston.

Columnists prize their special, personal relationships with presidents and other high government officials. Arthur Krock of the Times and Walter Lippmann of the Herald Tribune were confidantes of FDR and other world leaders, Charles Bartlett and other friends of JFK received insider tips, and James Reston has had his exclusive sources.

Reston's most controversial friendship was with Spiro Agnew, which started in 1968 with columns which were unusually friendly to the vice president.

The Press section of Time magazine on October 15, 1973, concluded that "Reston does not write puff pieces for the Veep. Rather, in most cases he seems inclined to give Agnew the benefit of the doubt. When asked if he could recall writing a single column strongly critical of Agnew, Reston said that he could not."

Nick Thimmesch, of the Los Angeles Times Syndicate, admits that Reston generally reflects the mood of the nation and is must reading. Thimmesch, who is in his forties, says that the ideal age for a political columnist is about 35, a time when a journalist is likely to be experienced but not tired. "It's exhausting to try to come up with fresh ideas three times a week," says Thimmesch, though he still manages to do it quite well.

Thimmesch does not have a Washington outlet, but excerpts from his column often appear in the daily news summary circulated to the President and other administration officials. A similar influence is wielded by Jeffrey St. John, Kevin Phillips, and other columnists, many of whom do not appear in the two Washington dailies.

Clippings often are mailed by key people to Congressmen and government officials, thus extending the influence of columns which do not have capital outlets. The impact of political columnists thus often is measured as barometers of public opinion, having a witch doctor effect on politicians who perennially seek to divine the winds.

Milton Viorst, when he was writing for the Washington Star Syndicate, assessed the impact of capital columnists as having some influence on government officials.

"Outside Washington, I don't know," said Viorst. "I suspect that members of the press are the last to be able to measure their power, if it exists. Occasionally, I get a letter which buoys my spirit but often I feel as if I'm writing into a vacuum. Maybe television has intensified this, though I suspect it has always been the case."

In 1964, Karl Meyer compiled a list for Esquire magazine of the most powerful journalists in Washington. The selection included editors, bureau chiefs, foreign correspondents, wire service reporters, newspaper and magazine writers and broadcasters, and, the largest category, syndicated columnists. Meyer's selection of columnists was: Joseph Alsop, Charles Bartlett, Betty Beale, Marquis Childs, Roscoe

Drummond, Rowland Evans and Robert Novak, Doris Fleeson, John Herling, Marguirite Higgins, Arthur Krock, David Lawrence, Walter Lippmann, Peter Lisagor, Jim Lucas, Mary McGrory, Edward P. Morgan, Drew Pearson, James Reston, Richard Strout, Walter Trohan and Richard Wilson.

In 1973, Jack Limpert undertook the same assignment for the Washingtonian magazine. Of course, the power elite now included more network television people and more Washington Post editors and staffers. Limpert again gave great credit to syndicated columnists, in numbers and influence, including many who were on the 1964 list.

Still on the 1973 Washingtonian list of columnists were Peter Lisagor, Joseph Alsop, Evans and Novak and Strout. Additions to the columnist section of the power elite list were Jack Anderson, Russell Baker, David Broder, Art Buchwald, Maxine Cheshire, James J. Kilpatrick, Joseph Kraft, James Reston, Carl Rowan, Hobart Rowen and Nicholas von Hoffman.

Limpert noted in the 1973 Washingtonian article that "new presidents often spawn new columnists, but none of the Nixon disciples has made it big."

The Nixon group included Nick Thimmesch, Kevin Phillips and William Safire. Thimmesch and Phillips lacked the clout of a Washington outlet. Safire was in The New York Times but his well-written essays generally were of greater interest to semanticists than politicians.

In 1975, another Nixon aide, Patrick J. Buchanan, became a columnist, with such major outlets as The New York News and St. Louis Globe-Democrat. Safire and Buchanan try not to be labeled as Nixon apologists, but post-Watergate newspaper subscribers and readers find it hard to accept them. When he was in the White House, Pat Buchanan stated, "It's all over if you get chopped up on the networks. You never recover. The newspapers can beat the hell out of you and you've got no problem."

Since it was The Washington Post and other newspapers which were responsible for Buchanan's ouster from the White House, perhaps he's changed his mind about the power of the press.

James J. Kilpatrick, the stylish conservative of The Washington Star, is in a good position to evaluate television and newspapers, as a result of his weekly debates on CBS-TV's Sixty Minutes. The two-minute duel with Shana Alexander generates more mail than the columns, but the programming gimmick generally makes Kilpatrick predictable, and he comes off better in print.

Predictability is the bane of columnists. It's hard not to look like other columnists, or, worse still, to avoid repeating past columns. Fans of Kilpatrick and others who try to be different are more tolerant as newspaper readers than they are as TV viewers, and recognize that one stimulating column out of three a week is a commendable average.

Others with high averages for getting off the beaten track are Jack Anderson, Russell Baker, David Broder, Art Buchwald, Ernest B. Furguson and Carl Rowan. In this era of consumerists and investigative reporters, pioneer muckraker Anderson has trouble engendering excitement, though he tries very hard and still manages to score occasionally. Furguson is extremely intelligent, but his Baltimore Sun column is not widely syndicated and he is relatively unknown.

Many of the 1964 stars still are around, but most not only are older but appear to be tired. Marquis Childs of the St. Louis Post-Dispatch still is praised by his colleagues, Charles Bartlett has overcome the image of a "Kennedy flash," and James Reston still is one of the world's most famous and respected journalists. Though columnists have longer career lives than athletes or TV personalities, it's awfully hard to expect anyone to be as vigorous or competitive today as compared to 25 years ago.

Among the 1964 group, the one who has tried hardest to become world famous, in the tradition of Walter Lippmann, is Joseph Kraft. He has left the safety of Washington more often than his colleagues, and traveled around the world in an attempt to develop contacts and expertise on foreign policy. Meeting with world leaders sometimes produces a pretentiousness in Kraft, though he has remained consistently lively. His articles in the New Yorker, New York and other magazines often are better written than the columns, and have added considerably to his reputation. Of course, he has his critics. In 1971, Kraft worked for presidential candidate Ed Muskie, and this has remained to haunt Kraft, particularly among the Carter people.

In March, 1975, James Fallows wrote an 8000-word analysis of Joseph Kraft in The Washington Monthly. Titled "The Most Famous Journalist in America," Fallows noted that Kraft has days on which he's as good as he egotistically thinks he is, but too often too little time to prepare and too much deference to the powerful produce dullness and predictability. He concluded that "by his ability and his drive, Kraft has made himself probably the best of the columnists' whole bunch, but that is primarily an indication of how much more they all have to do."

In 1963, Joseph Kraft took over the upper left corner of The Washington Post op-ed page, the coveted position long held by Walter Lippmann, and this started a chain of articles in which Kraft was compared to the old master. Lippmann himself called Kraft "the most promising commentator of his generation."

Kraft and Lippmann had amazingly similar backgrounds. Both were children of affluent New York families, both benefited from private schools and higher education. Lippmann made Phi Beta Kappa at Harvard, Kraft was 1947 valedictorian at Columbia and then went on to Princeton. Most important, both shucked their Jewish backgrounds and achieved a WASP-ish demeanor. Numerous other similarities exist. Kraft operates out of his home in Georgetown and summers in East Hampton. Lippmann's base was his Manhattan townhouse, but political leaders trekked during the summer to his houses in Maine and Long Island.

Kraft started at the top, as an editorial writer at The Washington Post, and went on to The New York Times and then succeeded William S. White as Washington correspondent of Harper's. Lippmann's first newspaper job also was as an editorial writer, at the New York World, which in 1920 was one of the world's great newspapers.

Kraft has written many books and magazine articles, as did Lippmann, and the total output has established his erudition and literary skill. Though Kraft now ranks with Reston, Wicker and Lewis of the Times as a leading liberal analyst, he (in fact, none of them) has not come close to the fame and importance of elitist Walter Lippmann. Kraft's foreign dispatches in The New Yorker are his best, not only because of the greater length and details and more careful writing as compared to his newspaper columns, but also because of the more careful editing which is the sine qua non of the New Yorker and which rarely applies to newspapers.

What Kraft lacks, noted James Fallows, "is the time to devote himself properly to his columns, without cutting corners and without driving himself at the same frantic pace that gave him his first heart attack long before he was 50."

When Mao Tse-tung died in 1976, Newsweek proudly declared in its September 20 cover article, "Among the few outsiders visiting China at the time of Mao's death was former U.S. Defense Secretary James Schlesinger; in his party was columnist Joseph Kraft, who filed an exclusive eyewitness report to Newsweek."

Kraft's report was limited to a description of the funeral week and a short-term prediction of relative calm and stability, and Newsweek coyly omitted mention that the Schlesinger entourage also included Jerrold Schecter, diplomatic editor of Time.

Ben H. Bagdikian, former assistant managing editor of The Washington Post, believes that in the last few years there has been a decline in importance of syndicated columnists, "partly because of the growth of alternative expressions of political and social analysis."

Bagdikian has studied political columnists, and he may be referring only to this type of writer, though even this category has not declined in number of columnists and outlets.

In a 1966 analysis of the role of syndicated public affairs columnists, Bagdikian concluded that their primary impact was not on the general public but rather on a few hundred key people, mostly political leaders in Washington. Among his observations, published in the Columbia

Journalism Review, was that columnists who are not published in Washington have reduced effect on national policy, and afternoon columns are less influential than those published in the morning. Thus, the columnists of The Washington Post are of supreme importance. The Washington Star is published in the afternoon, after the day's work has begun, and in competition with the evening TV news programs, and the Washington News was almost out of the running as far as political prestige, even before its demise in the summer of 1972.

The current elite groups of syndicated political columnists at The Washington Post includes Jack Anderson, Rowland Evans and Robert Novak, Joseph Kraft, William Raspberry, Nicholas von Hoffman and George F. Will, and this makes these writers extremely important, regardless of their number of other subscribers.

To this distinguished group must be added the lineup of The New York Times, which also appears on many important Washington breakfast tables. Current Times columnists include Anthony Lewis, William Safire, James Reston and Tom Wicker.

When a columnist is friendly with a President and is read by him, states Bagdikian, "the columnist's influence is multiplied beyond the intrinsic power of his words."

On this basis, most of the Washington Post and New York Times columnists were most influential during the Kennedy administration and lost considerable esteem during the Johnson and Nixon periods, while William Buckley, John Chamberlain, Barry Goldwater, James Kilpatrick, David Lawrence and other conservatives assumed increased importance. Newcomers to the conservative pack who have achieved fame and respect are William Rusher and George Will.

For many years, through Republican and Democratic administrations, the two columnists most often ranked as most influential were Walter Lippmann and James Reston. Foreign officials often exaggerated their importance, assuming that these columnists reflected the views of the President.

Perhaps a more logical explanation of the importance of Reston and other top columnists is their influence on the editorial writers around the country. The editorial page of the New York Post, for example, often appears to be tremendously influenced by Reston and other Timesmen.

Flora Lewis, a former columnist and now a Timeswoman in Paris, believes that columnists have some influence in focusing public attention on issues, and in clarifying them. "I don't think our comments have any real influence on government officials," she says. "They don't tailor policy to please writers, they only tailor their presentation of their policy in hopes of putting it in the best possible light. But facts dug out and interpreted by columnists and other newmen do influence policy decisions and the behavior of politicians.

That is why the framers of the U.S. constitution considered it essential to democratic process that our freedom to dig out and publish facts be unrestricted. Freedom of comment is important too, but I don't think government is much affected by it except where that freedom is denied. It makes a difference in the behavior of the Soviet government that adverse comment is routinely suppressed. I don't think the adverse comment of American political columnists makes much difference in the behavior of the U.S. government, though it can eventually change the national political climate if the general public becomes convinced that the criticism is valid and should be heeded," says Flora Lewis.

Joseph Alsop also wavered in his appraisal of the power of columnists. In the May, 1972, issue of The Washingtonian, Tom Kelly quoted Alsop's evaluation of the impact of political columnists as "zero," except with people who already agree with the columnist and "as a reporter bringing important facts which cause impact."

"If we had national newspapers with real editorial pages, we wouldn't have columns," continued Alsop, who pointed with pride to The Washington Post as "a glorious exception."

Managing editors often prefer daily columns in order to establish a habit forming appeal. It's not too hard to do a daily question-and-answer column, such as those turned out by the health and advice columnists, but it's much more difficult for a political columnist to do a five- or six- or seven-times-a-week column in which he is supposed to be profound and provide insights different from those found in wire service news articles. Jack Anderson does it, but the trend, ever since Walter Lippmann broke the five-columns-a-week habit, it to three-times-a-week political columns. In 1975, for example, Bill Buckley switched from six to three columns a week.

Several hundred foreign press correspondents are stationed in New York and Washington, and American columnists are extremely influential with this group, which in turn affects the attitudes of foreigners toward Americans and the relationship of foreign governments to the United States. Most newspapers rotate their correspondents every few years and a newcomer to the U.S. often looks to James Reston's columns, for example, for guidance about trends in American politics.

Many foreign correspondents are overwhelmed by the task of trying to cover an entire country, or are lazy, or don't understand English too well, or don't fathom American customs, or, for various other reasons, rely heavily on a few Washington columnists. Perhaps their colleagues or predecessors have told them that Joseph Kraft is perceptive, or that Marquis Childs is in tune with their readers back home, or that they can copy or rewrite Mary McGrory and their editors will never know it, or that Evans and Novak are astute trend spotters. Regardless of their motivations, the fact is that the foreign press corps in the U.S.

carefully read American columns.

Evans and Novak, Marquis Childs and other columnists who are highly respected by their journalistic colleagues often have their greatest effect in terms of stimulating their subscribing newspapers to query the wire services or their own Washington bureaus for follow-ups on items originated by these columnists. This snowball effect has resulted in changes in votes, investigations and other effects in Congress and elsewhere.

Many columnists are forever hustling and extolling their accomplishments to readers, and more important, to current and potential publishers. Walter Winchell and Drew Pearson were the most blatant in reminding readers of their exclusives and, of course, were the first to point out predictions which had become reality. Even the somber Walter Lippmann often repeated earlier appraisals and predictions in order to emphasize his trend-spotting skills. This recycling of columns, as practiced most artistically by Joseph Alsop and Joseph Kraft, also helps to fill space during vacations and slow news periods.

There's nothing wrong in doing this, and those columnists who thrive on extolling their scoops and pointing out errors made by their colleagues, produce a zesty competitiveness which has a useful press-watchdog effect. An example is Jack Anderson, the loner maverick who, for example, pointed out that the glowing reports of the Greek government written in 1972 by James Kilpatrick, Ralph de Toledano and other conservative columnists emanated from a red carpet junket financed by the Hellenic Industrial Development Bank.

Press junkets are common among travel, entertainment and other writers, but they do present problems, particularly for political columnists. The Associated Press, The New York Times, The Wall Street Journal, Time and a few other publications ban free trips, but the syndicates rarely intervene in this aspect of their columnists' work, and, in general, have rather loose controls because the columnists often are the equivalent of free lancers, rather than employees.

One newspaper which made an attempt to monitor columnists was the New York Star, a liberal tabloid published by Bartley Crum, which made a very brief twinkle on the New York newspaper scene during the six months that it was published. From June 23, 1948, to January 28, 1949, a dime bought such comics as Pogo and Barnaby along with columnists Albert Deutsch (science), John S. Wilson ("New York, N.Y."), Tom Meany (sports), John Horn (radio-TV), Leonard Feather (music), Heywood Hale Broun, I.F. Stone, and, appearing adjacent, Max Lerner and Wax Werner.

The Star assumed that its readers read one or more other New York papers, and since the carping of columnists with each other was in vogue, Tim Taylor set out to review the columns in a column titled "SO They Said." Using the protection of a pseudonym, Frank Columbine, free-lancer Taylor studied three dozen columns daily at his home in Stamford, Connecticut, and then attempted to put the record straight.

For example, in his Star column of Monday, December 6, 1948, Columbine spotted a Dorothy Kilgallen item in the Journal-American of the previous week about Lya De Putti, who is "trying to get her daughter (also an actress) over to this country from Hungary." Columbine noted that Lya De Putti died in 1931.

Columbine found faults among almost all of the columnists, though he also gave credit for scoops. It was a near-impossible task, since the New York columnists in 1948 included Lucius Beebe, John Crosby and Mark Sullivan in the Herald Tribune, David Lawrence and H.I. Phillips in the Sun, Bugs Baer, Bob Considine, Frank Conniff, Bill Corum, Leslie Gould, Dorothy Kilgallen and Cholly Knickerbocker in the Journal-American, Danton Walker and Ed Sullivan in the News, George Dixon, Dan Parker, Victor Riesel and Walter Winchell in the Mirror, plus Dr. Frank Kingdom, Louis Sobol, Drew Pearson, Elsa Maxwell, Earl Wilson, Marquis Childs, Leonard Lyons and on and on.

Kilgallen was a favorite target. Columbine noted that she loved items about the illnesses of celebrities and she set some sort of record when, during the first week of January, 1949, she used 14 items about the medical problems of various prominent people, ranging from "seriously ailing" to "battling the flu."

Columbine also corrected Danton Walker of the News, who had asked "Has Stanton Griffis, Ambassador to Egypt, purchased the Brentano bookstores?"

"The answer is yes," wrote Columbine, "Ambassador Griffis did purchase the book chain—about 14 years ago."

The Truman upset victory over Dewey in the 1948 election embarrassed lots of columnists, as gleefully noted by Columbine. George E. Sokolsky in the Sun had been disgusted by Truman's campaign tactics and had nominated Emily Post as election campaign czar. Paul Gallico in the Journal-American had said it would be a joke if Truman won. The Post's George Fielding Eliot analyzed the Truman voters and said that they were endorsing Secretary of Defense James Forrestal, but Sokolsky, Joseph and Stewart Alsop in the Herald Tribune and others predicted that Forestal was on the way out. Westbrook Pegler concluded, "The people have made ghastly mistakes before. The people have booted another one."

But Samuel Grafton, on the same day, said that "the people have not lost confidence in themselves."

The Star was the only New York newspaper which supported Truman. The Post came close but equivocated. Editor Ted Thackerey supported Henry Wallace and his wife, and boss, Publisher Dorothy Schiff, wrote a last minute endorsement of Truman. A few years later,

Thackerey lost both his job and marriage.

The 1948 post-election mortems provided significant insights into the pontifications of political columnists. Walter Lippmann had been a New Dealer but in the summer of '48 he advised the Democrats that they couldn't win and should aim "to survive as the national party of opposition, to be critical, vigilant, but good-humored about the return of the Republicans and the rise of Dewey."

After Dewey and others woke up to find that Truman had won, a stunned Lippmann meditated a day and then wrote that "there was never any doubt that in this political generation there are more Democrats than Republicans." Sokolsky remained a sore loser and columned that Truman's "speeches were in bad taste and if they won him votes, it can only mean that good manners are not of our times."

David Lawrence somewhat illogically suggested that Truman "should thank the pollsters—and also those members of the Un-American Activities Committee who made Communism and the Wallace cause so unpopular as to drive almost all the Wallace vote back into the Democratic Party from which it had strayed."

The death of a prominent person is somewhat of a windfall to the student of newspaper columns, as dozens of byliners simultaneously rush into print with their postmortems.

Within hours after J. Edgar Hoover died on May 1, 1972, Leonard Lyons had yanked a collection of anecdotes and personal reminiscences from his files and turned in a 800-word column which predictably opened, "I first met John Edgar Hoover during the Hauptmann trial in New Jersey in the '30s. I saw him last at the Banshee luncheon last week."

Bob Considine had been master of ceremonies at the Banshee luncheon for newspaper publishers and he and others noted that Walter Winchell had printed more items about G-man Hoover than anyone else.

Just a few days before Hoover died, Jack Anderson nastily related the delight which Lyndon B. Johnson had taken in reading the FBI confidential reports on the sexual and other personal details of prominent individuals. The Anderson obituary opened with homage ("J. Edgar Hoover died, as he would have wished, in harness"), devoted a few paragraphs to the accomplishments of the FBI under the 48-year reign of Hoover, and then got rolling with, "But we would be hypocritical if we didn't also make note of the FBI's excesses under Hoover."

Harriet Van Horne was less polite with this opening, "To many admirers of John Edgar Hoover, his tragedy was that he did not die before his shield was tarnished and his laurels withered." Van Horne followed with such jabs as "It's safe to say that there will be no drearier reading in the next decade than his collected speeches and letters . . . Over his private life, let us draw a veil." She then went on to sympathetically discuss Angela Davis.

Evans and Novak were not concerned with looking backward, but rather in impassionately analyzing the future role of the FBI and accusing Hoover's successor, succinctly calling acting director L. Patrick Gray, III, "competent and colorless."

The end of the Vietnam war was the occasion for analytic looks backward and forward by every political columnist. Most, particularly those who had been critical of the war, remained gloomy. Reston predicted social turmoil resulting from the President's "indifference and paternalism toward the black and the very poor." Anderson predictably foresaw "a national revulsion at too much corruption." Joe Kraft was cheerier about the self-confidence of the country and zeroed in on income distribution as the major domestic problem, as did Robert Novak, who charged that the Administration was ignoring the problems of international competition and the economy.

James Keogh, who was a Nixon assistant, claimed that most columnists were unfair in their massive distortions of facts about Richard Nixon and Spiro Agnew. In a 1972 book, "President Nixon and the Press," Keogh stated, "As commentators, they had an unchallengeable right to express their opinions. But what responsibility did they bear for being certain that the 'facts' on which they based their comments were accurate? Whatever the professional answer to that question, columnists often compromised truth and enhanced myth by rather casually making a statement as fact when it was far from fact and then constructing a major point or even a whole column on it. Here, again, the key to distortion and error frequently was the prevailing point of view in the fraternity of journalists," wrote Keogh.

"Mr. Nixon is the first President in political memory who can't be caricatured," wrote San Francisco Chronicle columnist Art Hoppe in his book, "Mr. Nixon And My Other Problems."

"Roosevelt, Truman, Eisenhower, Kennedy and Johnson were easy. Each had a human quality you could lovingly exploit—flamboyance, temper, fatherliness, elan, or folksiness. Some, like Mr. Kennedy, wanted to be admired. Some, like Mr. Johnson, wanted to be loved. But Mr. Nixon, it seems to me, wants, above all, to be respected. For twenty-five years, the press has kicked him around. Now he's on top. He wants, above all, the respect he feels he has rightfully earned . . . "

James Reston seriously disagreed with Keogh. Speaking at the April, 1972, meeting of the American Society of Newspaper Editors, Reston said that, "never, since before the last world war, not even in Lyndon Johnson's time, have I seen a trickier Administration than this one.

"Overwhelmed by their problems, they have sought to deal with the consequences of their failures by adopting all the techniques of

70

commercial advertising and by trying to manipulate, or intimidate, or discredit their critics," said Reston.

Referring to columnist Jack Anderson and Neil Sheehan of The New York Times, Reston said, "The trouble is not that we have too many Andersons and Sheehans, but that we have too few of them."

Journalists have a tough job, continued Reston, to attempt to give a true account of what goes on in Washington, either overtly or covertly, and dispel the doubts and distrusts that seethe in the public mind. Reston, ever the optimist, expressed confidence that the skeptical veterans of the Washington press corps, and the ambitious new-comers, could do the job.

Speaking at the same convention, ex-missionary Jack Anderson dramatically boomed that the First Amendment to the Constitution gives journalists "the right and the duty" to pry into government secrets in order to inform what bureaucrats are doing without being intimidated by threats of censorship or prosecution.

A few days later, Anderson testified at a House of Representatives Subcommittee on Government Information and urged passage of a law to require the automatic declassification of Government documents that are two years old.

At the same time, Jim Bishop columned that, "Nixon's greatest mistake, in my opinion, was to retreat into secrecy. This forced the well-paid White House reporters and columnists to speculate—not on what was news, but on what might happen. The so-called background story often drove Nixon, Keogh, Herb Klein and Ron Ziegler up a wall.

"A good percentage of the press has been fair—indeed biased— toward the President. Agnew has never acknowledged this," stated Bishop.

Every President has his friends and foes among the columnists. Abraham Lincoln read Artemus Ward and Theodore Roosevelt enjoyed "Mr. Dooley."

Herbert Hoover in private was alleged to be warm, witty and forceful, but this was not conveyed in his somber public presentations and his relationship with the press was pedestrian and uncongenial. One of his fans was New York Timesman Arthur Krock, who, in his "Memoirs," lauded Hoover's "contributions to the relief of the miseries of mankind that were greater and more durable than any in his time" and called him "a great American, a great citizen of the world."

Franklin D. Roosevelt closely followed the news, developed the press conference and Fireside Chat radio broadcasts as part of his dual desire to manage the news and inform the public, and granted important exclusive interviews with Arthur Krock, Walter Lippmann and other columnists whose views he regarded. He also enjoyed trading jokes with Walter Winchell and occasionally fed him items, and corresponded with Arthur Brisbane, Raymond Clapper, Robert S. Allen, Heywood Broun, Franklin P. Adams and others.

Harry Truman was explosive in his views of Drew Pearson, thin-skinned with regard to critics of his daughter (particularly with regard to her musical ability), but generally was more relaxed with regard to the press than his predecessor.

Eisenhower was even less of a student of the press and was indifferent toward most columnists.

The Kennedy era was the golden age of the Washington press. Renowned for his phenomenal 1200-word-a-minute reading speed, John F. Kennedy scanned several newspapers every day and followed the leading columnists more avidly than any other President. He assiduously cultivated all segments of the press and enjoyed a social relationship with several columnists.

FDR had been a reporter on the Harvard Crimson and Kennedy had been a sporadic newspaperman and author of two books, "Profiles in Courage" and "Why England Slept," which was an expansion of his Harvard senior thesis. The columnists read most carefully by President Kennedy were said to be Joseph Alsop, Walter Lippmann and James Reston. Joseph Kraft had been a speech writer of Kennedy's during the 1960 campaign, but Kraft didn't start columning until 1963.

Jacqueline Bouvier had been an inquiring photographer at the Washington Times-Herald and she too became a close student of the press, though with less intensity than her husband. One of her favorite columnists was Igor Cassini, the Hearstman who wrote as Cholly Knickerbocker. His brother, Oleg, was one of Mrs. Kennedy's couturiers.

Lyndon B. Johnson's early courtship of the press floundered amidst charges of news management and he became increasingly abrasive as he failed in his heavy-handed attempts to cajole favorable treatment. During his first year as President, Johnson granted long, relaxed private interviews to James Reston and Walter Lippmann, and courteously solicited their advice, but the Bobby Baker case and other press exposés, and the shifting of opinion on the conduct of the Vietnam war, soured the relationship, and most columnists became extremely hostile.

Washington columnists generally assume an adversary relationship with the President and his administration, with the notable exceptions of the honeymoon periods when Franklin D. Roosevelt and John F. Kennedy assumed office. The liberals generally outnumber the conservatives among the columnists, for a variety of reasons. Among the old-timers, a factor may be a regard for the New Deal and its support of the labor movement, including the Newspaper Guild. Among others, a factor may be the attraction of political analysts to leaders in the academic and arts communities, many of whom are vocal liberals and radicals. Still another factor is the traditional affection of journalists for the poor, handicapped, minority groups and other underdogs. Though the Republicans have made major advances in welfare reform and other support of neglected groups, the Democrats are more likely to be associated by journalists with progressiveness in these areas.

In a 1977 column, Michael Novak speculated that the "40-year phase (of liberal columnists) has exhausted itself." Though James Kilpatrick, William Buckley and other conservative columnists indeed are popular, Mr. Novak's generalization is not accurate.

Columnist Eleanor Roosevelt once wrote, "The only hope for a really free press is for the public to recognize that the press should not express the point of view of the owners and the writers, but be factual; whereas the editorials must express the opinions of owners and writers."

A trend in the "new journalism" is for newspaper reporters to include interpretive comment, so that it's sometimes hard to distinguish between "straight news" and columns.

Feature writing may improve the readability of a newspaper, and since most people increasingly get "hard news" from radio and television, a major function of today's newspaper is to provide background information and commentary.

However, the diminished number and variety of newspapers has weakened the influence of this medium. A few decades ago, a person could read a daily diversity of opinion expressed by the editorials and columnists of several newspapers, and then make up his own mind. Today, it's a rare individual who reads more than one newspaper on a regular basis.

A smattering of the diversity of political ideas expressed by columnists is provided by a few newspapers, such as the St. Petersburg Times, which publish one paragraph excerpts from the columns of William F. Buckley, Evans and Novak, and others on their editorial pages.

For more than 100 years, newspaper syndicates have contributed to the standardization of the American press. At first, this was an enormously valuable boost to publishers, particularly in small cities. News, information. literature and entertainment were brought to millions of Americans, at fantastically low cost, via newspaper syndicates.

The pendulum then shifted to the negative, and the surfeit of syndicated columns weakened editorial initiative by reducing local news and features.

Today's newspaper syndicates are as important and influential as ever, and greater in quantity and diversity than their predecessors.

Their responsibility to newspaper readers is enormous.

In a survey such as this, it is impossible to single out the most widely read or most influential newspaper column.

Jack Anderson's record of scoops and their impact certainly comes to mind, along with other Washington Post byliners, as well as The New York Times roster of columnists. On the lighter side, in 1976, "Suzy" was the only reporter at the Palm Springs wedding of Frank Sinatra and Barbara Marx.

For many millions of readers, the most surprising and memorable column in recent years was the "sad and personal message" written in 1975 by Mrs. Jules Lederer. It started, "In my 20 years as Ann Landers *this* is the most difficult column I have ever tried to put together."

And then came the announcement "that after 36 years of marriage, Jules and I are being divorced."

The column was a journalistic first in that it ended with a request from Ann Landers to editors to leave a blank space "as a memorial to one of the world's best marriages that didn't make it to the finish line."

The column, with a blank space, appeared in the New York Daily News and hundreds of other newspapers on July 2. But the wire services picked up the news as soon as the column was mailed, and New York's other morning newspaper, the Times, thus scooped the News, on July 1, with a three-column headline, Ann Landers Is Being Divorced.

In 1978, the Washingtonian magazine reported a new survey of the Washington press corps. This time, the surveyors were graduate students at American University who asked members of the press corps to rate their colleagues. As with the other surveys, David Broder was described as most respected. The other ratings may be more debatable. Least respected: Evans and Novak. Most overrated: James Reston. Most pretentious: Joseph Kraft. Most thoughtful: Patrick Buchanan and Tom Wicker.

It's easy to quibble with surveys of this kind. Any columnist who has been writing as long as Reston is likely to lack freshness or be out of touch on some days. Kraft still is looked upon as the ambitious successor to Walter Lippmann, and this is annoying to some competitors.

Thomas Griffith commented on the survey in his Newswatch column in Time magazine of July 10, 1978. Under the apt headline, "Trying to Be Wise Three Times a Week," Griffith agreed that there has been a decline of the Washington columnist and described his own survey of newspaper editors around the country. He noted that Michael Gartner, editor of the Des Moines Register, subscribes to many syndicates and pays only $25 a week for Kraft and $20 each for Broder, Will and McGrory. At these prices, the Register, and other newspapers, can afford not to run every column which they receive, or merely to print excerpts.

Griffith concluded with a comment by Clayton Kirkpatrick, editor of the Chicago Tribune, "The Washington column is more complex, the issues are more varied. Mark Sullivan used to write fundamentally about politics, but that was before politics became so embedded in science, in economics, in sociology."

76

FAMILY COLUMNISTS

It used to be called the Women's Page. Now it's called Style, Neighbors, Lifestyle, Family, Weekend or various other names. More important than the name change is the increased size. Many major newspapers, such as The New York Times, Chicago Tribune and Washington Post, have daily separate sections, with more articles than ever before on food, fashion and lots of consumer advice, including a variety of old and new syndicated columns.

Among the small-circulation daily newspapers, most women's pages still are a collection of local society items, commercial news releases, and syndicated columns of a more traditional nature. The country's top nonpolitical columnists, such as Erma Bombeck, Jeane Dixon, Heloise, Ann Landers and Abby, generally have more female than male readers, but are not always "relegated" to the women's section.

In 1970, Russell Baker opened his New York Times column with this comment:

"One field in which the oppression of women has been healthy for the common good is the newspaper column. Here the rule that a woman must be at least twice as good as a competing man to get the job they both want has spared the reading public at least a modicum of twaddle.

"The rare woman who succeeds to a newspaper column is so extraordinarily good that, unlike her male competitor who prospers on smaller ability, she never seems obliged on days when her brain is marking time to fill space with material about her pets, her family or her household."

Newspaper publishers thrive on department store, supermarket and other retail advertising aimed mainly at women. They are reluctant to tamper with the women's interest columns, particularly those which use them as convenient space-fillers between the ads. It's not the sexual demographics which bother publishers, but it's the ages of their readers which give many of them nightmares.

A key aspect of these "family columns" is reader involvement and response, and the most common format is based on letters.

The syndicates claim that the published letters are authentic and are from readers. That generally is true, but many columnists often make up letters as lead-ins to topics which they want to discuss, and a very common procedure is to edit letters for brevity, clarity and improved grammar.

Whether the mail counts issued by syndicates are accurate (they probably are exaggerated), and regardless of the ethics of using fictionalized letters, no one can dispute the enormous circulation of such advice columnists as Abby, Ann Landers and Elizabeth Post. They surely influence many people, perhaps less so now than with earlier generations of readers, and they most certainly have a high fascination and entertainment value, as attested by numerous readership surveys.

The advice column is one of the oldest types of newspaper feature, and several women advisors have made journalism history.

Large numbers of women entered the newspaper field in the 1880's and two of the most prominent were "stunt reporters." Elizabeth Cochran, as Nellie Bly, circled the world in a race conducted in 1889 by the New York World and "Dorothy Dare" rode in a horseless carriage in 1896, for the same newspaper.

Publishers (almost all were male chauvinists) generally felt that women writers were not as likely to remain on their staffs as men, and therefore set up "house names." Mrs. Marie Manning Gorsch, a plump matron who had come from Fairfax County in northern Virginia, was the first advice columnist. As "Beatrice Fairfax," her column first appeared around 1900 in the New York Journal, and was immensely popular in the 1920's. The column was continued by several writers, notably Mrs. Marion Clyde McCarroll Booth, who wrote it for 21 years, from 1945 (when Mrs. Gorsch died) to 1966. Earlier in her career, in the 1920's, Miss McCarroll had written "Women in Business," a column in The Commercial, a New York City business daily. Miss McCarroll, who died in 1977, at the age of 84, was outshadowed for many years by another Hearst advisor, Dorothy Dix.

The Dorothy Dix column, titled "Advice to the Lovelorn," appeared in about 300 newspapers in the thirties. The first Dorothy Dix was Elizabeth Meriwether Gilmer, who started as a news reporter in 1896 for the New Orleans Picayune. Her husband, George, was the brother of her stepmother. They were childless, had various marital problems and George O. Gilmer became mentally ill. He died in a sanatorium in

1929, and during the peak of her career the widow provided cheerful practical advice to young women, including a 1939 book, "How to Win and Hold a Husband."

Dorothy Dix' syndicate history was more cheerful. Her first column in the Picayune was a sermonette titled "Sunday Salad," for which she was paid $5 a week. In 1901, Mrs. Gilmer moved to the New York Journal, where she covered a succession of murder trials and other sensational news events, while writing the three times a week column, "Dorothy Dix Talks."

In 1917, John Wheeler lured her with the offer to write a daily column, with no more gore. Not feeling able to produce a daily essay, she decided to publish some of the reader mail. The format clicked, and she switched to the Philadelphia Ledger Syndicate.

When Elizabeth Gilmer died in 1951, the Dorothy Dix column was continued by Muriel Nissen for the Bell Syndicate, and, in 1959, she was succeeded by Helen Worden Erskine. A former New York World-Telegram reporter, she was married to William H.H. Cranner, a wealthy Utah mining executive, and she commuted between her Utah home and New York apartment. She tried hard, and for a while revitalized the column, but it simply was no match for Abby and Ann Landers.

When psychologist Joyce Brothers achieved fame as a TV quiz show contestant, Bell-McClure dropped Beatrice Fairfax and promoted Dr. Brothers as a new type of advice columnist, one with professional qualifications.

Another pioneer advisor to the lovelorn was "Doris Blake," who wrote "Speaking of Love" in the New York News. The Chicago Tribune-New York News syndicated it for more than 30 years under various names such as "Heart to Heart Talks." The identity of the various authors was highly secretive, but the writer who held the position for the longest tenure was Antoinette Donnelly, who was beauty editor of the News.

Of course, women news reporters have not had to use pseudonyms and several have achieved fame as political and general columnists without name changes. For example, Peggy Hall (Mrs. Harvey Deuel) of Cleveland covered the First World War for the Newspaper Enterprise Association and the Second World War for the American Newspaper Alliance. The first woman columnist on The New York Times was Anne O'Hare McCormick, who covered the European scene from 1937 until her death in 1954.

Dorothy Roe (Mrs. John B. Lewis) of Rowayton, Connecticut, started as a newspaper reporter in 1925, and became known to millions of readers for over 30 years, first as women's editor of the Associated Press, from 1941 to 1960, and then for a decade as author of "Women Now," a daily column syndicated by the Chicago Tribune-New York

News.

Mary Haworth, whose practical advice was syndicated by King Features for 30 years (starting in 1944), wrote with a straightforward frankness and without any jibes and "asides." "Mary Haworth's Mail" appeared in only about 25 newspapers, but one of them was the prestigious Washington Post, where she worked.

A typical letter to Miss Haworth included this common problem: "Guy had said he loved me very much. But when I mentioned pregnancy, his love died instantly."

Born in Ohio, Mary Haworth Reardon (she subsequently divorced and used her maiden name) attended college briefly in Ohio before moving to Washington. (It appears that more columnists were born in Ohio than any other state—James Reston, Earl Wilson, Phyllis Battelle, and many others.)

Another type of advice column which generated a great deal of reader mail was handwriting analysis. The undisputed pioneer was Muriel Stafford, whose column was syndicated by Bell, Los Angeles Times, the New York Herald Tribune, and then, finally, by herself, from her home in Fort Lauderdale. In New York, the column variously appeared in the Journal-American, World-Telegram and Sun, Mirror and Herald Tribune. More than two million readers sent in their handwriting to be analyzed for "personality, character, emotional nature, temperament and abilities." In addition to a stamped, self-addressed envelope, and a note penned on unlined paper, the writer enclosed a fee, which ranged up to the dollar charged by the Journal-American in 1964.

In spite of the income, which was split with Miss Stafford, most publishers remained wary of the column, "Cissy Patterson had turned me down, through her editors," noted Miss Stafford, "but started my column in the Washington Times-Herald the following Monday when I managed to reach her and analyze her writing."

Other subscribers included the Detroit News, Buffalo News, Toronto Globe and Mail, Baltimore News-Post, Miami News, Indianapolis Star, Newark Evening News, Columbus Dispatch, Louisville Courier-Journal, as well as series in Parade and Look.

A typical column was the 1964 analysis of Doris Day, "whose handwriting shows a very gifted and emotionally restrained personality . . . Originality and independence of thought and action are pronounced in Doris' writing. Her capitals are high, unique, and gracefully curved. The small letter "i," when given attention, is an expression of the writer's ego image, just as the capital "I" is . . . You are both charming and discreet if you write like Doris Day."

Among the voluminous collection of famous names whose handwriting she analyzed, Miss Stafford cited the Duchess of Windsor as the most memorable.

As for her analysis of this author's handwriting, here it is, complete and verbatim:

"Richard Weiner

"Your handwriting reveals an unusually gifted mind. Those who write as you do are usually engaged in some creative field such as music, invention, drama, some form of art work, or as an "idea man." Many of the successful people in the arts write as you do.

"Unless you have some suitable outlet for your gifts you become restless and moody and may be inclined to do nothing but use your imagination to tell fantastic tales.

"You have a deep self-reliance. You dislike to have to do anything according to a set pattern and generally find a way of your own that is quicker, better and more efficient. When interested, you have much initiative. When bored, you become restless and impatient.

"Too much restriction arouses inward rebellion. You are individualistic and so often far ahead of others in your thinking that you frequently have a feeling of loneliness. Seek congenial companionship of your own caliber.

"Your individualism can cause you to seem egotistical to some but you know exactly how to charm them when you wish. You have an intuitive feeling for the right word at the right time and can almost read minds. Your hunches are so accurate they are almost frightening. You are better off when you act upon them without discussion because others cannot always see the possibilities that you envision.

"You should not be tied too closely to routine. Given the chance to use your gifts you can achieve unusual success."

Thank you, Miss Stafford!

The longest running advice column was started by Emily Post. Born in Baltimore in 1873 as Emily Price, Mrs. Post became the world's authority on standards of dress, manners and speech. Her book, "Etiquette," was first published in 1922 and successive editions have kept it up-to-date as it both influenced life styles and, in turn, was influenced by changing mores. Mrs. Post also achieved fame as a novelist, basing many of her themes on the contrasts between European and American social ideas, and as an authority on interior decorating. Her book, "The Personality of a House," had many revised editions since its first publication in 1930. When Emily Post died in 1960, her name had become a household phrase, but few were aware of the colorful details of her life. Her first book, a novel, was "The Flight of a Moth," published in 1904, and one of her important books was "Children Are People and Ideal Parents Are Companions."

A tall beautiful socialite, she was the only child of Bruce Price, who was the architect of most of the posh homes in Tuxedo Park, New York. She married Edwin Main Post, a banker, and they lived in an apartment on East 79th Street in Manhattan. She divorced him, a bold act at the time, especially in New York State where the only grounds were adultery.

Mrs. Post's two sons, Edwin Jr. and Bruce, both went to Harvard. Bruce, who became an architect, died in 1927.

In the thirties. Emily Post did a daily network radio program, in addition to the daily column, which appeared in about 150 newspapers. The advice and writing style were prim and proper. In person, she was a nonsmoker and teetotaler, but did allow herself such conversational words as damn, godawful and lousy.

Following the death of Emily Post at the age of 86 in 1960, the column, what had started in 1930, was managed by her son, Edwin. In 1965, when he retired to live in Italy, Funk and Wagnalls asked Elizabeth L. Post, wife of Emily's grandson, to edit the 11th revised edition of "The Blue Book of Social Usage," and in 1966, she took over the column, then syndicated by Newsday and now distributed six times a week by the Chicago Tribune-New York News.

Elizabeth Post's philosophy is that etiquette is neither strait jacket, nor a relic of Victorian manners, but rather a realistic code of conduct which makes relations with others as pleasant as possible.

In the original book, guidelines were suggested on how to refuse a cocktail gracefully without hurting the host's feelings. In the recent versions, socially acceptable methods are outlined for dealing with the delicate problem of speeding the departure of a cocktail party guest who is unaware that the party is over.

The prolific etiquetist was born in Englewood, New Jersey, and attended a socially correct boarding school, the Masters School in Dobbs Ferry, New York, from which she graduated cum laude. Her first husband, George E. Cookman, died in naval action in 1943. The widow and her two-month-old son, Allen, moved to Washington and worked in the Navy Department where she met and married William Goadby Post.

After the war, the Posts lived for six years in Bogota, Columbia, where they had four servants to help the family, which included daughter Cindy and three sons, Allen, Bill and Peter.

The children have grown up and no longer live at home, which is in Rye, New York, in the winter and Martha's Vineyard in the summer. The Posts are avid sailors and Elizabeth is a long-time artist, tending toward impressionistic landscapes.

Informality may have completely submerged most of the bygone etiquette rituals but Elizabeth Post believes that the mark of the educated and well bred individual is still perfect manners but without appearing to be "stiff." However, perfect etiquette is a cooperative endeavor. It is essential to let those about you feel that they are equally well-mannered.

She believes the keys to achieving compatible relationships are consideration and unselfishness; two basic requisites for establishing human friendship and understanding.

Readers' questions have become more involved with personal relations between people rather than strictly queries about manners. The majority ask about weddings. This is the one time in a woman's life when she wants everything to be right, says Elizabeth Post.

The column, now in fewer than 100 newspapers, still generates considerable mail, which is sent to The Emily Post Institute located at 120 East 36th Street, New York 10016. The postal meter slogan is "Courtesy is contagious—let's start an epidemic."

The symptoms of the epidemic have changed considerably since the reign of Emily Post, and one major arbiter, and benefactor, has been Mrs. William or Ms. Elizabeth Post.

For many years, the only other columnist authority on etiquette and "gracious living" was Amy Vanderbilt. Her books and articles made her name a household word, though she never quite achieved the autocratic position of her archrival, Emily Post. Amy Vanderbilt said that Emily Post "told people how to behave," whereas her role as a journalist was to "tell how the best people are usually behaving."

Born in Staten Island (which in 1908 was the rural part of New York City), Amy Vanderbilt's genealogy went back to the Revolutionary War. The first Vanderbilt in America was Jan Aoersten van der Bilt. Amy's parents were Joseph and Mary Vanderbilt. Not a college graduate, Amy Vanderbilt attended a girl's school in Brooklyn and a boarding school in Switzerland, and took journalism courses at New York University for two years.

She started her newspaper career at the Staten Island Advance in 1927, worked as a publicist and advertising agency executive for four years and joined International News Service in 1933. She then was a consultant to many companies and organizations, hosted a TV program called "It's Good Taste," and, in 1963, started a monthly series of publications called "Amy Vanderbilt's Success Program for Women." Her column appeared in McCall's, This Week, Better Homes and Gardens, and, from 1965 to 1975, in Ladies' Home Journal. A top author at Doubleday, her first book, "Amy Vanderbilt's Complete Book of Etiquette," was published in 1952. Others include "Amy Vanderbilt's Everyday Etiquette" and "Amy Vanderbilt's Complete Cookbook."

Her list of husbands was equally impressive.

First was Robert S. Brinkerhoff in 1929.

Second was Morton C. Clark in 1935. They had a son, Lincoln.

Third was Hans Knopf in 1945. They had two sons, Paul and Stephen, and lived in Westport, Connecticut.

Fourth was Curtis B. Keller in 1968. Amy and Curtis Keller lived for many years at 438 East 87th Street, New York, and were active in international society.

Amy Vanderbilt was far from extravagant, however. In the April 3, 1972, issue of Moneysworth, she revealed that she soaked off and reused stamps, made soap out of the outside leaves of lettuce, and gave this hint:

"When my lipsticks get down to the last one-eighth inch, I dig out the residue with an orange stick and put it into a little porcelain patch box I obtained from the great porcelain works of Viste Alegre in Portugal. The eventually makes an interesting mix, which I then apply with the help of a lipstick brush."

(Another good-to-the-last-speck user of lipstick is Ann Landers, who uses a hairpin to scoop it out.)

United Features syndicated Amy Vanderbilt's advice from 1954 to 1968. The daily column then was syndicated by the Los Angeles Times and appeared in about 150 newspapers, including The Los Angeles Times, Long Island Press, Newark Star-Ledger, and Providence Journal. A sample, from her column of January 28, 1972:

"Question: What is the correct etiquette in the wearing of gloves to public functions—church, theater and so on? Should they be kept on at all times or not?—Mrs. G.J., Buffalo, N.Y.

"Answer: Today, because it is more practical and comfortable, gloves are frequently removed in church, at the theater and even at balls for dancing. In fact, at many big functions, long evening gloves are checked with coats. They are difficult to manage during the evening, are lost or soiled from falling on the floor and almost nobody wears gloves for dancing any more. They are removed at the theater and always before eating, drinking or smoking."

As might be expected, the column often offered advice which is more prim and formal than Amy Vanderbilt was in person. In June, 1972, she told Life magazine that she believed in "Keeping up with what is actually happening in society."

"Let's face it," said Miss Vanderbilt, "there are virtually no virgins left and I think it all right for a couple in love to live together."

It would have shocked Emily Post, Dorothy Dix, Beatrice Fairfax, Doris Black, and all of Amy Vanderbilt's ancestors.

In 1974, at the age of 66, Amy Vanderbilt jumped or fell to her death.

The Los Angeles Times Syndicate column has been continued, under the title, "Contemporary Living," by Letitia ("Tish") Baldrige, former social secretary to Jacqueline Kennedy, who operates a public relations agency in New York.

For many years, a touch of intellectual class was added to the advice column genre by Mortimer J. Adler. The weekly column, syndicated by Publishers-Hall, was called, "Great Ideas From the Great Books." A typical column started this way:

"Dear Dr. Adler:

"One of man's problems is the preservation of his environment if he is to live. Was this a problem in the past? What did the great thinkers say on this matter?"

Dr. Adler's answer was a deft blend of history and contemporary philosophy, based on his experience as the primary developer of the Great Books movement.

Born in New York in 1902, Mortimer Jerome Adler received a Ph.D. degree in psychology from Columbia University in 1928. Though he was awarded a Phi Beta Kappa key, Dr. Adler never received a bachelor's degree—he refused to take the required swimming test. He taught at Columbia, and in 1929, started his movement westward. For 23 years, he was an educational rebel at the University of Chicago, where he helped President Robert Maynard Hutchins in a curriculum reorganization which greatly added to the intellectual luster of the institution. During this period, Drs. Adler and Hutchins helped to develop the "Great Books of the Western World," which was introduced in 1945. In 1952, he resigned as professor of philosophy of law at the University of Chicago and established the Institute of Philosophical Research in San Francisco.

The author of many books on religion, history and philosophy, Dr. Adler's first book, "Dialectic," was published in 1927. His first popular book, "How to Read a Book," was published in 1940, followed in 1944 with "How to Think About War and Peace." In 1958, he co-authored with Milton Mayer, "The Capitalist Manifesto," which established his fame as a popular philosopher.

The more typical advice column is the one which provides answers to questions about beauty, fashion, decorating, food and other subjects which are considered to be of primary interest to women. For many years, one of the most popular columns of this type was unusual in its focus on young women. The ahead-of-its-time column, Youth Parade, was authored by Reba (she's the brunette) and Bonnie (she's blonde) Churchill, beautiful, blue-eyed, look-alike sisters whose motto was "Two heads are better than one." Their 200-word weekly illustrated column concentrated on beauty tips and self-improvement ideas. It was distributed by the National Newspaper Syndicate to about 285 newspapers.

Readers obtained a variety of self-help booklets, including tips on art, diet, fashion, hobbies, literature, music and vocabulary. "We tell the reader how to be attractive," said Reba, "but not how to catch a mate or how to be sexy—we never use that word."

Reba, born in 1933, and Bonnie, born in 1936, are the daughters of a beauty columnist. While still in high school in Los Angeles, the Churchill sisters started interviewing movie stars for several local weeklies. They did not drink or smoke, and believed in hard work and good grooming. Bonnie started in college when she was 15 and the two sisters were honor students at the University of California at Los Angeles. They co-authored over a thousand magazine and Sunday supplement articles and a book, "Reba and Bonnie's Guide to Glamour and Personality." In the sixties, they received over 10,000 letters a week.

Other columns in the sixties for young women were written by Jean Adams (Teen Forum, United Features), Ele and Walt Dulaney (Teen Age Dateline, Bell-McClure), Ellen Peck (The Column, Chicago Tribune-New York News), Elizabeth Weiner (Youth Enterprises Syndicate) and Elinor (Ellie) and David J. Lavin (Teenage Corner).

One of the youngest columnists was Steven Levine of the Denver Post, who started writing the weekly commentary, "Speaking Out," for the Register and Tribune Syndicate in 1969, when he was 17 years old. He was recruited by Allan Priaulx, managing editor of the syndicate, who at that time was 29.

Of all the youth columns, the Nancy Gilbert page had the largest circulation. It was sent by mail in the sixties to more than 1000 Associated Press subscribers and emanated from a New York company, Gilbert Youth Research. A competing company, Greenwich Research Center, also produced a column, College Poll, which was based on surveys of 1000 students on 200 campuses. Formed in 1968 by attorney George F. Foley, the company was operated by his sons, Robert and James, and the column was edited by Bill Papp, who formerly worked for Dr. George Gallup.

In 1970, National Newspaper Syndicate started "Over and Under Thirty," a weekly column by John L. Sinn, in which the views of the author (then in his mid-50's) were commented on by an under-30 reader.

Born in Cincinnati in 1914, Sinn started as a radio soap opera writer in Cincinnati, went on to become a successful author and executive in television and motion pictures and produced the 1955 TV series, "Sea Hunt."

Another columnist of the defunct National Newspaper Syndicate was Arnold Arnold (that's his actual and complete name), a graphic and industrial designer who is an expert in the design of play and learning materials for children. Educated at London University, Pratt Institute, the American School of Design and Columbia University, Arnold taught in New York and wrote a three-times-a-week column called "Parents and Children." A prolific author, his books for adults include "Violence and Your Child," "Career Choices for the Seventies," "Teaching Your Child to Learn from Birth to School Age," "The World Book of Children's Games," and the most popular, "Your Child's Play." Books for children include "The Arnold Arnold Book of Toy Soldiers," "Tongue Twisters and Double Talk," and "The Yes and

No Book."

The column grew out of these activities and the author's conviction that "the culture of childhood determines, as much as it reflects, the society in which we live."

Mrs. Arnold, who illustrated the column, writes and illustrates children's books under the professional name of Gail E. Haley. Her books include "A Story, A Story" and "Noah's Ark."

The collection of children's toys and learning materials amassed by Gail and Arnold Arnold has outgrown their house in Virginia and now is in the Children's Museum in Jacksonville, Florida.

The Arnolds have two children, Geoffrey (born 1970) and Marguerite (born 1968). Arnold also has a son, Francis (born 1950), from his first marriage. When the Arnolds moved from their apartment on the West Side of Manhattan, he wrote:

"Since urban life is no longer conducive to health or to a happy childhood, we have moved to Virginia. Here our children can still run barefoot in the grass and among the trees, laugh, play, learn and survive the minor mishaps of childhood without disastrous consequences."

Advice to parents in the early seventies also was dispensed, three times a week via the Los Angeles Times Syndicate, by Theresa H. Stanley, a mother of five children who received a degree in journalism from the University of Maine.

Because of her husband's work as a resort hotel manager, Terri Stanley and her children lived in such places as Phoenix, Arizona, and Kennebunkport, Maine. The enjoyment of her family was warmly conveyed in the column, titled, "Creative Mothering," in the Phoenix Republic, Portland (Maine) Telegram and other newspapers.

In 1968, Ernie Fladel, a New York advertising executive, and his nephew, Richard, a student at Columbia University, co-authored a McGraw-Hill book, "The Generation Gap." The book influenced many people, particularly as a result of a cover story in Life. Its greatest influence, though, was on the senior author. In 1971, Fladel resigned his partnership in his advertising agency and moved, with his wife, son and daughter, to Canada.

In 1971, King Features started a column, "The Generation Gap," to perform a similar function as the Fladel book, to present views on the same problem from the viewpoint of a parent and teenager. The authors are Helen Bottel and her daughter, Suzanne, who at that time was a student at Luther Burbank High School in Sacramento, California. Sue Bottel now is married and became a mother in 1978.

Mrs. Bottel also is the author of a companion King Features advice column, "Helen Help Us!," which has a high proportion of mail from under-25 readers. The orientation of the Helen and Sue Bottel columns is not as "swinging" as that of the Fladels, nor as humorous as

Abby and Ann Landers, and the "arguments" between the mother and daughter are generally moderate in the nature of the problem and the solution.

Born in Beaumont, California, in 1915, Helen Alfea Brigan married Robert Edwin Bottel in 1936. They have four children, Robert, Rodger, Roberta and Suzanne.

Another advisor to teen-agers is Elizabeth Winship, who writes "Ask Beth" three times a week for the Los Angeles Times Syndicate.

The most common question which teenage girls ask Beth is "How do I get that certain boy to like me," and the single most asked question from boys is "What do girls like to talk about."

In general, says Elizabeth Winship, the biggest problem which teenagers have is not getting along with their parents but simply relating to each other, particularly with regard to the sexual aspects of going steady. As for the generation gap, the most voiced complaints are variations of "They treat me like a baby, they won't let me date who I want and why can't I stay out late."

Girls send more letters than boys, with adolescent problems of face and figure and crises about bosoms (too little), height (too much) and complexion, high on the list. Other letters deal with shyness, depression, drugs, venereal disease, pregnancy and school. Fashion and grooming are discussed by very few correspondents.

Syndicated since 1970, "Ask Beth" appears in many major newspapers, including the Boston Globe, which is edited by her husband, Thomas. When the column started in the Globe, Mrs. Winship provided advice to readers of all ages, but most of the letters were from teenagers, so that became the focus.

The Winships, who were married in 1942, have three daughters and a son.

Born in Pittsfield, Mass., in 1921, Elizabeth Coolidge graduated cum laude in psychology from Radcliffe. In 1972, Houghton Mifflin published "Ask Beth, You Can't Ask Your Mother."

A typical Beth column consists of one or two questions answered in a detailed, straightforward manner. There are no one liners or wise cracks. A girl who wrote that she felt "grungy" because her school was "pathetic" was respectfully encouraged with a reply which started:

"Dear May:

"I think the school is failing you rather than the other way around. Teachers and parents are sometimes quick to blame kids for having a poor attitude or not working up to their potential. Both may be true, but perhaps it is poor teaching that is making the student lazy and inattentive.

"If your school is boring and inadequate, it is vital for you to realize it is not your fault. You squawk that the school stinks, but deep down you feel it is you who are the failure. If you go through your days lugging a burden of disrespect for your own abilities, of course you feel grungy."

Today, one of the most popular types of advice column deals with home repairs and household problems. The leaders are Erma Bombeck and Heloise, though there also are several specialists whose columns have very sizable circulation. One of the pioneers was Roger B. Whitman, who wrote "First Aid for the Ailing House" for over 40 years, starting in the early thirties in the New York Sun.

A specialist in this profitable business is the U-B Newspaper Syndicate in Van Nuys, Calif., headed by Russell Steinpfad and Stephen W. Ellingson. U-B, which provides a daily pattern service, do-it-yourself column and other household services, is the country's largest do-it-yourself service. The articles, which appear in the Washington Post and about 400 newspapers, combine a homely philosophy and easy humor with detailed drawings, illustrations and other material produced at Gopher Gulch, the name given by the author to his "pattern ranch" in the San Fernando Valley.

Specialized columns, such as those about antiques, often are syndicated by the writers, who occasionally are able to operate more efficiently and lucratively in this way than by working with a major syndicate. One such example was Dorothy H. Jenkins, a former New York Times gardening editor, who operated a successful specialized syndicate from her home in Connecticut until her death in 1972.

Outside the house also was the domain in the sixties and early seventies of George Creed (Landscape, Publishers-Hall), J. Finletter (Miracle Gardening, Singer), Irwin and Martha Jones (Dispatch), and Katherine B. Walker (Indoor Gardening, Publishers-Hall).

Self-syndicated columns included Down to Earth, written by Walter Masson at his home in Needham, Mass. George and Katherine Graham in Naples, N.Y. (near Syracuse) operated a syndicate with a delightful name, The Green Thumb, and Cindy Smith and Pat Almond operated Creative Features in Harmony, Rhode Island (near Providence, like every town in Rhode Island), where they wrote two gardening columns.

One of the most popular gardening columns (about 175 newspapers) currently is "Plants in the Home," a King Features weekly column by Elvin McDonald.

With regard to other women's interest columns, fashion is not as big a category as one might guess, possibly because much of this is covered by local women's editors via trips to New York and other fashion capitals, supplemented by a continuing deluge of publicity materials. For many years, the major fashion columnists have been Bostonian Marian Christy (United) and New Yorkers Eleanor Lambert, Eugenia Sheppard and Tobe, all of whom are syndicated by the Field Newspaper Syndicate, which has a corner on the fashion market. Mrs.

Lambert conducts a multitude of fashion promotion projects, Mrs. Sheppard was the fashion editor of the New York Herald Tribune, and Tobe operates a service for retailers and others in the fashion field.

Fashion and beauty columns are introduced and dropped with almost as much frequency as hemline lengths are changed. Columnists who were popular in the fifties and sixties included Florence de Santis (Bell-McClure), Ida Fried (E.P.S.), Helen Hennessy (NEA), Monique (Chicago Tribune) and Berta Mohr. One of the best-known was Edith Head, who created, since 1936, the fashions worn in several hundred motion pictures. Her considerable influence, particularly in the "golden days of Hollywood," produced a fame and respect among show business peers and millions of movie and television viewers.

Miss Head was born in Los Angeles and lived and worked in or near Hollywood all of her life, except for a colorful childhood in Mexico and on Indian reservations in the southwest. An inspiration to those who believe in formal education, Miss Head received a B.A. degree from the University of California, a M.A. from Stanford, and *then* took design courses. Starting as a sketch artist at Paramount, she became head designer in 1938.

In a 1959 book, "The Dress Doctor," she described her role in "telling a story with clothes" and as personal stylist to such stylish stars as Ingrid Bergman, Claudette Colbert and Marlene Dietrich.

Her beauty and fashion hints were syndicated for about ten years by Newsday Specials, prior to its acquisition by the Los Angeles Times, under the title "How Do You Look."

Other celebrities who became beauty columnists were Eileen Ford, Mr. Kenneth and Arlene Dahl. Eileen Ford started her modeling career almost by accident in 1946 when she began taking appointment calls for two busy friends who were professional models. In 1947, with the assistance of her husband, Gerald, she opened an office in New York which has become one of the largest modeling agencies in the country. The semi-weekly column, appropriately titled, "Model Beauty," was distributed in the early seventies by the Chicago Tribune-New York News Syndicate to about 50 U.S. newspapers, plus such overseas subscribers as Kvallsposten in Malmo, Sweden and Sanomat in Helsinki, Finland.

For years, international socialites were coiffed by Mr. Kenneth at his beauty salon at 157 East 57th Street, New York, but it wasn't until one of his patrons, Jacqueline Kennedy, brought him to the White House that the hairdresser became a celebrity. As is common among hairdressers, Syracuse-born (1927) Kenneth Battelle dropped his last name when he became a beauty artist. Among other hair-raising accomplishments, Kenneth invented the bouffant hairstyle.

The illustrated weekly column for the Chicago Tribune-New York News Syndicate was written with the assistance of Joan Rattner

Heilman, a well-coiffed blond resident of Mamaroneck, New York, who was women's editor of This Week, the newspaper supplement.

Actress, business executive and journalist are the triple successes of Arlene Dahl of Beverly Hills, California. Born in Minneapolis in 1928, Arlene Dahl studied fashion design at the University of Minnesota. Her first stage role, at the age of 17, was in "Mr. Strauss Goes to Boston," and her first movie, two years later, was "My Wild Irish Rose." Among several unmemorable movies which followed was one, in 1954, called "Women's World." Miss Dahl used this is 1967 to name her company, which became part of the Kenyon and Eckhardt advertising agency. Her books include "Always Ask A Man" and "Beauty Scopes."

The illustrated, three-times-a-week column, called "Let's Be Beautiful," was started in 1950 and was syndicated for over 20 years by the Chicago Tribune-New York News Syndicate.

One of the long-running beauty columns which still is successful is "A New You," a three-times-a-week illustrated article distributed by King Features and written by Emily Wilkens.

In 1965, in recognition of her achievements, the Fashion Institute of Technology in New York established the Emily Wilkens Chair in External Impressions. It was an odd name, but the honor was deserved, because New Yorker Emily Wilkens has promoted beauty, grooming and fashion in thousands of self-improvement lectures to young women. Her other honors include the coveted Coty American Fashion Critics Award and her popular books include "A New You," "Here's Looking At You" and "Secrets from the Super Spas."

For many years, King also syndicated a beauty column by Jeanne D'Arcy, which was the pen name of Joan D'Arcy O'Sullivan, a New Yorker who currently writes "Living Today" and is a senior editor of King. The "Living Today" page includes beauty, fashion, furnishings and interviews.

The other prominent long-time fashion columnists are Eugenia Sheppard and Eleanor Lambert.

One of the country's leading fashion and society columnists, Eugenia Sheppard in person is refreshingly informal. She started as a home furnishing writer at the New York Herald Tribune in 1939, shortly after graduating from Bryn Mawr College, and for years was fashion editor. A widow (her husband was Walter Millis), she lives in a fashionable apartment in Manhattan and a house in Glenhead, Long Island.

Eleanor Lambert is a unique triple-star in the fashion world. She is a publicist who represents designers and manufacturers. She conducts the American Designers Series Press Week, the Coty Awards and other projects for the fashion industry. And, she is one of the few publicists who also is a syndicated columnist. (Others are Betty

Yarmon and Letitia Baldrige.)

The indefatigable Miss Lambert also produces the International Best Dressed List, which has been issued in the U.S. since 1940, and has written a syndicated column since 1964.

Born in Crawfordsville, Indiana, Eleanor Lambert studied art in Indianapolis and Chicago, did fashion drawings for department stores and worked as a newspaper reporter and fashion columnist. In the thirties, she started a New York public relations agency, specializing in art and fashion. "I believed then, as I do now, that fashion is an art form," says Miss Lambert.

The Lambert color is red. She owns dozens of red gowns and other red clothes. Red heels on black patent leather shoes are a Lambert trademark. "I perk myself up after a hard day by wearing red," says Miss Lambert.

The home-sewing boom has produced several new columns, and the sale of patterns, pamphlets and books by syndicates is a sizable business. The two leaders in this field are King Features and NEA. Most of the features include mail-order coupons, and newspapers share in the revenue. Many newspapers devote large space to these illustrated features in their Sunday comics section.

An example of the size and importance of these patterns-for-sale columns can be seen in the Sunday edition of the Miami Herald. The King Features one-third page "Let's Sew" feature appears in the color comics section, Pat Trexler's "Pointers" is given almost one-quarter of a page in the women's section, and Steve Ellingson's do-it-yourself plans appear in a 3-column by 10-inch space in the real estate section.

Food columns were one of the staples of McClure and other early syndicates, and the subject still ranks as one of the major categories. One of the few to add a dash of humor to the recipes was Hymen Goldberg, a long-time New York Mirror reporter who wrote "Our Man in the Kitchen" for the New York Post and other Register-Tribune subscribers.

(One of the few beauty columnists who incorporated humor with advice was Henry Spinelli, a retired hairdresser who wrote in the sixties for the San Francisco Chronicle under the pseudonym of Count Marco.)

Among the food columnists, the leaders in the sixties were Poppy Cannon, Johna Blinn, Craig Claiborne, Aileen Claire (the psuedonym of Aileen Snoddy of NEA), Alice Denhoff (long-timer at King), Jeanne Lesem (UPI), Cecily Brownstone (AP), Gaynor Maddox (long-timer at NEA), Myra Waldo, Jean Nidetch (founder of Weight Watchers); several veteran wine writers, notably Bob Balzer (Los Angeles Times), Bill Sonstein and Bob Misch; and nutritionists Dr. Frederick Stare (Los Angeles Times) and Dr. Jean Mayer (Chicago Tribune).

Poppy Cannon, who died in 1975, wrote "The Fast Gourmet" three times a week for General Features (now incorporated into the Los Angeles Times Syndicate). She wrote over a dozen cookbooks, hundreds of articles in the Ladies' Home Journal and other magazines, and over a thousand newspaper columns on food, but her spiciest literary work was not culinary. It was a 1956 biography, "Gentle Knight," about Walter Francis White, the Georgia black who was secretary of the National Association for the Advancement of Colored People for 24 years until his death in 1955. White's biographer was a white woman, his wife. After Walter White's death, Poppy Cannon worked tirelessly in a kitchen and office in a charming apartment on lower Park Avenue in New York. She became one of the deans among food writers, with contributions to encyclopedias and such historical books as "The President's Cookbook" and "The Anthropology of Food." Her popular books included "Wine, Women and So On," "The Frozen Food Cookbook," "The Electric Epicure," "The Bride's Cookbook," "The ABC's of Cooking" and "Eating European," all of which were related to the theme of the column, which is that good eating does not require elaborate training or preparation. Her first book stated part of her philosophy in its title, "The Can-Opener Cookbook," which was such a success that it was followed by "The New Can-Opener Cookbook" and "The New, New Can-Opener Cookbook." Honestly. Honestly.

For several decades, another dean among food writers was James Beard, a big, heavy, jovial man who is an excellent cook and writer.

Food writers are among the most finicky and competitive of all journalists. Some of them tend to be carping and bitchy in their evaluations of other gourmets. Purists often are critical, perhaps because of jealousy and sometimes for more valid reasons, of food writers who endorse products or become "commercial." Jim Beard attained fame and mass appeal, and though he had his critics, in general, he ranked quite high among his peers as well as the general public.

James Andrews Beard was born in Portland, Oregon, in 1903. He attended Reed College for a year in 1920 and returned to college 10 years later, first to the University of Washington and then, in 1931, to Carnegie Institute of Technology where he studied drama.

Beard appeared on the stage and on radio programs in the twenties, and started in the food field as an announcer of food commercials on a Portland radio station. He moved east in 1938 and became co-proprietor of a restaurant in New York and also was associated with a farm in Pennsylvania. His first big break came in 1946 when he hosted a food program on television, called "Elsie Presents," sponsored by Borden's, whose trademark at the time was Elsie the Cow.

The daytime program lasted only a year, but Beard's radio and television career blossomed with frequent appearances on various programs. He became a lecturer and consultant to various companies, including the Restaurant Associates chain, and started conducting cooking classes in his home.

Beard's first book, "Hors D'oeuvre Canapes," was published in 1940. Since then, he authored about 20 books, including paperbacks on barbecue and outdoor cooking, as well as other popular appeal subjects, such as cooking for entertaining. His autobiography,"Delights and Prejudices," was published in 1964. The weekly column was syndicated by the Washington Star from 1970 to 1978.

By combining two popular subjects—celebrity interviews and recipes—Johna Blinn created a virtually unique column. (An earlier version of this idea was done by Helen Dunn.)

Each week, Miss Blinn interviews a show business personality, generally in the person's home. Most of the questions, but not all, are about cuisine and the recipe usually is the celebrity's own creation or merely a favorite food.

From its start, when it was syndicated by Newsday, and appeared in the New York Post, "Celebrity Cookbook" had all the looks of a winner. The column has appeared in the Boston Herald Traveler, Chicago Tribune, Detroit Free Press, Cincinnati Enquirer, Richmond Times-Dispatch, Washington Post, Houston Post and other major newspapers.

Celebrities in the column included Bette Davis, Justice William O. Douglas, Woody Allen, Jack Benny, Phyllis McGinley, Danny Kaye, Richard and Pat Nixon, Art Linkletter, Sammy Davis Jr., Patricia Neal, Rock Hudson, Barbra Streisand, Andy Williams and about 400 others.

The author of Celebrity Cookbook was Helen Dorsey, who wrote with the pen name of Johna Blinn for several reasons, one of which was that her boss was her husband, Thomas Dorsey. In 1976, when Tom Dorsey moved, from editor of the Chicago Tribune-New York News Syndicate to editor of the Los Angeles Times Syndicate, several columnists switched with him, including Johna Blinn. About a year later, Tom Dorsey left the Los Angeles Times Syndicate, but "Celebrity Cookbook" was retained.

Here then, for the historical record, are the alleged favorite recipes of a few celebrities, who, for purposes of impartial billing, are listed alphabetically:

Victor Borge—braised pork tenderloin
Billy Casper—fried rabbit
Carol Channing—German pot roast
Bill Cosby—omelet
Bette Davis—spinach-stuffed filets
Phyllis Diller—stuffed mushrooms

94

William O. Douglas—trout
Jimmy Durante—umbriago salad
Eileen Farrell—lasagne
Mahalia Jackson—stuffed crabs
Burt Lancaster—beef curry
Guy Lombardo—lobster
Sophia Loren—pizza
Shirley MacLaine—lamb stew
Richard Nixon—meat loaf
Joan Rivers—duck
Kate Smith—rock cornish hens
Barbara Stanwyck—steak tartar
Gloria Swanson—broth
Jonathan Winters—tuna bake
Natalie Wood—beef stroganoff

One of the spriteliest interviews was with Buddy Hackett. After kibitzing about his mother's cooking ("Once when I was home on furlough, I said if the Army were exposed to her cooking, we would blow the war."), he gave the heretofore secret recipe for Buddy Hackett's Chinese chile. It involved mixing ground beef with onion, green pepper, white pepper, red peppers, garlic, chile powder, water chestnuts, mushrooms, and bean sprouts. Hackett told Miss Blinn to be sure to taste along the way and add the sprouts near the end.

The increasing popularity of wines has produced several columns exclusively about wine. Among the xonophile columnists of the sixties were David Purslove of Washington, D.C., Ruth Ellen Church of The Chicago Tribune, and William Clifford, an Englishman who produced a weekly column, "Wine on the Table," from his home at the delightful typically British address: The Lookout, Branscombe (near Seaton), Devon, England.

The nation's longest running wine columnist is Robert Jay Misch, author of many books and articles on wine and recipient of various awards and honorary memberships, including Chevalier du Tastevin.

A magna cum laude graduate of Dartmouth College, Bob Misch is a native New Yorker who resides on the West Side of Manhattan. In a delightful little book, titled "Quick Guide to Wine" (Doubleday, 1966), Misch disabused the uninitiate of some of the cliches, pronouncements and dogmatisms of the wine snobs, recommended a permissive policy of common sense, and concluded with a 200-year-old couplet by J.H. Voss:

"Who loves not woman, wine and song—
Remains a fool his whole life long."

Among the current food columns one of the most successful is "The Slim Gourmet," written for United Features by Barbara Gibbons, an ex-heavyweight, who went from 208 to 125 pounds. Started in 1971,

"The Slim Gourmet," evolved from a column Mrs. Gibbons wrote in Family Circle magazine, called "Creative Low-Calorie Cooking."

"I was a lifelong fatty," explains the 5-foot, size-9 columnist. "I was so fat that I graduated from grammar school in a nurse's uniform because I couldn't find a white dress in a size 20½. Over the years, I tried everything to lose weight, but it wasn't until I decided to tackle my weight problem in the kitchen that I finally succeeded. Like most homemakers who really love to cook and enjoy good food, I found it almost impossible to stay on a diet—dieting deprives you not only of the foods you love, but your hobby as well!"

Born in 1934, Barbara Gibbons was a newspaper reporter for five years and an advertising copywriter for six years, before starting her column in the Elizabeth (N.J.) Daily Journal.

One of the appeals of "Slim Gourmet" is that Mrs. Gibbons combines recipes and other factual advice with comments about her life. This personal approach is the key to several super-successful columnists, such as Nancy Stahl and Erma Bombeck.

Another type of food column is the scientific approach, as expressed by nutritionists, such as Dr. Jean Mayer, Dr. Frederick Stare and Philomena Corradeno, and ecologists, such as Robert Rodale. There also are specialized columns, including one devoted solely to meat (by California butcher Merle Ellis).

The top ecological column in the early seventies was "Organic Living" by Robert Rodale, the son of the founder of Rodale Press, publisher of Prevention, Let's Live and Organic Gardening. The column was distributed by the Chicago Tribune-New York News Syndicate and was attractive to editors because of its unusual appeal to very young and very old readers of both sexes.

Several syndicates provide columns exclusively for family or women's pages. One of the oldest is Women's News Service, a package service which is operated by United Media Service. Fairchild Publications, publisher of Women's Wear Daily, also operates a syndicate in this field.

Any one of the major syndicates, such as King, United, Field, Los Angeles Times and Chicago Tribune-New York News turn out enough columns to fill an entire section of a newspaper every day. Some of the beauty and food columns are dull, repetitive and often clumsily written, and the fashion columns frequently are annoyingly haughty and egotistical. All have their fans, and most of these columnists have established their credentials by surviving years of competition from national and local writers who have fallen by the wayside. The leaders, in terms of longevity and number of subscribers, are Nancy Stahl, Erma Bombeck, Heloise, Abby and Ann Landers.

NANCY, ERMA AND HELOISE

Nancy and John Stahl and their daughter, Laurie, and son, Eric, and assorted pets (which at one time included a guinea pig, Delilah, a mouse, Daisy, a chihuahua-terrier mongrel dog, Duke, and a fish, Moby Dick) are the all-American family.

The Stahls and their menage have become a part of several million families in the U.S. who joyously declare that Nancy Stahl is the funniest, most realistic housewife-writer since Jean Kerr.

The column, called "Jelly Side Down," started in December, 1969, in Canada in the Calgary Herald, and was picked up for syndication as the first offering of the Universal Press Syndicate, when it was formed in March, 1970. Newspapers which stampeded to carry the semi-weekly conversations by Mrs. Stahl included The New York News, Chicago Tribune, Philadelphia Inquirer, Cleveland Press, Detroit Free Press, Rocky Mountain News, Hartford Courant, Baltimore News-American, San Francisco Examiner, Buffalo News, Cincinnati Enquirer, Fort Worth Press, Indianapolis Star and about 100 others. In Florida, "Jelly Side Down" appeared in the Tampa Times and also the rival St. Petersburg Times, the Miami Herald and also the nearby Fort Lauderdale News and Palm Beach Times, as well as the Jacksonville Times-Union.

In the years since its inception, subscribers have changed, of course, but the column continues to be fresh and appealing to readers of all levels of sophistication. For example, here is the complete text of one of the early columns:

"In most homes there exists among the children a periodic wish that one or more of their brothers or sisters would be staked out on the Nevada Salt Flats at high noon and trampled by a passing herd of heat-crazed elephants. This is known as 'sibling rivalry' because it's shorter and sounds nicer.

"Sibling rivalry is the direct result of being forced to share the same Mommy, Daddy, and red crayon, and making sure that you get equal time with each one. It usually begins when the new baby is brought home from the hospital (or in from the cabbage patch, depending on how you handle these things.)

"Suddenly the people who are nearest and dearest to a two-year-old, like her Grandma and the milkman, flock to her new brother and begin kissing his toes. The two-year-old begins to think that having a baby brother is going to be about as much fun as having chicken pox.

"Despite all the fancy footwork that we went through to make the blessed event seem as commonplace as the purchase of a new tea towel, our two-year-old was not fooled for a moment. Efforts to persuade her that the new baby was 'Her Baby, Too' are met with the cynical observation that she'd rather have had an Easy Bake Oven.

"When her brother began toddling, she carefully explained his place in the seniority system, then drew one chalk line down the middle of the playroom floor and another down my lap.

"Their separate but equal system has reduced sibling rivalry to a minimum though my husband and I are often called upon to act as the court of highest appeal in nebulous areas, such as who gets to keep the dog's baby tooth and whose turn it is to lick the stamp for the letter to Santa. We usually handle the more delicate chores, like cutting the odd cherry in a can of fruit cocktail into two equal parts.

"Handling sibling rivalry is not terribly difficult. All you need is the wisdom of Solomon, the patience of Job, and a stopwatch for timing the use of the red crayon."

"Jelly Side Down" is easy to take. Its gentle humor is distinctive and readers feel warmly toward the author. The column has a distinctive personality. These are essential attributes of any successful column, particularly one which deals with humor. Readers actually look for the column with eagerness, even though they somewhat know what to expect. This too is part of the ingredients of a newspaper habit.

The Stahl children remain unfazed by their mother's success. Laurie Ann, born 1960, and Eric, born two years later, used to be excited about seeing their names in the newspaper, but now they only read the column once in a while. "They just like to spend the money," says Nancy Stahl.

John Stahl, who still does read the column, is an economics professor at the University of Calgary. Nancy and John, who are U.S. citizens, met while they were attending the University of Massachusetts. Nancy was an art major and John was studying dairy technology. Married in 1958, the couple lived in several places, including Puerto Rico, in accordance with John's studies and his roving job with the U.S. Department of Agriculture. In 1967, they moved to Calgary and bought a modest two-story house, within walking distance of the University.

Among her family and friends, Nancy Stahl is not known as a comedian or even a story teller. She had no previous journalistic experience and writes the personal journal in long hand on long yellow pads. She also does the line drawings which accompany many of the columns. As for the title of the column, she says the name has no special significance.

Millions of housewives, particularly those who are known among their families as being witty, often have pipe dreams about the ease of doing a personal chatter column. "Jelly Side Down" may seem effortless and imitable, but it really is an art to sustain a personal column, and Nancy Stahl is a superb artist.

The better known and more widely syndicated columnist of this type is Erma Bombeck, a midwestern housewife who writes a humorous, helpful, informal journal about her family and home. It is a delightful, personal column which appears easy-to-do only because the author is a very competent, experienced journalist.

"I am big on manners," says Mrs. Bombeck. "Always have been. Somehow, you feel that a man who laughs with cottage cheese in his mouth will never head a large corporation."

Born in 1927, Erma Bombeck was a women's news reporter at the Dayton Journal Herald in Ohio, where, in 1965, she started her column. She is married to a former high school social studies supervisor. Bill and Erma Bombeck and their two sons and daughter, plus assorted dogs, horses and other animals, lived for many years on a farm in Bellbrook, which is near Dayton. In 1971, they moved to a plush house in Paradise Valley, Arizona, just outside of Phoenix.

The column, titled "At Wit's End," is one of the 10 most successful of any type. It is distributed by the Field Newspaper Syndicate to over 300 subscribers, including the Chattanooga Times, Tampa Times, Kansas City Star, Cleveland Plain Dealer, Philadelphia Bulletin, Miami News, Newsday and Boston Globe.

Mrs. Bombeck also writes a column in Good Housekeeping, and, in 1971, authored a Doubleday book, "Just Wait Till You Have Children of Your Own." Several bestsellers followed, and the biggest, in 1978, was "If Life Is A Bowl of Cherries—What Am I Doing in the Pits?"

A typical Bombeckism: "Every time there is a successful flight to the Moon, there is a lot of static from women who want to be Feminauts. As I told an aspirant the other day, 'Honey, I don't have to leave home to look at that much dust.' "

It's difficult to rank columns, because syndicates do not divulge accurate figures, but the country's top columns probably are Abby, Ann Landers, Jack Anderson and Heloise. Hints from Heloise, which appears in over 500 newspapers, is perhaps the most extraordinary, in that the author is the daughter of the column's founder, Heloise Bowles, who died on December 28, 1977. Heloise had been married three times and Ponce Cruse, her daughter from her first marriage, has continued the seven-times-a-week King Features column.

Subscribers, including the Buffalo Courier Express, Chattanooga Times, Cleveland Plain Dealer, Miami Herald, Jacksonville Journal and Philadelphia Bulletin, publish the column under various titles, such as "Dear Heloise," "Here's Heloise," and simply, "Heloise."

In 1971, Heloise I was honored in her home state by the Texas Press Association in a resolution which called her "First Lady of Home-makers . . . Our beloved Mrs. Fix-It, Mother's Friend, Housewife's Helper, Husband's Consolation." The award commended Heloise for "her unequalled love of home and homemakers and for her untiring efforts to communicate this love through her renowned syndicated column and through her personal answers to thousands of letters from readers weekly."

"Hints from Heloise" was, and still is, a collection of practical, innovative tips from readers which are passed along in a chatty, witty style.

The ingenious tips by America's champion housekeeper include letting a blender wash itself, slicing pies before freezing, and packing clothes in cleaners' bags.

Born in Fort Worth in 1919, Heloise Bowles was part Indian. She attended business college and Texas Christian University, and started the column in 1959 in Honolulu, where her first husband, Lt. Col. Marshall ("Mike") H. Cruse was stationed. With no previous journalistic experience, Heloise edited an exchange column in the Honolulu Advertiser, in which readers answered each other's questions, and Heloise simply acted as a sort of literary umpire. The format changed, with added comments by Heloise, but the column remained oriented to reader mail.

She once received what postal authorities claimed was the largest single mail delivery in Hawaii's history. After the war, the family, including daughter, Ponce, and son, Louis, lived in various military locations, including Arlington, Virginia. Heloise moved with her second husband to San Antonio, and lived until her death in an apartment in north San Antonio.

A glamorous brunette who varied her hair color through the years, Heloise definitely was not a women's liberationist and believed that a woman's place is in the home. An early riser, she was joined by a staff of several women who plowed through the mail, which totaled well over a million letters a year. Ponce Cruse assisted her mother since 1974.

Heloise I and II indeed have become an American institution. The first of Heloise's five books, "Heloise's Housekeeping Hints," published in 1963, was one of the top 10 bestselling hardcover and also paperback books.

All of which proves that Heloise has earned a place in history, ranking with Heloise of the 12th century, who is famous for her exchange of letters with Peter Abelard.

ANN AND ABBY

Ann Landers and "Dear Abby" have been called the most widely read and most widely quoted women in the world. Mrs. Eppie Lederer who is Ann Landers, and Mrs. Morton Phillips, who is Abby, took the lovelorn column, which was in danger of becoming extinct, discarded its reticences, trimmed it, and, most important, gave it a sense of humor. Ann Landers and Abby spawned a slew of imitators and made this type of column an essential part of almost every newspaper. Many major newspapers carry two or more "family advisors" and the mail to each of the leading columnists numbers in the many thousands each week.

The Ann Landers-Abby formula is not a slapstick trick and is far more difficult to achieve than is obvious to the casual observer. It is based on research, hard work and careful, shrewd judgment on the part of the writer. Of course, a staff is required to plow through the mailbags crammed with letters and postcards. Ann Landers and Abby spend the largest part of their writing time answering letters which never appear in the column, and referring problem cases to professional agencies. They take their work extremely seriously, though their contribution to this type of newspaper journalism is the frequent insult and putdown, an absolute departure from the primness of Dorothy Dix, Beatrice Fairfax and other predecessors. Their vaudeville-like, earthy sarcasm and abrasive wit would have shocked Dorothy Dix, but they were right on target for the times, when they started in the fifties.

Mrs. Lederer and Mrs. Phillips are somewhat stereotyped Jewish mothers. Their lack of inhibition in discussing sexual problems, which was more unusual when they started the columns than it is now, belies their own conservative views. They both are strong on family ties, and

103

an analysis of their advice indicates that they are conventionally moralistic. During the early years of their marriages, both moved around the country a great deal, in accordance with the job changes of their husbands. Mrs. Lederer lived in Sioux City, St. Louis, Milwaukee, New Orleans and Chicago. She was divorced in 1975 and has continued to live in an apartment in Chicago. Mrs. Phillips lived in Eau Claire, Minneapolis and currently lives in Beverly Hills.

Readers are eager to learn about the personal lives of these twin celebrities, and Life and other magazines satisfied these yearnings with a barrage of articles about the competitive feud between the sisters. For many years, items and articles about them stated that they didn't talk to each other, and there was quite a bit of sniping as to which had the larger number of subscribers and other measures of popularity.

In a personal letter in 1978, Abby declared, "For the record ... there NEVER was a time that my sister and I did not speak to each other. We have a warm and loving relationship, but most people prefer to believe that we are not on good terms."

She added in a P.S., "I am going to Chicago to speak next week, and I will stay with my twin."

There are a few differences between the sisters, but very few. Both are packed with energy, exuberant, extroverted, early risers, well organized, beautifully coiffed and attired, and are non-smokers. Each is 5'2", weighs about 110 lbs., with black hair and green-blue eyes.

Ann has dimples, which are less obvious with Abby. Some years ago, Ann bobbed her nose, but though the difference may be obvious to a plastic surgeon, the ladies still look similar. Abby probably is more flippant.

Ann denies the cosmetic surgery and it's a good example of the fascinating behavior of the twins. Ann Landers was, and still is, extremely attractive. She is a strong proponent of many types of medical care and is also renowned for her candor, and it's puzzling when she denies her plastic surgery.

Well, of course, there is no desire to hurt or embarrass Ann Landers. The fact is printed here not for any low-shot journalistic scoop, but rather to illustrate the style of the two women. Both of them still are promoting, in spite of their much-described fabulous success. Their aggressiveness comes out in various ways, including angry rebuttals to critics and occasional snipes at each other.

According to Abby, "there NEVER was a time that my sister and I did not speak to each other."

According to Ann, "We are good friends, visit each other often and have for several years. The 'feud' was vastly exaggerated and was of short duration."

The sisters' first column was a collaborative effort in the Campus Rat, when they were students at Morningside College in Iowa. The gossip column was called PEEP, an acronym formed from the initials of Pauline Esther and Esther Pauline. However, this linkage was very brief.

In 1965, Abby switched to the Chicago Tribune-New York News Syndicate because she was unhappy with the McNaught Syndicate. The rumor in the newspaper business was that McNaught didn't promote her enough, were underpaying her, and were selling her column only to subscribers which agreed to take lesser features.

McNaught was predictably shocked by the loss of its number one columnist, though president Charles V. McAdams agreed that Abby's column sometimes was sold as part of a package. "But when she started out, we used Joe Palooka to promote her," said McAdams, referring to the syndicate's number one comic strip. McNaught's sales manager Peter Boggs bitterly added, "When you take them from nothing and make them bigger, they're unappreciative."

Now, here's Abby's version:

"I credit my speedy recognition and success to the fact that Edward R. Murrow was an admirer of mine from the very beginning of my career—and when I had been writing less than a year and a half (October 1958), Murrow did a Person to Person TV show of me and my family when we lived in Hillsborough, California.

"It brought me instant fame . . . and, as I recall, after that TV show I had editors and publishers writing directly to ME, asking how they could buy the column. All I did was stuff their letters into an envelope and send them to McNaught. They really FILLED orders for my column. They didn't have to 'sell' it.

"I rather resent the stories they put out when I refused to renew my contract with them. I never complained about not getting enough money, ever. My only complaint was their selling me in a 'package' deal. Then editors all over the country would tell me that they had to buy six 'dogs' in order to get my column . . . and they never ran the dogs—only my column, but they paid for the whole lot."

Under the aegis of the Trib-News Syndicate, Abby's column proliferated into more than 700 newspapers, though Ann, who stayed with Publishers-Hall (now called Field Newspaper Syndicate) kept pace, principally because in many cases a morning newspaper would take one twin and the afternoon paper would almost be forced to take the other twin.

The twins haven't drastically changed the strict moralistic code set up by the early lovelorn advisors. Abby and Ann turn out a type of short order psychology which often appears to be the Ten Commandments jazzed up with wisecracks.

In recent years, Ann and Abby began to see some minor competition from a new breed of ultra-permissive advice columnists, but most of them have fallen by the wayside.

105

One columnist spawned by Ann Landers was her daughter, Margo, who wrote an interview and personal commentary column for the Chicago Daily News in the early seventies.

At the time of the column, Margo was married to Chicago mortician, Jules L. Furth, but she used the name Margo Coleman, from her first marriage to financier John Coleman. She and Furth lived in a 17-room apartment overlooking Lake Michigan with Margo's three children from her first marriage, Abra, Adam and Andrea.

Margo now lives in California and no longer is columning.

A few columnists, such as Walter Winchell, Leonard Lyons and Earl Wilson, referred repeatedly to their families in their columns.

Abby and Ann do not do this, though there have been a few exceptions.

In her column of February 18, 1972, Abby printed a letter from an identical twin who argued that twins should dress alike. Abby disagreed and wrote that as soon as twins are old enough to express themselves, their individual preferences should be respected and encouraged. "Twins who dress themselves identically," said Abby, "are saying, look at us, we're twins! (P.S. I asked my twin and she agrees with me.)"

As to the competition in number of outlets and circulation, it's difficult to declare the winner.

"Dear Abby" has become part of our vocabulary and Abby has become better known than any other advice columnist in the world.

Abby is the creation of Mrs. Pauline Esther Friedman Phillips, who started the column at the San Francisco Chronicle in 1956.

Born in Sioux City, Iowa, on July 4, 1918, Pauline Friedman acquired the nickname of Po-Po. She and her sister both married businessmen, in a double wedding ceremony on July 2, 1939. Pauline married Morton Phillips who was executive vice president of National Presto Industries, a company owned by his family which manufactured pressure cookers in Eau Claire, Wisconsin. The family lived in Minneapolis and Eau Claire, and then moved to San Francisco, where Phillips was president of M. Seller Co., a housewares distributor.

When Pauline learned that her sister had landed a job as advice columnist at the Chicago Sun-Times, she quickly jumped' into the newspaper business, with no previous experience, and took over the Molly Mayfield advice column in the San Francisco Chronicle.

.The Abby first name was picked by Mrs. Phillips from the Old Testament—"and David said to Abigail, blessed be thy advice." The last name comes from Martin Van Buren, our eighth President, and was selected because it sounded aristocratic.

The McNaught Syndicate picked up the "Dear Abby" column three weeks after it started at the San Francisco Chronicle and only three weeks later it started in the New York Mirror, thus giving Abby the jump on sister Ann, who didn't get a coveted New York outlet until 15 years later, in the World-Telegram and Sun. But Ann Landers one-upped Abby by writing seven columns a week, as compared to Abby's six. She also may have topped Abby with more secretaries, and these and other instances added to their competitive feud. The twin tigresses now are more relaxed, as they both bask in their international fame.

Not too relaxed, though.

"I don't understand why you say Ann has the 'jump' on me because she writes seven days a week," states Abby.

"I was offered a seven-day-a-week column but turned it down. I think six days a week is plenty. My papers run me either on Saturday or Sunday—not both. Saturday readership is very thin, and it's not worth the effort to me. The pay is the same.

One advantage which Mrs. Phillips has is that she owns the name, Abby Van Buren. "I dreamed it up, copyrighted it and it belongs to me ... NOT my syndicate. It's a tremendous advantage. If they ever want to say 'bye bye' to me, I'll take my name with me," notes Abby. On the other hand, the Ann Landers name is owned by Field Syndicate.

For a while, Abby and Morton Phillips maintained homes in Minneapolis and Hillsborough, a suburb of San Francisco, but they now have settled in Beverly Hills.

Mrs. Phillips is active in several charities, particularly in the mental health field.

She carries two cards in her handbag—one requesting that upon her death her eyes be given to an eye bank, and the other making a similar request with regard to transplanting her kidneys. "No matter what else I leave behind," she states, "these, I think, will be the most precious."

She has two children, Jeanne, born in 1942, and Edward Jay, born in 1944. For six years, Jeanne assisted in the "Dear Abby" radio program, which was broadcast six times a week on the CBS network for 12 years.

Jeanne is married to attorney Luke McKissack of Los Angeles and Edward, an attorney, is president of Ed Phillips and Sons, a Minneapolis company. He's married and has two children.

So Abby and Ann are grandmothers.

Ann Landers also had a radio program, on the rival NBC network.

The balance of power between the two is measured solely in terms of the newspaper column. Abby has more subscribers because of a reason which is an integral part of the syndicate business. The Ann Landers column was started before Abby, and Publishers-Hall sold exclusive territorial rights for the Ann Landers column to several large newspapers.

When Abby came along, she picked up several smaller newspapers in various Landers' territories, thus giving her the edge in number of papers but not always in total circulation.

February 28, 1966, was a momentous date in the history of newspaper syndicates, because on that historic day Abby switched from McNaught to the Chicago Tribune-New York News Syndicate. Her new syndicate generally does not follow the territorial custom, nor does it give away columns as part of package deals involving several items. The Trib-News picked up quite a few major circulation outlets for Abby, and her annual income has been well over $100,000 for many years.

One measure of a column's popularity and importance is reader mail. In 1971, Abby published a letter from a woman with an unusual problem. The reader had been invited to a party at the home of her husband's boss, and she refused to go because the married employer was living with his girl friend. Her husband, who felt that his job was at stake, disagreed with his wife and wanted to go to the party.

Abby wavered between two opposite solutions, and asked her readers for guidance. 877,091 readers wrote to Abby with their views about this monumental issue.

The tally: 566,001 (predominantly female) said, "Don't go." 311,090 (predominantly male) said, "Go."

Of the several million letters allegedly sent each year to Abby, about 1200 are published in the column. A typical Abby question and answer:

"Dear Abby: My wife had a hysterectomy. Does that mean it is the end of her sex life? She is only 34. WONDERING.

"Dear Wondering: Absolutely not! In fact, it could very well be the beginning of a better sex life because she no longer has to worry about becoming pregnant."

Certainly not all of the questions which Abby prints deal with sex, nor are her answers always terse and amusing. However, it is this breezy style which gave Abby her initial fame.

Prior to Abby and Ann Landers, advice columnists generally had been prim and proper. Abby and Ann Landers were hailed as the first to break out of the square formula. By today's standards, Abby is not old-fashioned. On the other hand, she certainly is not mod or avant-garde. Her advice therefore is acceptable, and often lauded, by teachers, clergymen, parents and others. Her primary appeal probably is to the lower and middle classes, including children as well as adults of all ages. Millions of people look to her for guidance, carefully save specific columns and post them on office bulletin boards or mail them to friends and relatives who have similar problems as the readers quoted by Abby. Intellectuals often deprecate Abby, but, even among this group, readers find her column to be light and entertaining, if not edifying and uplifting. Hence, Abby has an almost universal appeal.

Abby and Ann Landers have spawned a slew of imitators but none has come close to their success.

A theology professor asked Abby how she arrived at her answers and how long it took her to write them. Her reply (March 10, 1972):

"I think my answers are simply common sense in a capsule. And it took me about 1 hour and 53 years to write today's column."

In 1978, Abigail McCarthy wrote a newspaper column (part of the "One Woman's Voice" series) in which she described Dear Abby as "diminutive, funny, charming, witty, shrewd, down-to-earth, kind, warm, compassionate . . . one of the most powerful social forces in the country."

As important as is the column, Abby perhaps should be commended mostly for her behind-the-scenes work in helping people. She maintains lists of legal aid, drug abuse and other agencies in every city where she has subscribers, and constantly consults with lawyers, physicians, clergymen and others in order to answer the problems of readers. A staff of 10 secretaries is kept busy with a flow of personal and form letters.

One of the most glowing tributes to Abby came from the late Louis Cassels, religion editor of United Press International, who, in 1973, nominated her as "the best moral theologian in America today."

Now, let's take a look at Abby's look-alike, Ann Landers.

"Truth Is Stranger," a 1968 best-selling book, was dedicated to "Jules, who continues to do the impossible . . . he keeps two women happy—Ann Landers and Eppie Lederer."

The explanation, of course, is that Ann Landers is the pen name of Esther Pauline Lederer, whose nickname is Eppie. Her husband, Jules W. Lederer, was head of the Budget Rent-A-Car System, which was founded by Morey Mirkin, a cousin of Ann and Abby. The Lederers were divorced in 1975, but Eppie still uses the Lederer name—she was married 36 years.

Born in Sioux City, Iowa, on July 4, 1918 (her parents were Abe and Rebecca Friedman), Mrs. Lederer has lived in the Midwest all her life. She attended Morningside College in Sioux City, but dropped out shortly before graduation.

The column has been syndicated since she started it in 1955 at the Chicago Sun-Times, where she replaced nurse Ruth Crowley, the original Ann Landers advice columnist, who had just died. Mrs. Lederer had had no previous journalistic experience, or any job experience. Each of the 28 eager applicants for the Ann Landers job were given a few letters and one week in which to compose replies. Mrs. Lederer won the competition and has been known as Ann Landers ever since.

She plunged into the job with intense vigor and treated every letter with utmost respect and importance by calling doctors, dentists, lawyers, clergymen and other experts for guidance. Lawrence Fanning, the editor of the Sun-Times Syndicate helped her considerably for ten years, as did John G. Trezevant, Wilbur Munnecke and other executives at Field Enterprises and Publishers-Hall. Will Munnecke retired to Michigan and Larry Fanning moved to Alaska to become publisher of the Anchorage Daily News. (Fanning died in 1971. Among the columnists whom he nurtured were Mike Royko, Peter Lisagor and Nicholas von Hoffman.) John Trezevant has been her editor since Fanning moved.)

The principal source of the column's success has been the passionate care given to it by Ann Landers, combined with a pithy writing style, which was radically different from the heavy prose of many older advice columnists.

"I do not consider myself a journalist and it is self-evident that I am not an intellectual," wrote Ann Landers in a November 12, 1966, article in The Saturday Review. "I am at once flattered and surprised when professional writers ask me how I get through to people. They say I have a direct line to the masses, to the average American. But I have never met a mass and I have yet to meet anyone who will admit he is average. I address myself to individuals, not masses. People who suffer, suffer alone."

In "Truth Is Stranger," Ann Landers wrote, "My readers are unpredictable, supersensitive, warmhearted, irascible, sharp-eyed, sharp-tongued, fiercely critical and beautifully loyal."

A few of the letters are attempts to evoke witty replies, some are anonymous, others are illegible, but most are genuinely honest pleas for help, including many which are heart breaking. Eight secretaries (there have been more) sort the mail and provide replies under Miss Landers' supervision. Perhaps the most disturbing letters are those from homosexuals, states Miss Landers, because "I can give them so little hope for a cure."

She closely follows the mail count from each newspaper, and if it falls off, she's immediately on the phone, calling the editor to find out if the column has been buried or other reasons.

The subjects of the letters include just about every conceivable problem, but the wittiest and often most poignant usually deal with sex. Women complain about sex more often than men, notes Ann Landers. "Their gripes fall into two major categories: 1) not enough, 2) too much."

Many of the marital problems concern adultery. "The cheating husband is insecure and needs to keep proving himself," she counsels. "The wise wife understands this. She doesn't rush to the divorce court, although she may well have more than adequate legal grounds."

"I've been told to drop dead, get lost, stop playing God, and quit making up crazy letters," states Ann Landers. "I've been called a crummy broad, a square from Iowa, and a broken-down museum

110

piece. The cocktail set insists I am a reformed drunk who is determined to dry up the world. I've been accused of being a public relations agent for the American Medical Association and a mouthpiece for the American Psychiatric Association."

Through the years, the specialists Ann Landers regularly consults with, mostly by telephone, include Dr. Mary Griffin (Northbrook, Ill.); Drs. Robert Stolar (dermatologist) and Zigmond Lebensohn (psychiatrist) in Washington, D.C.; Dr. John P. Merrill (kidney specialist at Harvard); Dr. Michael De Bakey (Houston heart specialist); Dr. George Pollack (Chicago psychoanalyst); Dr. William Simpson (psychiatrist at the Menninger Foundation); Dr. Jordan Block (Chicago dentist); Chicago attorneys Harold Katz, Newton Minow and Morris Leibman, and a large group of religious experts, including Rabbi Balfour Brickner (New York), Rev. Theodore Hesburgh (president of the University of Notre Dame) and Bishop John J. Paul in La Crosse, Wisconsin.

Most of the advisors are men. In the past, the advisors included such distinguished physicians as Philip Soloman (Boston), Edwin M. Litin (Mayo Clinic) and Maynard Cook and Chicago attorneys Lowell Sachnoff and Jack Pritzker.

Most readers simply are unaware of the enormous research effort involved in the Ann Landers column.

The Landers office is at the Chicago Sun-Times and The Boss lives in a nearby luxury apartment house, where the furnishings include Picasso and Renoir paintings and a collection of owls. For years, whenever readers and friends heard of her interest in owls, they would send her replicas of owls in glass, bronze, ceramic, plastic and just about every conceivable material, including, of course, the real thing.

The intertwining of Abby and Ann Landers is indicated by the fact that Jules Lederer worked for his brother-in-law, Morton Phillips (Abby's husband) at National Presto Industries. Mr. Lederer then became president of the Autopoint Company in Chicago, one of the first ballpoint manufacturers. Married on July 2, 1939, their daughter, Margo, was born the following year.

A pert, glamorous brunette, Ann Landers Lederer doesn't drink or smoke, plays the violin—though not in public, doesn't care for parties, and is active in various civic and charity organizations.

In a TV interview on the David Frost Show, Ann Landers said that the most commonly asked questions from her readers are from parents about their children, and teen-agers about their parents. Describing herself as a "Jewish, small town, conservative, middle class square," Miss Landers noted that she has changed her views through the years due to changing moralities.

Even before her own divorce, she stated that she had become more accepting of divorce (her daughter Margo is divorced), but strongly opposed to premarital intercourse ("it violates the moral and ethical rules of our society.") When we disregard rules, we pay a penalty, and the penalty for premarital sex is usually guilt, self-deprecation, worry, and a sullied reputation. Sometimes the penalty is V.D. or pregnancy.")

She is in favor of legalized abortion, and equal rights for women, somewhat accepting of mixed faith marriages ("It's risky, but the decision is highly personal.") and frowns on the use of marijuana. A Democrat, she supported Eugene McCarthy and Edmund Muskie, but criticized aspects of the McGovern platform, including the women's liberation issues.

She told Christianity Today in the March 13, 1970, issue, "I have noticed definite trends in permissiveness on the part of parents. Perhaps a better word is abdicated."

A typical letter started, "I am in love with the man I plan to marry in a few months. He is in love with his former girl friend." The reader asked if she should marry him and Miss Landers provided the answer with her usual forthright brevity:

"Not unless you are willing to live a lifetime knowing you are second choice."

In the Saturday Review article, Miss Landers concluded, "There is an enormous need for such a column, and I view it as one of journalism's great challenges, a unique opportunity to spotlight ignorance, fear and stupidity. I pray only that I am equal to the task."

Reader mail to Ann Landers is consistently among the highest of all columnists. In 1970, Miss Landers set some sort of record when she offered readers a free American Cancer Society booklet on breast self-examination. About 350,000 requests were received by the society.

Various Ann Landers' booklets, including "Necking and Petting—What are the Limits," "The Bride's Guide" and "Marriage: What to Expect," are sold as part of a publishing operation which produces considerable income.

Almost all of Miss Landers' correspondents write to her in care of their local newspaper and mail generally gets to her, even from non-subscribing newspapers, in about two weeks. Occasionally, Miss Landers directs readers to write to a particular organization, and the reaction is overwhelming.

On May 1, 1972, Miss Landers published a letter from a reader who complained about cruel insults to handicapped people on television programs. Miss Landers responded by urging readers to complain to the television networks, and gave the names of the presidents of the three networks and their addresses. Typographical errors resulted in incorrect zip codes for all three, but her intentions were laudable, and several thousand people sent copies of the column to the TV executives.

Miss Landers also has written several books, including "Since You Asked Me," "Ann Landers Talks to Teen-Agers About Sex," "Truth Is Stranger," and, in late 1978, "The Ann Landers Encyclopedia—From A to Z."

Of all the questions asked her, one of the most common subjects is women's health. In this category, Miss Landers says that the two most-asked questions are:

"A woman will outline some symptoms and ask me if she's pregnant.

"A woman will ask me what is the 100% safe way to keep from getting pregnant."

On Christmas Day each year, Miss Landers writes an essay in which she reviews the problems of our society. In 1971, her message concluded:

"I realize that many people who write don't want advice, they merely need someone to listen.

"I have been entrusted with the largest reading audience in the world. What a magnificent opportunity to shine a spotlight on ignorance and fear. There is no greater satisfaction than to serve, and I will continue to do my best. May the new year bring peace, good health and contentment to you all."

THE DOCTORS

The "Bill of Rights" currently being distributed to patients at many hospitals, the open discussion of euthanasia, the increase in malpractice litigation all are evidence of the changing attitudes of large segments of the public toward medicine. Health education can be annoying to physicians who are unaccustomed to being questioned by patients, but it is part of the consumerism movement.

Medical and scientific articles always have been a bulwark of the Reader's Digest, and a few other publications, such as the National Enquirer and the women's magazines, turn out a steady stream of articles about new medical research, drugs and treatment. Some of it, such as wonder diets and cancer cures, can offer false hope or be misleading and doctors often are annoyed at patients who ask them why they don't prescribe some of the new remedies.

The largest source of medical information for the lay person is the local newspaper. Health columnists are one of the oldest and most lucrative categories in the newspaper syndicate business. They also are among the most influential.

In 1977, the Register and Tribune Syndicate introduced "After Divorce," a column by Dr. Melvyn Berke; the Los Angeles Times Syndicate launched "Food & Fitness," by Dr. Lawrence Power of Wayne State University College of Medicine, and a sex- and marriage-counseling column by Los Angeles psychologist, Irene Kassorla; and Princeton Features started a sex column by Dr. Robert Long of the University of Louisville School of Medicine. The subjects reflect changing mores, as well as the continuing dominance of health columns. Other new columns in 1977 were started by Leonore Feinstein ("Medical Frontiers," Chronicle Features), Dr. Allen W. Mathies Jr. of the University of Southern California School of

Medicine (Inter-Continental Features) and Dr. Elizabeth Morgan of Yale New Haven Hospital.

The leaders among the health columnists are Dr. Lester Coleman, Dr. Frank Falkner, Dr. Lawrence Lamb, Dr. Jean Mayer, Dr. Neil Solomon and Dr. George C. Thosteson. Dr. Solomon, a psychiatrist with M.D. and Ph.D. degrees, is relatively new, but most of the others have been columning for a decade or more.

Many of these authors are the equivalent of old fashioned general practitioners and their house calls are viewed with the absolute respect and fidelity which many patients no longer accord to their own physicians. Sophisticated readers may mock the homey advice of Dr. Thosteson, and some of his other cronies, but their prejudices are likely to be unfounded. The average age of the health columnists is rather high, but almost all of them keep abreast of the current professional journals, and serve as science reporters.

Those who are turned off by the folksy bedside manner of medical columnists with old fashioned values can read Dr. Lawrence Lamb and others who advocate sexual permissiveness and candidly discuss contemporary social issues.

The styles and subject preference varies among the health columnists. Dr. Lester Coleman is an eye-ear-nose-throat specialist, Dr. Michael Halberstram is a cardiologist, and along with most of the other specialists, they tend to favor their special interests. This occasionally produces sharp differences of opinion between two medical columns, but generally, the viewpoints are unified and relatively conservative.

Newspapers are a family medium, with almost all sections rated G, to be read by all ages, and only recently have a few non-underground newspapers broken out of this mold. The health columnists were talking about venereal disease, drug abuse, alcoholism and unwanted pregnancy long before other mass media, and their current role in education in and beyond the health field tends to be grossly underestimated by those who are unfamiliar with them.

The first *syndicated* medical column was written by Dr. William Brady, an upstate New York general practitioner who started a column in the Elmira Star-Gazette in 1914.

When he died in Beverly Hills in 1972, he was 92 and thus was America's oldest columnist, in age and in number of years of syndication. The National Newspaper Syndicate tried to set a few more records by continuing to distribute the column, without changing the name of the late author, but it finally petered out.

The homespun general practitioner had turned out, with the aid of a researcher, a solid *daily* dose of old fasioned, no-nonsense medical advice, called "Personal Health Service," for 58 years. Dr. Brady sometimes is referred to as the country's first medical columnist, but

116

that distinction belongs to Dr. William A. Evans, a Chicago health commissioner and professor at Northwestern, who wrote for the Chicago Tribune from 1911 to 1934. Another pioneer was Dr. Joseph G. Molner, whose Chicago Sun-Times Syndicate column appeared in more than 300 newspapers.

One of the foremost popularizers of medicine was David Dietz, who became the science editor of Scripps-Howard Newspapers in 1921, the first newspaperman with that title. He started a daily column on science and medical research in the Cleveland Press in 1923, which appeared in the New York World-Telegram and other major newspapers. He estimated that he wrote nine million words as a columnist. Deitz proposed the organization of the National Association of Science Writers in 1934 and became its first president. He received a Pulitzer Prize in 1937. His first book, "The Story of Science," was published in 1931, and he wrote eight books since then.

Born in Cleveland in 1897, David Henry Dietz has lived in the area all his life and is a big booster of Cleveland. He received a B.A. degree from Western Reserve University and 29 years later was awarded a doctorate in literature.

The most famous medical columnist was Dr. Morris Fishbein, editor of the Journal of the American Medical Association from 1924 to 1949 and then editor of Medical World News, who wrote a newspaper column for 27 years.

When he was honored in 1969 at a banquet in Chicago to celebrate his 80th birthday, Dr. Fishbein was greeted by medical leaders from around the world, including South Africa's Christian Bernard, who said, "When I look at Morris Fishbein's accomplishments, I develop an inferiority complex."

Dr. Fishbein died in 1977, at the age of 88.

The elder statesman of the psychological advice columnists for several decades was George W. Crane, an anomalous combination of psychiatrist (an M.D., he still sees patients at his Chicago office), psychologist (a Ph.D., he is author of one of the most widely used applied psychology college textbooks), and Sunday school teacher (thousands of his Bible booklets have been distributed and he received the Religious Heritage Award for 35 years of Bible class). But if that isn't enough to worry anyone, Dr. Crane also is an advertising expert, and taught the subject at George Washington University and Northwestern University.

The father of five children, Dr. Crane generally is conservative in his views on sex, marriage and family problems, though he has been known to boldly attack "scalpel-lazy surgeons," "soporific clergymen," and teachers who rely on tenure instead of ability.

One of Dr. Crane's early rooters was William Randolph Hearst Sr., who urged him to "needle stodgy wives. Then they'll flood us with red-hot letters. We'll print them and this will become the best-read page in the newspaper."

The column, called "The Worry Clinic" was one of the most successful of the advice columns, indeed of any columns. It appeared in about 300 newspapers and, surprisingly, was not distributed by one of the major companies, but rather by the Hopkins Syndicate, located in Mellott, Indiana, a small town near Indianapolis.

Subscribers included the Indianapolis Star, Boston Globe, and Miami Herald. Among the thousands of letters sent by readers, mostly women, to Dr. Crane, the largest from any newspaper generally was the Santa Ana Register, which forwarded about a thousand letters a month from its 173,000 circulation.

Dr. Crane's Quiz, also distributed daily by Hopkins, appeared in the comics and feature sections of many major newspapers.

Garry Cleveland Myers, who had a Ph.D. in education, was editor-in-chief of Highlights for Children, a publication he started with his wife, Caroline Clark, and other members of his family in 1946 in Honesdale, Pa. His column, "Parent Problems," was syndicated by King Features to Chicago Today and about 100 newspapers six times a week for more than 40 years, until his death in 1971.

Other child-care advisors who were prominent columnists were New York pediatrician Dr. Milton I. Levine, who wrote for General Features, and Myrle Meyer Eldred, author of "Your Baby and Mine," which was syndicated daily and Sunday by the Register and Tribune Syndicate from 1922 to 1971. At her retirement in 1971, Mrs. Eldred was the mother of three children, grandmother of six, great grand-mother of seven, and "honorary mother" of many thousands. Though she had some relevant training (at Teachers College of Columbia University and the pediatrics clinic of St. Luke's Hospital in New York), her basic orientation was common sense motherly advice.

Another prominent psychologist-columnist was Haim Ginott, who died in 1973, at the age of 51. The King Features weekly column, "Between Us," was continued for a few years by his wife, Dr. Alice Lasker Ginott, also a psychologist.

"No parent wakes up early in the morning planning to make his child's life miserable. No mother says to herself, "Today I'll yell, nag and humiliate my child whenever possible.' On the contrary. In the morning many mothers resolve: 'This is going to be a peaceful day. No yelling, no arguing, and no fighting.' "

Thus begins "Between Parent and Child, New Solutions to Old Problems," by Haim G. Ginott, Ph.D. Published by Macmillan in 1965, the book was a succinct, delightful, easy-to-read collection of illustrations of "childrenese," a new way for parents to get through to their children. Subsequent Ginott books were "Between Parent and Teenager" and "Teacher and Child."

Born in Israel in 1922, Haim Ginott received bachelor's, master's and doctorate degrees from Columbia University, was an elementary school teacher and psychologist in Jacksonville and a professor at Adelphi University and New York University. He became particularly well-known as "resident psychologist" on the Today television program and as the author of a column in Family Circle. He had two daughters, Mimi and Roz.

The syndicated column, which started in 1970, developed a faithful following among young parents, an audience which is highly regarded by newspaper publishers.

The prolific writer and incredibly busy teacher said that he wrote as a necessity. "If I don't write," Dr. Ginott told Publishers Weekly, "the tension to say something builds. I enjoy the struggle of putting into succinct, practical terms a complex, clinical concept. And it isn't only the process of putting words on paper that I enjoy. I want to write beautifully as well. My native tongue is Hebrew, and for me there is a special joy in having mastered the English language in all its nuances."

Advice to parents also was provided by Louise Bates Ames, whose "Parents Ask," was distributed five times a week by Publishers-Hall.

A prominent child psychologist (Ph.D., Yale University), Dr. Ames was research director of the Gesell Institute of Child Development in New Haven. From 1968 to1975, she authored a question-and-answer newspaper column, with child psychiatrist Dr. Frances L. Ilg.

The late Dr. Arnold Gesell, a pioneer in research in child development, developed a new approach to the problems of child guidance and behavior. His orientation, based on the observation and charting of normal behavior, was carried on by Drs. Ames and Ilg in books, magazine articles and newspaper columns.

As might be expected, most of the health columnists are M.D.'s. Leaders in the fifties included Dr. Herman Bunderson; Dr. H.L. Herschensohn of the Los Angeles Mirror-News (later syndicated by the Los Angeles Times); Dr. Edwin Jordan, who appeared in the New York World-Telegram and Sun and many other NEA outlets; and Dr. Albert Edward Wiggam of the National Newspaper Syndicate, who appeared in the New York Mirror, Long Island Press, Long Island Star-Journal, all of which are defunct.

The leaders in the sixties, in terms of number of subscribers, were Drs. Walter Alvarez, S.L. Andelman, Peter Steincrohn, George Thosteson and Theodore Van Dellen. None of them were young men, and the oldest was a phenomenon among columnists—Walter Clement Alvarez, who was born in San Francisco in 1884 and died in the same city in 1977, at the age of 93.

For many years, his syndicate, the Register and Tribune, avoided discussions of his age for fear that subscribers would feel that Dr. Alvarez was old fashioned. Publishers who are potential new subscribers are wary of any columnist over sixty, not just for fear that the author may not write in a lively manner, but rather that the columnist might not be alive long enough to establish an audience.

"Some men may wonder if I have driven myself all these years because I was ambitious for wealth or position," stated Dr. Alvarez. "I asked myself that question, and I think that the answer is that what has motivated me and led me on is no more than curiosity, and the desire always to know and understand more, not only of medicine, but of life in general. In fact, my father worried when he saw that I had no interest in making money. The only ambition that I can remember was to become a well-informed physician so that I could have the fun of making difficult diagnoses, and the pleasure of having fine friends whom I respected."

In 1972, at the age of 88, Dr. Alvarez summarized his experience in the treatment and understanding of epilepsy in "Nerves in Collision," a Pyramid book which contended that there may be 10 million Americans who suffer from the myriad, mild, non-conventional forms of epilepsy which often are undetected.

The affable Dr. Alvarez, who lived for many years in a Michigan Avenue hotel along Chicago's near-North Side, looked and talked like a man who is several decades younger. "Whenever I get the time," said Dr. Alvarez, "I peek at Ann Landers' column to see how she handles situations. I think that the lovelorn columnists have great wisdom and do a lot of good."

Other health columnists in the early seventies included Dr. William G. Crook ("Child Care"), Dr. Frank Falkner ("Young and Healthy"), Dr. A.L. Herschensohn ("Medical Memos"), Dr. Alfred A. Messer ("Eye on Your Family"), Dr. Irwin J. Polk ("Men and Medicine"), Dr. Paul Popenoe ("Your Family and You"), Dr. Leonard Reiffel, Dr. Eleanor Rodgerson, and Dr. Lee Salk.

The family doctor advice of Dr. Alvarez appeared for over 25 years in the Jacksonville Journal, Chicago Tribune and more than 60 other newspapers.

A graduate of Stanford University Medical School, Dr. Alvarez took over his father's practice in Cananea, Mexico, a small city near the Arizona border, and became fluent in Spanish. His first research paper, on syphilis, appeared in the Journal of the American Medical Association in 1907. By 1925, he had published 75 papers, including a controversial article in 1919 titled "Protest Against the Reckless Extraction of Teeth." Dr. Alvarez produced the first charts of stomach activity, called electrogastrograms. From 1925 until his retirement in 1950, Dr. Alvarez was a researcher at the Mayo Clinic in Rochester, Minnesota, where he became an authority on the physiology of the digestive tract and was editor of two journals, Gastroenterology and also the American Journal of Digestive Diseases. Dr. Alvarez was a pioneer in recognizing the psychological influence in producing disease symptoms and his specialties included migraine headaches, food allergies, and strokes.

In 1907, he married Harriet Smith, who died in 1973. Their two sons and two daughters include Dr. Luis W. Alvarez, who received a Nobel Prize in 1968 for physics research at the University of California.

It may be coincidental that the American Medical Association is headquartered in Chicago, but it is a fact that quite a few health columnists were long-time Chicago residents.

Another generality is that a majority of the top columnists are super-educated, with graduate degrees in addition to the M.D. degree. A good example is Samuel Louis Andelman, who was born in Chicago in 1916 and has a B.S., M.S., and a Master's degree in public health (M.P.H.), as well as an M.D. degree.

Born in Chicago in 1911, Dr. Theodore Robert Van Dellen was active for many years in various Chicago health organizations, was a lecturer at Northwestern University Medical School, and, in 1945, became medical editor at The Chicago Tribune. In addition to the general medical advice column, he also wrote, with the aid of a researcher, a semi-weekly column for parents, titled "How to Keep Your Child Well."

Both of his columns appeared in The Chicago Tribune and New York News, and one or both were in more than 100 newspapers, including The Tampa Times.

A key feature of many health columns is the availability of booklets. Distribution generally is handled by mailing houses, but the income is split between the author and the syndicate and often is extremely sizable. One of the most successful bookleteers was Dr. Peter J. Steincrohn, author of McNaught's six-times-a-week column, "Stop Killing Yourself."

In the sixties, after about 40 years as an extremely active internist and cardiologist in Hartford, Connecticut, Dr. Steincrohn took the advice he had given to thousands of patients and retired to Coral Gables, Florida. Readers of the Philadelphia Bulletin, Hackensack Record, Kansas City Star and about 100 other newspapers can obtain booklets by Dr. Steincrohn for 25 cents and a stamped self-addressed envelope. Subjects include acne, arthritis, diet, stomach trouble, skin problems, change of life, sleep and others. The most popular are the first two written by Dr. Steincrohn, "22 Ways to Prevent and Treat Coronary Disease" and "How to Stop Killing Yourself." Hypoglycemia is the most common misdiagnosed disease, according to Dr. Steincrohn, and he attempted to rectify this in a 1972 book, "Low Blood Sugar."

Dr. George C. Thosteson, chief endocrinologist at Harper Hospital in Detroit and prominent internal medicine specialist, was proud to be known as the author of what probably was the country's most widely syndicated health column. But for years, Dr. Thosteson kept his literary life a secret.

"To Your Health" originally was bylined by Dr. Joseph C. Molner, a Detroit health official, but actually written by Dr. Thosteson and Jack Pickering, a science writer. Dr. Thosteson was concerned that a popular column would tarnish his reputation among his medical colleagues. As he achieved increased recognition for his work in medical research and treatment, and as the column became increasingly respected by health professionals and laymen, Dr. Thosteson started to acknowledge his role as a ghost writer. Dr. Molner had been ill for years when Publishers-Hall finally decided to replace the Molner byline with that of Dr. Thosteson. Some readers complained that Dr. Thosteson was not as good a writer as his predecessor, while others praised the "new writer." The syndicate resisted the temptation to tell the behind-the-scenes story, though many Detroiters and others knew about the minor intrigue. Dr. Molner died in 1968.

Born in Detroit in 1906, George C. Thosteson was one of the founding members of the American Diabetes Association, and was an authority on metabolism. He died in 1978, and the column has been continued by Dr. Paul E. Ruble.

"To Your Good Health" appears in the Detroit Free Press, Chicago Sun-Times, Newark Star-Ledger, St. Louis Post Dispatch, Cleveland Plain Dealer, San Francisco Chronicle, Philadelphia Inquirer, Boston Herald American, Los Angeles Herald-Examiner, and more than 200 newspapers. The column occasionally promotes the sale (35 cents) of booklets on diabetes and other medical problems, and the response is sufficient to increase the metabolic rate of any columnist.

The preponderance of readers of medical columns are women, and it therefore was logical for the National Newspaper Syndicate (whose superstar was Dr. William Brady) to introduce, in the sixties, a semi-weekly health article titled "For Women Only." The author was Dr. Lindsay R. Curtis, a University of Utah specialist in obstetrics and gynecology who has pioneered in the field of natural and "satisfying" childbirth. The Curtis column, which then was distributed by NEA, was not very different from other medical columns, particularly since he is interested in drug addiction and other general interest problems. He has written six books and his more than a dozen booklets include "Smoking or Health," "After Hysterectomy, What," and two which have been used by the U.S. Navy, "VD: America's Growing Threat" and "Alcohol: Fun or Folly."

Another logical development among health columns was the introduction in the sixties of a column about nutrition by Dr. Frederick J. Stare, whose qualifications indeed were astounding. Born in Columbus, Wisconsin, in 1910, he received B.S., M.S. and Ph.D.

122

degrees in biochemistry from the University of Wisconsin, an M.D. degree from the University of Chicago and a doctor of science degree from Trinity College in Dublin. The triple-doctor has been a researcher at various hospitals and has been at the Harvard Medical School and School of Public Health since 1947, where he is chairman of the department of nutrition.

The semi-weekly column was syndicated by the Los Angeles Times to the Philadelphia Inquirer, Miami Beach Sun-Reporter and over 100 newspapers unitl 1977. For 25 years, Dr. Stare's column, "Food and Your Health," was an important source of criticism of the nutritional deficiencies of candy, bread and other foods.

In 1972, Dr. Stare "welcomed" another nutrition columnist, none other than a professor in his department, Dr. Jean Mayer.

An amazing trait almost universally common to super-successful individuals is their ability to handle many major activities almost simultaneously. Perhaps it's something they eat. A prime example is the ubiquitous Jean Mayer, who now is president of Tufts University, in Medford, Mass., near Boston. He writes "Food for Thought" with the assistance of Johanna Dwyer, director of the Nutrition Center of Tufts-New England Medical Center.

Jean Mayer (pronounced My-air) has written over 400 research papers, 50 popular articles, and several books. He was a pioneer student of obesity and the physiology of hunger (his 1968 book was titled "Overweight: Causes, Cost and Control"), organized and was chairman of the 1969 White House Conference on Food, Nutrition and Health, founded the National Council on Hunger and Malnutrition in the United States, worked for the United Nations Food and Agricultural Organization, and has extensively studied and crusaded against poverty and malnutrition in Africa, Asia and the United States.

Jean Mayer was born in Paris in 1920 into a family of scientists. Both parents were physiologists and his father was president of the French Academy of Medicine and one of the creators of the United Nations Food and Agricultural Organization.

Young Jean received four degrees from the University of Paris, including a doctor of science in physiology, and a Ph.D. in physiological chemistry from Yale University in 1948, where his thesis was on Vitamin A.

His activities during the Second World War are as dazzling as his academic credentials. He was in the French underground as a British intelligence agent, fought with the Free French and Allied forces in North Africa and Italy, and earned numerous decorations and the rank of Captain. A U.S. citizen, Dr. Mayer became a professor of nutrition at Harvard University Graduate School of Public Health in 1950. His research focused on glucose and phosphorus levels in the blood and other physiological studies related to appetite, diet and nutrition.

A frequent witness at congressional hearings, Dr. Mayer is credited with persuading President Nixon to include a food stamp program in his welfare plan. He married a Bostonian, Elizabeth Van Huysen, and the Mayers, who live in Boston, have five children. Presumably, all are well fed.

The semi-weekly newspaper column, started by the Chicago Tribune-New York News Syndicate in 1972, raised a few eyebrows at Harvard because the "competitor" was Dr. Frederick J. Stare, who, as chairman of the department of nutrition was Dr. Mayer's boss. In Philadelphia, for example, Dr. Stare was in the Inquirer and Dr. Mayer was in the Bulletin.

"Food for Thought" answers readers' questions and stresses the Mayer philosophy, which is that much of our food has degenerated in quality, the diet of most Americans is dangerously imbalanced, rich in fat and poor in nutrients, and that we are being harmed by an epidemic of nutritionally unbalanced fad diets with confusing claims. The average American, says Dr. Mayer, gets too little exercise, has peculiar eating habits, and "enters middle age upon graduation from high school."

A sample of the Mayer straightforward style:

"A quiet revolution is taking place on the shelves and in the freezers of supermarkets across our country. It amounts, on the face of it, to nothing more than a simple difference in the labels you see on the food packages. Yet many nutritionists, including myself, regard this as the key to upgrading the quality of our national food supply, promising better balanced meals for everyone."

The effervescent Dr. Mayer drinks coffee (could that be his energy secret?), lots of fruit juices, scorns such additives as wheat germ ("useful but with no particular magic virtue") and says of starchy snack foods, "fried worms would be better. At least you'd get some protein."

Dr. Mayer is very practical about foods which he advocates. He admits that "hamburgers and French fries are not bad foods for a physically active youngster," though he urges that it be supplemented by other items.

As for a good wine, French or American, now that's food for thought.

Perhaps the most commonly asked question of Dr. Mayer, particularly by male readers, is the relationship of fatty meats and other foods to heart disease.

"During the next year, millions of men will suffer from painful, often fatal heart attacks. Ironically, many of these attacks could be prevented by one very simple, very cheap, and very pleasant treatment: more sex."

124

Readers of Drs. Brady, Crane, Van Dellen and most other medical columnists would be shocked at the advice that sex not only is here to stay but it can help you stay here longer. That was the message for years of Dr. Eugene Scheimann, a sexologist who believed that sexual activity is good for your heart, can enhance your health and lengthen life. The column, "Let's Stay Well," was syndicated by United Features from 1968 to 1974.

Dr. Scheimann, a stern-looking, white-haired general practitioner who, in spite of his seniority (he was a practicing physician for about 50 years) was one of the new breed of medical columnists.

Dr. Scheimann's office on the near north side of Chicago, near a Skid Row area called Bughouse Square, became almost a spiritual home for people with social, sexual and medical problems. "The Clark Street blight has begun to spread over our entire contemporary society," says Dr. Scheimann. "Frustration, apathy, drug addiction, venereal disease and drunkenness are no longer confined to the social outcasts of Bug House Square."

Chicago columnist Mike Royko succinctly reaffirmed, "The whole country has become Bughouse Square."

In addition to his specialty as an emergency doctor for residents of flophouses and tenements, Dr. Scheimann pioneered in palmistry, astrology, graphology, psychic research and parapsychology. This endeared him to fans of Long John Nebel and other radio and TV programs on which he was a frequent guest, but it also produced occasional explosions, or at the least, quizzical appraisals, from some of his scientific colleagues.

Dr. Scheimann published articles in the Journal of the American Medical Association and other medical journals, but he was better known as a frequent contributor to Sexology, Forum, Cosmopolitan, Pageant and other magazines, and as author or co-author of several popular books, including "A Doctor's Guide to Better Health Through Palmistry" and "Sex and the Overweight Woman."

Almost all of the advice columnists are conservative with regard to homosexuality, group sex, mate swapping and almost anything offbeat. For years, most of the health and advice columnists discouraged premarital sexual relations, or avoided taking positions on almost any controversial social issue. In addition to Dr. Scheimann, a notable exception was Dr. Eugene Schoenfeld, who wrote a weekly column in the sixties called, "Dr. Hip Pocrates."

Hippocrates, the ancient Greek physician, was the "father of medicine," whose oath is a cornerstone of modern medical ethics.

Born in 1935 (2395 years after the first Dr. Hippocrates), Eugene Schoenfeld was a "hip" medic on the staff of the University of California student health services at Berkeley. He started his unusually frank, permissive column about sex and other health matters in 1967 in

125

the Berkeley Barb. It was quickly picked up by other underground newspapers and then emerged into the San Francisco Chronicle and other dailies as a sign of our less inhibited times, though the Chicago Sun-Times published it anonymously.

Gene Schoenfeld was married for about a year, when he was 19, but was divorced. During the summers of 1959 and 1960, he worked at the Schweitzer Hospital in Africa. He described Dr. Schweitzer as a "drop-out hippie who ran a commune" and was influenced by many of his ideas, particularly about ecology.

Many of the columns dealt with readers' questions about sex, were sprinkled with puns and editorials in behalf of national health insurance and improved nursing homes and in opposition to cigarette smoking and the habitual use of marijuana. Dr. Hip was the only syndicated columnist in the sixties who discussed and evaluated specific birth-control techniques. America's best-known sexologist, Dr. David Reuben, started a question-and-answer column about sex in late 1972. It was inevitable that this super-celebrity would become a columnist, but somewhat surprisingly, the Chicago Tribune-New York News Syndicate column was not successful, and was dropped after about a year. Perhaps some editors decided that the California psychiatrist already had told readers everything they wanted to know about sex, or at least, everything he had to say on the subject. More likely the problem was that the price to publishers appeared to be too high.

At about the same time that the Trib-News introduced Dr. Reuben, Dr. Joyce Brothers switched to King Features, and the Hearst company offered "Ask Dr. Brothers" to many newspapers at a much lower price than the Reuben column. If nothing else, at least Dr. Brothers avoided the male chauvinism which often seeped into the Reuben column.

Dr. Brothers also has the advantage of many years of column experience. She knows who her audience is and what they want to know.

For a few years in the early seventies, Dr. Brothers had minor competition from Dr. Lorlene Chase.

The tri-weekly Los Angeles Times Syndicate column consisted of questions and answers in the form of consulting-room dialogue. Trying to condense a complete problem and solution into 350 words often has inane results.

In Case No. 522, for example, the "Case," as the clients were called, was a mother whose 9-year-old daughter had witnessed a neighbor "exposing himself." Here's the dialogue:

"DOCTOR: Just what has he done?

"CASE: Sometimes he is in his garage when the children are playing near. He will attract the attention of my daughter and then expose

126

himself.

"DOCTOR: Have you done anything about it?

"CASE: I wanted to get some advice before saying something to him. I don't know how dangerous a person like this may be. If he does that, would he actually molest a child or peek in her window?

"DOCTOR: You have mentioned three different types of sex offenders in your question: the exhibitionist, the peeping tom—voyeur is the technical term—and the child molester."

Dr. Chase, not to be confused with Case, then went on to describe the three types and the column concluded:

"CASE: I see the difference now, but what can I do about this neighbor?

"DOCTOR: Assuming the child's report is accurate, first, you have to keep her away from him. Then the man should be confronted by an adult and made to realize he is in need of psychiatric treatment. His symptom is one which demonstrates deep-seated sexual confusion and immaturity which can often be solved if given proper care."

Lorlene Chase is a Californian who received three degrees (B.A., M.A., and Ph.D.) from the University of Southern California. Born in Sacramento in 1920, Lorlene Eck was a WAVE during the Second World War, married Leo Goodman-Malamuth in 1946, when she was an undergraduate at U.S.C., and was divorced five years later, when she was a graduate student. They had one child, Leo. She married Allen Chase in 1960. Dr. Chase has worked extensively with spastic children and psychic energizer drugs, and has conducted research on brain waves and extrasensory perception.

Comparisons with Dr. Joyce Brothers are obvious, including her TV fame. Dr. Chase was a "permanent guest expert" on "Art Linkletter's House Party" and had her own ABC-TV program. Viewers became familiar with her parapsychology views, which were highly controversial, but the one aspect of Dr. Chase on which there was absolute unanimity was that her beautiful appearance was an infallible psychic energizer.

The Los Angeles Times Syndicate takes no chances, however, and in its promotion piece to prospective subscribers, used a photo of Dr. Chase taken quite a few years ago.

Book publishers sometimes use outdated photos of authors on book jackets and in advertisements, so this kind of deception is not confined to the newspaper syndicate business.

Another of the new breed of health columnists is Lawrence E. Lamb, whose five-times-a-week column is frank, discusses sex, and even is occasionally humorous.

NEA started the column in late 1970 as a replacement for Dr. Wayne Brandstadt, who had been their long-time medical columnist. The Lamb column appears in the Philadelphia Daily News and about 100 newspapers.

A cardiologist and internal medicine specialist, Dr. Lamb is the author of many professional articles and books, and two general books, "Your Heart and How to Live With It," and "Dear Doctor: It's About Sex," a 1973 collection of his columns on sex. Born in 1926, Lawrence Lamb is an expert on exercise and diet, helped set up physical examination procedures for astronauts, was cardiologist for Lyndon B. Johnson, was professor of medicine at Baylor University in Houston, and now practices in San Antonio.

Of all "health columnists," the most famous is not a physician but rather a psychologist—Joyce Brothers.

In May 1972, Meredith, one of the regular characters on ABC's soap opera, "One Life to Live," was suffering from postpartum depression. She sought help from a clinical psychologist, Dr. Brothers, played by none other than Joyce Brothers, the psychologist whose initial fame had come from television.

Dr. Joyce Diane Brothers is a petite blonde vivacious genius who for years has produced a daily newspaper column and, at various times, also has had daily radio and TV programs, a monthly magazine and also lectured and made assorted appearances on the Tonight Show and other television programs.

She became a celebrity in 1956 when she won $134,000 on the TV program, "The $64,000 Question." Her category was "boxing."

In the sixties, the Joyce Brothers column was distributed by King Features to as many as 300 newspapers. In the early seventies, it was syndicated by Bell-McClure and appeared in about 100 newspapers, including the Long Island Press. When Dr. Brothers returned to King, a few more subscribers were added.

Dr. Brothers has received many honors and ranks high on "most respected people" polls and other barometers of public and professional opinion. She taught at Hunter and Columbia (her Ph.D. is from Columbia) and was a consultant to several companies. Among her many skills is an ability to read with amazing rapidity. Some of these secrets are revealed in her 1960 book, "Ten Days to a Successful Memory" and others are examined in the courses of the Reading Development Center, of which she was a part owner. Dr. Brothers also authored a 1962 book, "Woman" and many magazine articles.

Nowadays she tries to downplay or avoid discussion of her stint on "The $64,000 Question." Her many significant accomplishments as a teacher, author, lecturer and broadcaster make this understandable. Still, it's irresistible to ask her to name 25 heavyweight champions, and thrilling to hear her reply—John L. Sullivan, James J. Corbett, Robert Fitzsimmons, James J. Jeffries . . .

A few other topics are embarrasing to Dr. Brothers. One is the number of column subscribers. A 1972 ad for her book, "The Brothers

System for Liberated Love and Marriage" (with an introduction by Dr. Milton J. Brothers) stated that she received 5000 telephone calls a day from radio listeners and that her column appeared in 350 newspapers, which was an exaggeration.

Another grey area was the long-time ghost-writing role of Barbara Seamons. Also not-to-be-discussed is the American Psychological Association, which investigated her for unprofessional behavior. A few clinical psychologists complained that Dr. Brothers received her degree in experimental psychology, never practiced, and made unwarranted generalizations in her articles. To some outsiders, the carping seemed like sour grapes.

Though still youthful looking, Dr. Brothers avoids mention of her birthdate, in biographies and interviews. She was born in New York in 1928, and, in 1949, married Dr. Milton Brothers, an internal medicine specialist. They have a daughter, Lisa Robin.

Still another subject about which the less said the better was the 1972 movie debut of Joyce Brothers in "The War Between Men and Women," an alleged comedy.

Perhaps because she's so successful, and sometimes conveys a smugness in her broadcasts, Joyce Brothers has not been taken as seriously as she deserves. She's a charming, thoughtful, helpful, lucid columnist and has many loyal readers.

Other psychologists, physicians and science writers write a variety of syndicated health columns. Two of the most successful deal with the health of pets and are by veterinarians, Dr. Michael Fox of St. Louis and Dr. Frank Miller of San Francisco.

Surprisingly, there currently is no syndicated column by a dentist. There was one, in the sixties, and it was written by Dr. Sydney Garfield, a Beverly Hills, California, dentist.

"From the beginning THE TOOTH has been one with man. He evolved with him from the depths of oceans. From waters they crept over the land. Bound to the surface he lifted his head, then rising he spread, and breaking bounds, entered the skies. He's always been one with man—King and peasant alike—through sufferings and pains and agonies and death. And he joined his pleasures and loves, and wars and plagues, and orgies and feasts. And now THE TOOTH enters other realms, to moons and planets and the stars."

The noble prologue introduced a 448-page book, published in 1969 by Simon and Schuster, titled "Teeth Teeth Teeth." The incredible treatise was written and profusely illustrated by Dr. Garfield, who used the same triple-barreled title for a semi-weekly column which appeared in the Miami Herald and about 20 newspapers. It was a dental version of the typical medical advice column, and discussed peridontia, endodontia, pedodontia, orthodontia and other aspects of teeth in an easy-to-understand manner. A graduate of the University of Southern California School of Dentistry, Sydney Garfield studied engineering at the Cooper Union School of Engineering in New York and worked as an aircraft designer at Convair in San Diego and Lockheed in Burbank.

His book is replete with anecdotes about human dental problems but there's one about a baboon at the Los Angeles Zoo which is particularly memorable. It seems that the 11-year-old male was raping all the female baboons and terrorizing the other males. The zoo veterinarian finally decided that the solution was to extract the long upper canine teeth which the problem baboon was using in his ferocious assaults. Immediately after the extraction, the baboon lost all agression, and his virility ceased. He lost weight, his coat became shaggy and even old females picked on him.

Dr. Garfield quoted animal trainer Earl Chumley. "You've got to have teeth to be a fighter and you've got to be a fighter to be a lover. You can't have one without the other."

LYONS

The Lyons Den has closed. On Monday, May 20, 1974, just one day short of his 40th anniversary on the New York Post, Leonard Lyons wrote his farewell column.

It wasn't unexpected. The column had dwindled in length and frequency and many press agents and show business people were aware that Lyons had been ill. He died on October 7, 1976.

Leonard Lyons was genuinely liked by many thousands of people. He worked hard; he was never malicious; he was a family man. In summary, the opposite of the stereotyped columnist.

He probably made more errors than any other columnist. In almost every one of the well over 10,000 columns, there were misquotes, typos, screwed up punch lines and assorted errors. But they were unintentional and part of the Lyons style, so readers rarely were upset.

Whether they knew him only from the smiling photo atop the column or from seeing his bantam figure darting through a restaurant or elsewhere on his beat, New Yorkers felt a kinship with Leonard Lyons.

Through the years, Post readers grew up with Leonard Lyons, and his four sons, George, Warren, Jeffrey and Douglas, and their children.

Of course, the photo never changed, and the anecdotes often were repeated in the column, but never mind, it was good to be able to count on Lyons still being there. In fact, the familiarity was habit forming.

The Post always has been crammed with columns. These features are a smorgasbord, and the newspaper is a Jewish mother urging her children to eat. The Lyons Den was the longest of the columns but oh-so-much easier to read than Max Lerner, James Wechsler or any of the political oracles. The Lyons Den was a journalistic phenomenon, a heterogeneous collection of show business, literary and political news items, anecdotes and other easy-to-read, entertaining material zealously gathered by Leonard Lyons during a 12-hour work day.

In the thirties and forties—the golden era of New York columnists—the New York News, Mirror, and Herald Tribune in the morning and the Post, Journal-American, Sun and World-Telegram in the evening carried the columns of Frank Farrell, Hy Gardner, Mark Hellinger, Dorothy Kilgallen, Leonard Lyons, Lee Mortimer, Damon Runyon, Louis Sobol, Ed Sullivan, Danton Walker, Earl Wilson, Walter Winchell and many other New York-based writers.

Most of these column stars are gone now. Hy Gardner does a question-and-answer column with his wife Marilyn, from Miami. The only remaining New York gossiper who is widely syndicated is Earl Wilson. Born in Ohio in 1907, Earl Wilson still covers the New York scene with the enthusiasm of an out-of-towner who is in awe of the big City.

There are still a few gossip columnists, Suzy (Aileen Mehle), Liz Smith and Jack O'Brian in New York, plus Marilyn Beck, James Bacon and others in Los Angeles. The biggest, in number of subscribers, probably are Earl Wilson and Robin Adams Sloan (a pseudonym), who is syndicated by King Features to The New York News and other major newspapers. It's hard to relate to Sloan since the identity of the author (or authors) is a big secret. The others, particularly Wilson, certainly have their fans.

But Leonard Lyons was special. At its height, The Lyons Den appeared in only a relatively small number of newspapers (much fewer than claimed by the syndicate and the author), but Lyons achieved international fame as one of the few columnists who reached a select audience of influential people in the arts and politics.

The heyday of the gossip columnists was in the twenties and thirties when several hundred "flacks" earned their livings, in offices ranging from phone booths to elaborate suites, by providing items, tips and sometimes entire columns. Lyons used a great deal of material from public relations sources but he also tirelessly collected items from the dozens of celebrities he encountered as he toured his mid-Manhattan beat.

Born on the lower East Side of New York in 1906, Leonard Lyons graduated from the City College of New York and St. John's Law College. This was a supreme accomplishment. His father, Moses Leib Sucher, died when Leonard was a boy and his mother, a European immigrant who couldn't read or write English, ran a small candy store. The Lyons name was somewhat based on his father's middle name. If he had been literal, it would have been Love or, if had chosen the transliteration from the Yiddish of the last name, his name might have been Sweet.

132

Lyons practiced law from 1929 to 1934 (at the Wall Street firm of Armstrong, Keith & Kern) and maintained an active interest in the legal field, which partly accounted for his many exclusive interviews with William O. Douglas, Earl Warren and other Supreme Court Justices.

When the Duke of Windsor died in 1972, the column featured a collection of anecdotes which included the personal reminiscence that Lyons and the Duke had spoken in Spanish when they first met. Lyons, who had studied Spanish at the High School of Commerce in Manhattan, told the Duke that he had planned to practice law in Puerto Rico but his marriage and writing career intervened.

Lyons then quoted the Duke's reply, "You mean you had a career lined up, and you met a woman who changed your plans? How curious. Do tell me more."

The story probably was true, but even if it was altered or apocryphal, it was typically, delightfully, Leonard Lyons.

Married in 1934, he and his wife, Sylvia Schonberger, were inveterate travelers, with friends in almost every major capital. The family lived for many years in an apartment house on the West Side of Manhattan opposite the American Museum of Natural History. Other tenants who were friends included Mike Nichols, Isaac Stern, and Phyllis Newman and Adolph Green.

Lyons could have retired many years ago, could have bought a posh East Side townhouse (like Kilgallen) or a suburban estate (like Winchell). It was typical of him that he did not do any of these, and his zestful style of living remained that of a cub reporter. New Yorkers frequently saw him on the subway or dashing along the streets, from one favorite restaurant to another, constantly on the alert for quips, stories and news items.

Many articles were written about Leonard Lyons, and readers of The Wall Street Journal, Time, Newsweek, Holiday, and other publications were informed of such details as his income (once alleged to be $300,000 a year but probably considerably less) and the restaurants on his daily itinerary. Most of the articles grossly exaggerated the number of newspapers carrying The Lyons Den and erred, in Lyons' favor, on other details, but one aspect of his life which was chronicled with fidelity was the fastidious manner in which he covered his beat. New Yorkers bumped into him almost any day (except when he was on one of his several-times-a-year jaunts) on the street or even in the subway. His noon-time beat almost always included Sardi's, the Hotel Algonquin, the Ground Floor restaurant in the CBS building, 21, La Grenouille, Cote Basque, Four Seasons. The nighttime trek included most of the same places, as well as a few other celebrity hangouts.

Ports of call, particularly Le Pavillon, Billy Rose's Diamond

Horseshoe, the Latin Quarter, Cafe Society, Cotton Club and Stork Club, could count on Lyons to scan the house for VIPs and other sources of items. A non-drinker and prolific note taker, Lyons never ate at any of the restaurants on his beat, partly because of his peripatetic work schedule and partly due to his preference for kosher food.

"Imagine how much richer American history would have been had there been a Leonard Lyons in Lincoln's time!" Carl Sandburg once remarked.

Lyons was with George Bernard Shaw on the playwright's 90th birthday. He was the first reporter to whom Ingrid Bergman and Roberto Rosselini gave an interview after the birth of their son and before their marriage. Mrs. Ernest Hemingway selected Leonard Lyons to release to the world the news of the death of the Nobel prize-winning giant. Hemingway, an old friend of Lyons, once said: "In the 24 years of our friendship, Lyons never bored me once."

Lyons popularized fine artists and fashion designers. His column promoted Picasso, Braque, Dufy, Utrillo and Chagall. Famous songwriters played on the piano in his home the scores of their musicals and songs from their shows, not yet produced, but destined to be great hits.

The result of this lifestyle was that Leonard Lyons was genuinely liked by literally thousands of artists, performers, writers and publicists. Divorces and romances were not part of the Lyons style and he scrupulously avoided scandal.

Gossip columnist Jack O'Brian said that Lyons didn't always avoid raps and that he practiced "spit ball journalism," consisting of occasional neat little knocks handled with "a formal, almost Talmudic solemnity."

The Lyons name, The Lyons Den, was suggested by Walter Winchell, who helped Lyons get started at King Features, which also handled Winchell. Lyons switched to the McNaught Syndicate when he had a series of disagreements with William Randolph Hearst. One of the problems involved Lyons' many plugs for Orson Welles and his movie, Citizen Kane. However, McNaught then was syndicating O.O. McIntyre to more than 700 newspapers and many of the McNaught subscribers felt that they could not handle another "New York humor columnist," so Lyons moved to The New York Post Syndicate. The Post later merged with the Hall Syndicate, which merged in 1967 with Publishers Newspaper Syndicate to become Publishers-Hall. The name was changed to Field Newspaper Syndicate in 1975.

Lyons attributed his start as a columnist to J. David Stern, the publisher of The Philadelphia Record and The New York Post. When Stern died in 1971, at the age of 85, Lyons wrote, "He hired me for the New York Post although I had no newspaper experience, and had never been to a nightclub."

Leonard Lyons more than made up for his lack of newspaper and nightclub experience. He had an unusual loyalty to his readers, and to publicists. We miss you, Len.

MAJOR SYNDICATES
(Abbreviations in Parentheses)

Chicago Tribune-New York News Syndicate (CTNYNS)
220 E. 42nd St., N.Y. 10017, (212) 949-3400

Chronicle Features
870 Market St., San Francisco, Ca. 94102, (415) 777-7212

Columbia Features
36 W. 44th St., N.Y. 10036, (212) 840-1812

Copley News Service
Box 190, 350 Camino de la Reina, San Diego, Ca. 92112,
(714) 299-3131

Field Newspaper Syndicate
401 N. Wabash Ave., Chicago 60611, (312) 321-2795
N.Y. Office: 30 E. 42nd St., N.Y. 10017, (212) 874-2040

Gannett News Service
Broad & Exchange Sts., Rochester, N.Y. 14614, (716) 232-7100

King Features Syndicate
235 E. 45th St., N.Y. 10017, (212) 682-5600

Los Angeles Times Syndicate (LAT)
Times-Mirror Square, L.A. 90053, (213) 625-2345

137

Los Angeles Times/Washington Post News Service (LATWP)
1150 15th St., N.W., Wash., D.C. 20071, (202) 223-6173

McNaught Syndicate
60 E. 42nd St., N.Y. 10017, (212) 682-8787

The New York Times News Service (NYT)
229 W. 43rd St., N.Y. 10036, (212) 556-7087

New York Times Syndicate Sales Corp.—Special Features (NYT)
200 Park Ave., N.Y. 10017, (212) 972-1070

Newspaper Enterprise Association (NEA)
200 Park Ave., N.Y. 10017, (212) 557-5870
Also Enterprise Features (EF)

North American Newspaper Alliance (NANA)
200 Park Ave., N.Y. 10017, (212) 557-2333

Register and Tribune Syndicate
715 Locust St., Des Moines, Iowa 50304, (515) 284-8244

United Media Enterprises (also United Feature Syndicate)
200 Park Ave., N.Y. 10017, (212) 557-2333

Universal Press Syndicate
6700 Squibb Rd., Mission, Kansas 66202, (913) 362-1523

Washington Post Writers Group (Wash Post)
Washington Post, 1150 Fifteenth St., N.W., Wash., D.C. 20071
(202) 223-5171

THE KING

King Features is the country's largest newspaper syndicate. The company continues to grow, add new columns and is a vital force in the newspaper business, in addition to sizable, exciting activities in publishing, films and merchandising.

A profile of King Features really is seven decades of journalism history. Following are a few highlights.

King Features Syndicate was incorporated as part of the Hearst organization on November 16, 1915, in New York, with Moses Koenigsberg as president. Hearst already had the Newspaper Feature Service, which sold a package of features, called the budget system of sales. The concept of King Features was to sell features individually. The name connoted the superiority of the columns and the company, but actually was selected as the English translation of the first part of Koenigsberg.

The first King columnist was Herbert Kaufman, a Chicago advertising agency proprietor whose clients included National Cash Register and International Harvester. Herbert Kaufman's Weekly Page included a colloquial rhyme, a serious article, a treatise on advertising, an editorial by Kaufman, several short commentaries, and a few illustrations.

The Kaufman page was supplemented by a daily political commentary, so that within a few years, King sold the daily or weekly column to 165 newspapers, with Kaufman receiving 60% of about $70,000.

Within a decade, King Features became the largest syndicate, with over 1000 clients all over the world. The major income was from the largest staff of comic artists ever gathered. Harry Hershfield, an artist and humorist, called the office "The world's biggest fun foundry." The cartoonists and comic strip artists included George Herriman, ("Krazy Kat"), Billy De Beck ("Barney Google"), Russ Westover ("Tille the Toiler"), E.C. Segar ("Popeye the Sailor"), Rube Goldberg ("Foolish Questions"), Frederick Burr Opper ("Alphonse and Gaston"), Frank Willard ("Moon Mullins"), Percy Crosby ("Skippy"), and Jo Swerling ("Mr. Gallagher and Mr. Shean").

In 1928, George McManus' "Bringing Up Father," which starred Jiggs, appeared in more than 600 newspapers, the largest roster ever obtained for a comic, but the all-time record was held by Chic Young, whose "Blondie" still appears in over 1500 newspapers in several languages.

King was noted for its humor columns, with such early favorites as Arthur "Bugs" Baer, Kenneth C. Beaton, who wrote as K.C.B., J.P. Medbury, Ted Cook, W.F. Kirk, George E. Phair and J.J. Mundy.

King also syndicated, on a regular basis and as special series, the writings of Rex Beach, Gene Fowler, Kathleen Norris, George Norris, J.P. McEvoy, Ward Greene, Hendrick William Von Loon, George Bernard Shaw, Marshall Foch, Maxim Gorky, William Jennings Bryan, Fannie Hurst, B.C. Forbes, H.R. Knickerbocker, James J. Corbett, Jack Dempsey, Gene Tunney, and Lillian Lamferty, who was one of the succession of women who wrote as Beatrice Fairfax.

The sovereignty of King Features was established by its artists and writers, and also, though not as well known or heralded, its editors and executives. One such star was Emile Gauvreau.

An erudite high school dropout who studied Voltaire when he was a boy, Emile Gauvreau started as a cub reporter on the Journal-Courier in his native New Haven, Connecticut. His training included a study of the editorials of Hearst editor Arthur Brisbane, and years later, Gauvreau became one of the Hearst hierarchy.

Gauvreau spent seven years at the New Haven Journal-Courier, where he met and married the society editor, Sarah Welles Joyner. The managing editor of the rival Register was a cartoonist, H.I. Phillips, who went on to become a columnist at the New York Sun.

While still in his twenties, Gauvreau became managing editor of the prestigious Hartford Courant, but in 1924, in his fifth year at the newspaper, he was caught in a political struggle with the editor and business manager. On February 3, the day Woodrow Wilson died, Gauvreau lost his job and the second of his three sons, Peter, who died of pneumonia.

Emile and Sarah Gauvreau, and their two sons, Henry Welles and Alphonse, moved to New York and for the next five years, Gauvreau edited the Evening Graphic, the zany tabloid published by physical culturist Bernarr Macfadden. The staff included Fulton Oursler, Ed Sullivan, and other luminaries-to-be, including a $100-a-week gossip columnist hired by Oursler. He also doubled as drama critic, sold

140

theatrical advertising, and had other assignments. The boy wonder, who became the talk of the town and the Graphic's hottest property, was Walter Winchell. As Gauvreau stated in his autobiography, "My Last Million Readers," "No stranger phenomenon has yet appeared in the newspaper business. Gossip acquired such a tangibility, such a grip on his life, chiefly from the bare nucleus of a slim fact that many times, he was more often cleverly wrong than monotonously correct."

Gauvreau was more familiar with Winchell's copy than any other person; they both moved from the Graphic to the New York Mirror. At the Graphic, Louis Sobol succeeded Winchell as author of the "Your Broadway and Mine" column and Howard Swain succeeded Gauvreau as managing editor.

Winchell and Gauvreau had clashed continually and in 1929 Gauvreau fired him, much to Winchell's delight since Hearst had offered him a sizable salary increase.

Winchell and Gauvreau both had limited formal education— Winchell had dropped out of elementary school—but Gauvreau prided himself on his scholarly approach combined with extensive newspaper experience, whereas he referred to Winchell as a brash vaudeville hoofer.

Shortly thereafter, William Randolph Hearst hired Gauvreau as editor of the Mirror, starting at $500 a week, which was more than Gauvreau had made before, but still less than Winchell was paid. King Features then was headed by Joseph Vincent Connolly, who Gauvreau had known as a reporter on the New Haven Union.

The tabloid Mirror, originally published in downtown Brooklyn, moved to a new building at 235 East 45th Street in Manhattan, which also housed the Hearst Sunday supplement; American Weekly; Puck, the comics supplement, the various newspaper syndicates; and International News Service. It was a wildly colorful operation, which Gauvreau fictionalized in a novel, "Hot News."

The daily adventures at the Mirror rivaled the Graphic in their zaniness. Mark Hellinger, a Mirror columnist, decided to take a trip around the world to celebrate the return of his estranged wife, Gladys Glad, a Ziegfeld Follies beauty. King Features syndicated the reports of the global trip as "Broadway Around the World," only it wasn't a global trip. The Hellingers got as far as Vienna and decided to return to New York. It didn't matter, however, since Arthur James Pegler (father of Westbrook) ghosted the remainder of the series, and millions of readers learned of Hellinger's adventures in the Orient.

Hearst moved in Arthur Brisbane as editor of the Mirror and syndicated "Today," his daily editorial column. In 1934, two years before his death, Brisbane celebrated his seventieth birthday and The New York Times reported that his annual salary then was $260,000. Hearst trumpeted him as "The World's Foremost Commentator on

Public Events."

Brisbane's articles reflected his erudition, and, as editor, he tried to give class to the Mirror. He once memoed Gauvreau to "print photographs of as *few* prostitutes as possible unless they commit an interesting murder, or otherwise force themselves into the news, as they are bound to do."

Gauvreau and Brisbane disagreed repeatedly and Gauvreau joined a long list of axed Hearstmen. The specific incident which provoked the firing was Gauvreau's book, "What So Proudly We Hailed," a laudatory view of Russia resulting from an extensive tour. The articles on which the 1935 book were based previously had been syndicated by Hearst to about 300 newspapers, but bound into one volume, their criticisms of unemployment and corruption in the U.S. provoked critical reviews, and Hearst fired Gauvreau.

It was reminiscent of the resignation in February, 1928, by Moses Koenigsberg, who had been president of six of the Hearst news and feature services, including the King Features Syndicate. Koenigsberg had been honored by the French Legion of Honor for his efforts in keeping the League of Nations from restricting news. Hearst was furious about "any representative of our newspapers or news services receiving any decorations or honorarium from any foreign government," and said so in a strong editorial in the New York American and others of his newspapers.

William Randolph Hearst died in 1951, at the age of 88. His staff variously called him W.R., The Chief, The Old Man, The Boss. Biographers, notably W.A. Swanberg in his 1961 "Citizen Hearst," have examined the baroquely flamboyant life of Hearst the politician, publisher, tycoon, art collector, and worshiper of success. The New York Times obituary totaled about 20,000 words. Hearst's personal estate was valued at about $60 million. His legacy in the newspaper syndicate field is best attested by the following partial list of King Features columnists in 1967:

Celebrity—Mel Heimer, Jack O'Brian, Walter Winchell.

Commentary—Phyllis Battelle, Jim Bishop, William F. Buckley Jr., John Chamberlain, Bob Considine, Kingsbury Smith.

Financial—Sam Shulsky.

Human Relations—Helen Bottel, Mary Haworth.

Humor—Bert Bacharach, Bennett Cerf, Bob Cooke.

Movies—Harrison Carroll, Dorothy Manners.

Sports—Jimmy Cannon.

Travel—Temple Manning.

Washington—Henry Cathcart, Ralph de Toledano, Marianne Means, Ruth Montgomery.

Women's—Heloise.

And that's just a small part of the roster. King stars before 1967 included Elsa Maxwell, Cholly Knickerbocker, Dorothy Kilgallen, Westbrook Pegler, Louella Parsons, George Sokolsky, and many others. Recent additions have included John P. Roche, Kevin Phillips, Jeffrey Hart, Joyce Brothers, and "Robin Adams Sloan." The syndicate always has been a citadel of political conservatism, but even that is changing somewhat, with the 1972 addition of Washington Post maverick Nick von Hoffman.

The editor of King Features Syndicate formerly was Neal B. Freeman, a Yale man who worked at the Washington Star Syndicate, produced Bill Buckley's TV program, and was a book publishing editor. For many years, Buckley was distributed by both the Washington Star Syndicate and King Features, a novel arrangement. He currently is distributed only by the Washington Star and is its number one columnist.

The management of King Features currently is Joseph D'Angelo, president, Benson Srere, general manager, and Allan Priaulx, executive editor. D'Angelo has been with King for many years, Srere was a magazine editor and Priaulx was vice president of the Register and Tribune Syndicate.

One link with the early days was public relations director Joe Willicombe, who retired in 1977. His father for 22 years was secretary to William Randolph Hearst, and for many years was chairman of the Banshees, the social club sponsored by King Features.

At one of the famous luncheons of the Banshees, Damon Runyon, the guest of honor, was asked for his favorite newspaper story. Runyon said that "Bugs" Baer once wrote two columns simultaneously, under his name for the New York American and under a pseudonym, Graham Wire, at the Evening World.

Hearst was pleased with the Baer column and annoyed at the rival "Wiregrams by Graham Wire." He instructed King Features general manager Bradford Merrill to hire Graham Wire. Merrill gave Damon Runyon the assignment of locating the mysterious, but hilarious, Mr. Wire, thus thickening the plot since Runyon was one of the few who knew about the moonlighting ruse. The solution was evolved by Wire's "retirement," and Baer continued as one of the stars at King.

Born in Philadelphia in 1886, Arthur Baer was the seventh of 14 children. He started at 14 as a lace designer and, at 20 joined the Philadelphia Ledger, first as a copy boy and then as a sports cartoonist. His signature was a whimsical little bug in the corner, which soon was enlarged so that a satirical comment could be affixed to it. Arthur thus became known as Bugs Baer, a left handed sports artist who went to Stars and Stripes, the Washington Times, and then the New York American. He lived in Stamford, Connecticut, but usually could be found at Toots Shor's bar on West 51st Street and the syndicate office on West 45th Street.

Ring Lardner once wrote, "I don't care who runs the country as long as someone runs Bugs Baer twice a day." Irving S. Cobb said, "The Bugs Baers do not come in bunches like grapes. They appear but once in a millennium."

Which is quite a tribute from two humorists whose fame topped that of Baer. Bugs Baer, who died in 1969, had millions of fans among his readers but he was especially popular with his colleagues. He described Justice Charles Evans Hughes as being so impartial that he even parted his beard down the middle, and he called the International News Service the Uninternational News Service, suggesting that its slogans be changed from "Get it first—but first get it right" to "get it first—correct it later."

Another King humor columnist was George Dixon who wrote "Washington Scene" for about 20 years, starting in 1944. A Canadian, Dixon worked for several newspapers north of the border, including the Toronto Star and Toronto World, as well as several U.S. dailies, notably the Philadelphia Inquirer and New York News, where he was a sports writer. He married Ymelda Chavez, daughter of Senator Dennis Chavez of New Mexico. After his death, Ymelda Dixon started a society column, "Your Date With Ymelda," in the Washington Evening Star.

The all-time number one columnist at King Features was Walter Winchell. He was closely rivaled by several women, notably Dorothy Kilgallen and Louella Parsons. It thus is fitting that the current top columnist in the King roster is a female humorist, Heloise, whose column appears in over 500 newspapers. The column is written by Ponce Cruse, daughter of the originator of the column, Heloise Bowles, who died in late 1977. Some newspapers publish the by-line as Heloise II, while others have not changed the by-line.

Among the 1978 King roster is "Blondie," which appears in about 1,700 newspapers throughout the world and is the number one comic strip. Other bestselling comics from King are "Hagar the Horrible," "Barnie Google," "Hi and Lois," "Beetle Bailey," "Donald Duck," "Winnie the Pooh," "Flash Gordon," "Steve Canyon," "Prince Valiant," "Archie," "Bringing Up Father," "Henry," "Mickey Mouse," "Mandrake the Magician," "They'll Do It Every Time" and "Ripley's Believe It Or Not."

Most of these comics have appeared for many years, though there are a few newcomers, including "Inside Woody Allen."

The vast majority of income to King is from comics. However, the company still has an impressive lineup of text columns. Staffer Joan O'Sullivan writes six features a week, as does veterinarian Frank Miller. Other major columnists are gardener Elvin McDonald, consumerist Peter Weaver, adviser Helen Bottel, beauty authority Emily Wilkens, traveler Jane Morse, investor William A. Doyle, CBer

Dick Cowan, career counselor George Nobbe, nutritionist Philomena Corradeno, handyman Al Carrell, crafts expert Phyllis Fiarotta, architects John Bloodgood and Augustus Suglia and Dr. Lester L. Coleman.

Most of the political commentators are conservative, notably Ronald Reagan and Jeffrey Hart. Other editorial columns are written by Bert Bacharach, Jim Bishop, John Chamberlain, Marianne Means, Kevin Phillips, John Roche, Joseph Kingsbury Smith and Nicholas von Hoffman.

Robin Adams Sloan writes gossip, as do Dorothy Treloar in Hollywood and Jack O'Brian in New York.

Rolling Stone provides a feature service, including record reviews and other material for young readers; the pattern service has seven different items; Steve Scheuer provides the TV Key package; Jack Nicklaus and other athletes and sports experts provide lessons; B. Jay Becker writes a daily bridge column . . . and lots more as part of the something-for-everybody philosophy.

One of King's most famous columnists is Mrs. Arthur Van Horne, better known as Phyllis Battelle, author of "Assignment America." In 1947, after covering the police beat in her home town, Dayton, Ohio, for three years, Phyllis-Marie Battelle moved to New York. The chief of detectives told the Dayton Herald, "You never had a better man on the job."

"Newspaperman" Battelle was women's editor of International News Service from 1947 to 1954, where she joined the sometimes rough, highly competitive fraternity of Hearst reporters. "There's no place where a woman can feel more feminine than with a bunch of great newspapermen," says Battelle.

Females were an important part of the zestful life of William Randolph Hearst. He worshipped youth, energy, success, beauty, and sensation and, for the last thirty years of his life, his princess was Marion Davies, a blonde actress. Millicent Hearst, the mother of his five sons, refused to give him a divorce, and W.R. and Miss Davies settled for one of the most grandiose and poignant love affairs in history and fiction.

On October 31, 1951, ten weeks after Hearst died, Miss Davies, at the age of 51, married Captain Horace G. Brown Jr., a merchant marine officer who dramatically resembled Hearst in his younger days.

UNITED MEDIA

For many years, United Feature Syndicate and Newspaper Enterprise Association operated from different offices with separate staffs, as friendly rivals, though both were owned since their foundings by The E.W. Scripps Co. In 1978, United and NEA consolidated their operations in one office, in the Pan Am Building in New York, and formed a new company, United Media Enterprises Inc., which probably is the second biggest newspaper syndicate.

Robert Roy Metz, who was president and editor of NEA since 1972, now is president and chief executive officer of United Media, and William C. Payette, president of United Feature since 1969, now is chairman of the board of United Media.

A major difference between NEA and United is that the former company sells its columns as part of a package, rather than individually, as is the mode of operation of United Feature. Even before the merger, United Feature Syndicate was a giant in the syndicate business, notably a result of its acquisition in 1972 of Bell-McClure Syndicate and its affiliates, North American Newspaper Alliance and Women's News Service. Bell-McClure itself was the product of a major syndicate acquisition in 1952, when Bell, founded in 1912 by the late John N. Wheeler, bought McClure, the first of the major syndicates, founded in 1884 by Samuel McClure. North American Newspaper Alliance, which was founded in 1922 as a news cooperative by major independent newspapers, was later bought out by John Wheeler and brought under the wing of his Bell group. Women's News Service was established in 1946 and soon thereafter it, too, was bought by Wheeler.

Wheeler sold out in the mid-1950's, and the ownership of Bell-McClure, NANA and Women's News Service changed hands several times before their assets were bought by United.

Wheeler, who retired as chairman of NANA in 1964, died in 1973, at the age of 87.

Edward Wyllis Scripps entered the publishing field in 1878. When he died in 1926, at the age of 72, he had helped to establish the United Press Associations and a slew of subsidiaries and inter-related companies including, in 1923, United Feature, which was formed as a feature arm of United Press, initially to distribute the memoirs of Lloyd George.

Though not as prosperous as Scripps, Samuel McClure also was a publishing tycoon, who started one of the earliest syndicates, in 1884. More than any other single person, McClure, who died in 1949 at the age of 92, literally spanned the history of newspaper syndicates and was one of its geniuses.

When McClure died in 1949, the syndicate already had gone through several changes in ownership, and that pattern has continued. From 1959 to 1963 it was owned by columnist Ernest Cuneo. The editor for many years was George E. Lardner, a nephew of Ring Lardner. In 1965, three well-known individuals purchased the company, each owning one-third. They were columnist Drew Pearson, Washington attorney Leonard Marks and publisher Fortune Pope.

In the sixties, Women's News Service was headed by Anita Colby, beauty columnist, actress and model who, in the thirties, had been America's highest paid cover girl.

North American Newspaper Alliance promoted itself as the country's only completely independent supplemental news service, meaning that it was not a spin-off by a newspaper of its own features, nor was it subsidized or related to a newspaper chain or wire service. Many famous literary and political figures worked as war correspondents, stringers or short-term byliners of NANA, and the world's top newspapers purchased NANA series, which often were transmitted on the AP wire. The NANA specialty was long, magazine-type features which provided interpretation and a highly literary quality.

Perhaps the best known of the NANA quality writers was Ernest Hemingway, who, among other assignments, covered the Spanish Civil War in 1937. His writings rank among the world's journalistic masterpieces and were vivid glimpses of moments in history. The dialogue, colorful descriptions of "ordinary people," and personal involvement set new standards for eyewitness reporting.

United Feature's growth since 1972 has been marked not just by the acquisition of features, but, even more strikingly, by technological breakthroughs in the preparation and delivery of copy. United Features was first with an automated system of producing its text columns so that a typist can prepare a particular column in any number of formats without re-keyboarding. The Jack Anderson column, for example, is now produced in various camera-ready and scannable formats, as well as "hard copy" for hand setting.

Whereas a few years ago, United, like most syndicates, was cranking out copy on mimeograph machines, its editorial offices today are filled with computers, magnetic-tape typewriters, video editing terminals, and offset presses. The reason for this investment in computerized equipment is that newspapers are undergoing a technological explosion, each in a different direction, and United is trying to satisfy as many newspaper production needs as possible. Electronic feeds range from 83 to 1200 words per minute.

United is equally strong in comics and text features. Among the former are "Peanuts," "Nancy," "The Dropouts," "Dr. Smock," "Boomer," "Tarzan," and "There Oughta Be a Law." (The syndicate also has a wide range of specialty features, including many crossword puzzles, word games, and children's features.)

Among United's political columnists are Jack Anderson (the most widely syndicated text feature in the world), Marquis Childs, Ernest Cuneo, Col. Robert Heinl, Victor Lasky, Frank van der Linden, John D. Lofton Jr., Martin Nolan, Virginia Payette, Henry J. Taylor, and Gus Tyler. Business and finance are covered by Don G. Campbell (former business editor of the New York News), Lou Schneider and Dr. Herbert Stein (former chairman of the President's Council of Economic Advisors).

On the lighter side, United syndicates Norton Mockridge, Jim Fiebig, Sandy Teller (whose Senator Soaper, under successive authorships, is the longest-running newspaper column in America), and various filler items. Newcomer Fiebig is rare among humor columnists, in that he is a conservative. Food is covered by Marcia Burg (Chef Marcia), Barbara Gibbons (Slim Gourmet), and Robert J. Misch (Eat, Drink and Be Merry), while fashion and beauty are covered by Marian Christy and Florence de Santis. Margaret Dana, Sidney Margolius and Betty Yarmon cover consumerism.

United Features also syndicates columns on home decor (Genevieve Fernandez, Emily Malino), antiques (Anne Gilbert, Tom Bateson), and home repair (Roger Whitman). Dan Lewis previews the network TV shows and does TV interviews, while Barbara Lewis edits a complete package of youth features called Pop Scene Service. Miscellaneous columns include Dr. F.J.L. Blasingame on health, Stella Wilder on astrology, The Aces on bridge, Alice Scott on pets, Robert Irvin on autos, Jean Adams (Teen Forum), John Keasler (By George!) and Val Winsey who writes Susie Mac, the column originated by Susie MacDougall.

A United subsidiary, TV Data, of Glens Falls, N.Y., produces and sells TV log listings to newspapers and other clients.

Newspaper Enterprise Association—well known in the newspaper world as NEA—is one of the largest and most respected newspaper feature services. Founded by Ellen Browning Scripps in 1902, the NEA service has continued to expand and now includes interpretive articles, columns, cartoons and other graphic features serving over 700 newspapers with a combined circulation of more than 25 million.

Unlike those newspaper syndicates which are essentially sales agents for unrelated text and pictorial features, NEA in North America has always been an edited integrated service akin to a complete newspaper. Internationally, however, NEA features are sold individually.

NEA columnists include Ray Cromley in Washington, Dr. Lawrence Lamb on health, Oswald and James Jacoby on bridge, Bernice Bede Osol on horoscopes, plus Dick Kleiner, Joan Crosby, Aileen Claire Snoddy, Polly Cramer, Ellie Grossman and many others.

NEA comics classics include "Our Boarding House," "Alley Oop," and "Captain Easy," which are balanced by contemporary strips such as "Eek & Meek," "The Born Loser," "Frank & Ernest," and "Winthrop."

Cartoonists include Bill Crawford, John Lane and Ed Kudlaty. Then there's the panel cartoon, "Berry's World," which sits halfway between the editorial cartoon and the gag panel. Produced by Jim Berry, this feature rejuvenated thinking about editorial cartoons and comic art, and appears in more than 500 newspapers.

In addition to its daily service, NEA has created other, more specialized services to meet the changing needs of newspapers. They include TV Scout, a daily television preview service, ShowTime, a color cover service for weekend entertainment sections, Enterprise Science News, Enterprise Features, feature length stories, and Suburban Features, a specialized editorial service for weeklies.

In 1966, NEA acquired The World Almanac, the oldest and most popular book of its kind in the United States. The Almanac, now in its second century, is co-published in 130 major U.S. and Canadian markets by leading newspapers.

Acquisition of The World Almanac was a step in a unique concept of book publishing. In 1963, the company launched a program of reader service book publishing in which series of articles on self-help topics are run in newspapers and expanded versions of the series are simultaneously offered as paperback books. Enterprise Publications was formed in 1967.

Among the several famous NEA editors was Boyd Lewis. NEA sports department alumni include Sandy Padwe of the Philadelphia Inquirer, Dave Burgin of the San Francisco Examiner, Bud Benjamin of CBS, and its most famous columnist alumnus, Jimmy Breslin, who worked for NEA for five years before joining the New York Herald Tribune. In the forties, the NEA sports editor was Harry Grayson. His successor, Murray Olderman, moved to San Francisco, where he writes and illustrates features. Sports columns have been de-emphasized, primarily because local newspapers cover sports in depth. However, NEA has increased its sports-related series and books. The current sports editor is Howard Siner.

Enterprise Features offers social critic Jane O'Reilly, trivia expert Dan Carlinsky, soap opera columnist Jon-Michael Reed, business and financial columnists Phil Greer and Mike Kandel, "The Circus of P.T. Bimbo" by Howie Schneider and others.

TV Scout features Sketches and Reports by Dick Kleiner and Joan Crosby, Ask TV Scout by Joan Crosby, as well as the Daily TV Previews.

Suburban Features writers include Jean Nidetch, founder of Weight Watchers; Dr. James G. Price, past president of the American Academy of Family Physicians; campers Angela and Ford Bothwell; puzzler Tracy St. John; and editorial cartoonist Mike Gregory.

Newspaper syndicates were born in the midwest, and NEA in Cleveland was one of the pioneers. The company has changed considerably since its budget package days, and it still is one of the leaders and innovators.

CHICAGO TRIBUNE-NEW YORK NEWS

The Tribune Company is a communications conglomerate which includes The Chicago Tribune, whose motto was "The World's Greatest Newspaper." The New York News, which has the largest circulation of any U.S. newspaper; several newspapers, radio and television stations and the Chicago Tribune-New York News Syndicate, one of the world's largest newspaper syndicates.

Located in the News Building at 220 East 42nd Street, CTNYNS is a fascinating, complex operation which aggressively competes with other syndicates. Most of the CTNYNS columnists do not work at either the Trib or News. The articles and columns of many staff writers, such as Sidney Fields' Only Human, are sent out on the Knight Wire, which is sold by the syndicate as a feature package.

Syndicates, like TV networks and major sports teams, continually attempt to lure star columnists and this rivalry occasionally carries over to editorial and sales personnel.

Many years ago, a major coup for CTNYNS was attracting Al Capp's Li'l Abner from United Features. In the '60s, when the Los Angeles Times took over Newsday Specials, editor Tom Dorsey moved from Newsday to CTNYNS, taking a few columns with him. Ironically, Dorsey then moved to the Los Angeles Times Syndicate, where he continued his vigorous recruitment. For example, in early 1977, astrologer-seeress Jeane Dixon switched from the CTNYNS to the L.A. Times Syndicate.

Tom Dorsey no longer is at the Los Angeles Times Syndicate and the chief executive now is J. Willard Colston, who previously was president of the now defunct National Newspaper Syndicate in Chicago. Nothing is permanent in the syndicate business, except

153

perhaps Abigail Van Buren.

The current management at CTNYNS is Robert S. Reed, president, and Don Michel, editor.

The number one CTNYNS columnist is "Dear Abby," one of the most widely syndicated in the world. Abby and her twin sister, Ann Landers, both claim to have the largest readership of any columnist. Abby may have a slight edge, with over 900 newspapers, which would make her the country's number one feature columnist, with a lot of the credit due to former president Arthur Laro, who lured her from McNaught. Jack Anderson may have a few more subscribers than either Abby or Ann, but no matter how you count it, and it's extremely difficult in this hotly competitive, secretive field, Abby is the number one columnist at CTNYNS.

Laro is retired now, and it's hard to pin down the financial details involving Abby. One version of the saga is that the original contract with Pauline Esther Phillips, who is Abby, was at that time one of the most unusual in the journalism field, or in any business. Mrs. Phillips, whose nickname is "Popo," did not receive the traditional 50 per cent of gross income, nor the 60 or 70 per cent which a few celebrity columnists occasionally receive, but rather, she received considerably more. The explanation is simply that the CTNYNS signed her as a "loss leader," a superstar whose column has given the syndicate's salesmen entry into subscribers which previously preferred to deal with other syndicates.

It's hard to evaluate the benefit of the Dear Abby column to the Trib-News, but the arrangement certainly has been of great value to Popo-Abby. The current arrangements with Abby differ from the original contract (whatever that may have been), and everyone appears to be happy. Other similar special contracts exist with Abby's twin sister, Ann Landers (Field) and Jack Anderson (United).

Other CTNYNS celebrities are bridge and backgammon buff Omar Sharif, star bridge players Fred Karpin and Charles Goren, star watcher Rex Reed, consumerist Bess Myerson, needlepointer Erica Wilson, economist Eliot Janeway, etiquetist Elizabeth Post, society reporter Aileen Mehle (better known by her byline, "Suzy"), evangelist Billy Graham and pollster Louis Harris.

Nutritionist Jean Mayer switched from Harvard to Tufts University (he's president), but remained with the CTNYNS. His Tufts colleague, Joanna Dwyer, is co-author.

The comics include names which have been part of America for several generations—Brenda Starr, Dick Tracy, Gasoline Alley, Li'l Abner, Little Orphan Annie, Moon Mullins and Winnie Winkle. Other comics are "Broom-Hilda," "Dondi," "Rick O'Shay," "Catfish," "Animal Crackers," "Jumble," "Gil Thorp," "Lolly," "Motley's Crew" and "Casey."

Ed Fisher edits Toppix, a daily cartoon panel by one of 18 top editorial cartoonists. Jeff MacNelly of the Richmond (Va.) News-Leader is a Pulitzer Prize winning editorial cartoonist whose views generally are conservative and compatible with those of the Trib and News.

With few Washington or political columns, CTNYNS is best known for its features. The Washington roster is investigative reporters Jack Germond and Jules Witcover, who write six times a week from Washington, and former White House speech writer Patrick J. Buchanan, who writes three times a week.

In the late '60s and early '70s, the declining interest in Broadway celebrity columns was indicated by the almost total omission in the CTNYNS roster of any columnist in this category. Ed Sullivan was a prominent celebrity, but, in his last years The New York News was his only major column outlet.

Recently, the CTNYNS has returned to the red-hot gossip category with a bang. Liz Smith, a Cosmopolitan magazine writer who for many years ghosted and co-authored Igor Cassini's celebrity column, now writes under her own name in The New York News and other newspapers.

Maxine Cheshire of The Washington Post has been replaced by a tri-weekly gossip compendium, titled Ear, which emanates from the Washington Star. The column name is based in part on the long-time gossip column in Women's Wear Daily, which is called Eye.

For New Yorkers, and anybody else who loves colorful writing, the big news in late 1976 was the return of Jimmy Breslin, whose columns in the New York Herald Tribune still are fondly remembered, and the switch, in 1977, of Pete Hamill, from the Post to the News.

Newcomers to the CTNYNS include Lois Libien and Margaret Strong (home care), David Israel (sports), Gary Deeb (TV columnist of the Chicago Tribune), Roy Andries de Groot (wine and food expert), Stephen Birnbaum (successor to the late Richard Joseph, long-time travel editor of Esquire), Dr. G. Timothy Johnson (authority on preventive medicine), and Dr. David Bachman (who writes as "Dr. Jock").

Other CTNYNS columnists are Saul Kapel, M.D. (child psychiatry), Robert Mendelsohn, M.D. (People's Doctor), Jack Hurst (weekly country music commentary), and two New York News staffers, Dick Young (sports) and Gerald Nachman (satire).

The lineup of Drs. Bachman, Kapel, Johnson and Mendelsohn makes the CTNYNS particularly strong in the health category. One of the medical pioneers was Dr. Theodore Van Dellen, whose column appeared for many years in the Tribune, News and other newspapers.

Perhaps the most unusual CTNYNS columnist, in terms of name, is veterinarian Dr. Michael Fox. That's his real name.

L.A. TIMES

Established in 1948 and now one of the country's largest syndicates, the Los Angeles Times Syndicate is a subsidiary of the Times Mirror Company. In 1967, the syndicate absorbed the assets of General Features Corporation, and in 1975, General Features, as a separate entity, was phased out of existence.

The number one columnist, in terms of number of subscribers, is humorist Art Buchwald.

A reorganization in 1978, under the direction of J. Willard Colston, president, and Dan Byrne, editor, resulted in the dropping of several comics and the addition of text columns.

The comics roster, which is relatively small, includes "A Little Leary," "Luther," "Mr. Tweedy," "Splitsville," "Modesty Blaise," and several cartoon panels, notably Ed Nofziger's "Animalogic," Dave Eastman's "Carmichael," and Richard Guindon of the Minneapolis Tribune.

One of the largest collections of editorial cartoonists includes Ben Wicks (Toronto Sun), Lou Grant (Oakland Tribune), Hugh Haynie (Louisville Courier-Journal), Don Hesse (St. Louis Globe-Democrat), Paul Conrad (Los Angeles Times), Pat Oliphant (Washington Star), Taylor Jones (Charleston Gazette) and Charles Bassotti.

Los Angeles Times columnists include astrologers Sydney Omarr and Jeane Dixon, bridge expert Alfred Scheinwold, investment advisor David Sargent, do-it-yourselfer A.J. Hand, money advisors Carol Mathews and Milton Moskowitz, Eleanor Price ("All About Pets"), car doctors Ray Hill and Eugene Milmoe, religionist Rev. A. Purnell Bailey and numismatist Edward C. Rochette.

The lineup of more than 100 columns is extremely diversified and well balanced. The political opinion columns include Lt. Gen. Ira C.

Eaker, M. Stanton Evans, Roscoe Drummond, Paul Harvey, Jenkin Lloyd Jones and Max Rafferty, on the right; Max Lerner, Tom Braden, George Mair, Norman Cousins, Harriet Van Horne and Ron Hendren, on the left; and, somewhere in the middle, Ernest B. (Pat) Furgurson and Nick Thimmesch. Superstar Joseph Alsop retired in 1974. New columnists include Georgie Ann Geyer (formerly of the Chicago Daily News), Jack Cloherty (formerly of the Jack Anderson staff) and Retired Admirals Elmo R. Zumwalt and Worth H. Bagley.

Health columnists are veterans Frank Falkner, M.D., and Neil Solomon, M.D., and Ph.D.; Lasse Hessel, M.D., a Danish physician, produces a unique comic strip, The Family Doctor; Lawrence Power, M.D., writes about nutrition, and science writer John Brennan comments about drugs.

Beulah Collins has continued the columns of her late husband, Tom Collins (formerly of the Chicago Daily News), which are "Golden Years" and also "Senior Forum" (written under the name of Paul Hightower).

Humor is not neglected, and this category features four of the country's finest satirists: Art Buchwald, Mark Russell, Jim Fitzgerald and Marvin Kitman, as well as Today's Chuckle, a daily paragraph which brightens the front and editorial pages of hundreds of newspapers. The anonymous feature (one of the contributors is the prolific Beulah Collins) is one of the most successful syndicated items.

An extensive women's department includes advisors Miriam Landau, Susan Dietz and Beth Winship; beautician Jennifer Anderson; decorator Barbara Bradford; and gourmets Johna Blinn and Bob Balzer (wine). Julia Child no longer is columning, but others who are syndicated by the LAT include etiquetist Tish Baldrige (successor to Amy Vanderbilt), gardener Jack Kramer, photographer Albert Modvay, Susan Dietz ("Single File"), Cleveland Amory, Roderick Mann ("People") and John Clift, who writes City Editor's Tip Service.

Several of the columnists are on the staff of the Los Angeles Times, including Jim Murray (sports), Carolyn S. Murray (home), Marylou Luther (fashion) and Paul Henninger and Cecil Smith (TV).

The Los Angeles Times/Washington Post News Service combines the national and foreign staff of two of the country's most distinguished newspapers with other resources. Coincidentally, both "anchor" newspapers are associated with prominent families—the Chandler family in Los Angeles and the Graham (Eugene Meyer) families in Washington. The LAT/WP News Service has over 350 major subscribers all over the world, and also distributes on its wire the dispatches and features of Agence France-Presse, Newsday, the Dallas Times Herald and Manchester Guardian.

The Los Angeles Times Syndicate operation represents Big Business in the newspaper syndicate field. It is extremely efficient and its diverse output is sufficient to satisfy the needs of any managing editor. The reader is rarely aware of technical details of the origin of columns, and appreciate Art Buchwald, Paul Harvey and other long-time top columnists, regardless of their means of distribution.

FIELD

Field Newspaper Syndicate traces its recent history back to 1967 when, under the name of Publishers-Hall Syndicate, it emerged as one of the nation's top syndicates from consolidation of Hall Syndicate (formed in 1945 and acquired by Field Enterprises, Inc. in 1967) and Publishers Newspaper Syndicate (owned by Field since 1941). The name was changed, to reflect Field ownership, in 1975.

A wide distributor of comics and cartoons—including "Andy Capp," "B.C.," "Dennis the Menace," "Rex Morgan," "The Wizard of Id" and "Mary Worth"—Field Syndicate is equally well known for its editorial columns and such cartoon commentators as Bill Mauldin and Herblock. Approximately 80 Field comics, columns and other services are syndicated to more than 2,000 newspapers in the United States and abroad.

The old Publishers Newspaper Syndicate was a joint venture of Field Enterprises in Chicago, and Whitney Communications in New York, publishers of the now defunct New York Herald Tribune. Whitney interests in the Syndicate were acquired in 1967 by Field.

Field News Service incorporates the staffs of the Chicago Sun-Times, Newhouse News Service and the London Telegraph, and distributes Mike Royko (formerly of the Chicago Daily News) and various byliners in Chicago, Washington and New York.

The Chicago Daily News/Sun-Times News Service was America's oldest auxiliary wire service. Founded in 1898 as the Chicago Daily News Foreign Service, by pioneering journalist Victor Lawson, it listed a long roster of far-flung correspondents who contributed major stories in peace and in war. Pulitzer Prize winners honored for outstanding foreign reporting included Paul Scott Mowrer and Keyes Beech.

The morning Sun-Times was conceived as the Chicago Sun by Marshall Field, III, in 1941. The Chicago Times was acquired in 1947 and merged with the Sun. Field Enterprises, as the parent company is called, acquired the Chicago Daily News, an afternoon paper, in 1959. Marshall Field, IV, died in 1965; Field Enterprises today is headed by his son and namesake, born in 1940. The syndicate is headed by John G. Trezevant, chairman of the board, and Richard Sherry, president.

Among Field Newspaper Syndicate's political columnists are Charles Bartlett, Rowland Evans and Robert Novak, Joseph Kraft, Victor Riesel and Carl Rowan. Editorial cartoonists include Herbert L. Block ("Herblock," Washington Post), Jules Feiffer, John Fischetti, Bill Mauldin (Chicago Sun-Times) and Bill Sanders (Milwaukee Journal).

For women's and feature pages, the Syndicate offers Betty Beale (Washington social scene), Erma Bombeck (humor), Mary Sue Miller (beauty), Eugenia Sheppard (fashion), Pat Trexler (knitting and needlework), Carleton Varney (interior decorating), Bernie Meltzer (real estate), Drs. Frederick Stare and Elizabeth Wheland (nutrition), Jane Adler (indoor gardening), George Creed (landscaping), Lucille Rivers (sewing), Shirley Lord (beauty), Eleanor Lambert (fashion) and Tobe (fashion)—an extraordinary collection sufficient to fill a family magazine.

Other Field columns are its number one columnist Ann Landers, and also Sylvia Porter, Marilyn and Hy Gardner's "Glad You Asked That," Sydney J. Harris' "Strictly Personal," J.A. Livingston's "Business Outlook," Horace Sutton's "Of All Places," Dr. Paul E. Ruble's "To Your Good Health," Earl Wilson's "It Happened Last Night," Lisa Robinson's "Rock Talk," Lynda Hirsch's "Daytime Dial" and Mike Musick's "Heartline."

Field also distributes the famous Gallup poll.

Another service offered by Field Syndicate is Synergy, a program that serializes original work by well-known and promising authors, as well as adaptations of new books.

In 1977, Field Enterprises gave a big boost to Ann Landers by printing her column in the Sun-Times and the Daily News. As with other big city afternoon newspapers, the circulation of the Chicago Daily News had declined. In 1976, it was down to 358,000. In 1977, James Hoge, editor of the Sun-Times and the Daily News, said, "We're looking for a neater, cleaner, sharper, high-impact newspaper."

With due regard to Ann Landers, it takes more than repeating a column from the Sun-Times. It also was Hoge's thankless task to terminate the famous Chicago News foreign service.

Many changes still are going on at Field Enterprises. In 1978, part of the syndicate operation was moved to Newport Beach, California, which is near Los Angeles and reflects the company's emphasis on broadcasting. Field recently sold World Book-Childcraft and purchased five TV stations.

THE TIMES

The New York Times was founded in 1851. Adolph Ochs of Chattanooga bought the newspaper in 1896. The current publisher is Arthur Ochs Sulzberger. The company, which is publicly owned, has acquired Family Circle, Golf Digest and quite a few publishing operations, but the cornerstone is The Times. Its daily circulation of less than a million ranks it far behind the New York News in circulation. The western edition of The New York Times was a flop and the Los Angeles Times has surged ahead in circulation. These comparisons are relatively minor, however, because The New York Times for years has been, and still is, the newspaper of record and one of the world's most influential publications.

These are the bare facts; the details of The Times would fill several books. Meyer Berger, who used to write a column called "About New York," wrote the official biography of The Times in 1951 and Gay Talese wrote the unofficial version, "The Kingdom and The Power," in 1969.

The Times can be purchased in more cities than any other U.S. newspaper. Travelers who are regular readers of The Times, and who don't believe an event has really happened unless it's confirmed in The Times, exchange such lore as the price of The Times at the Washington National Airport newsstand (20 cents, same as in New York) and the time of arrival of The Times at resort hotels (about noon at Marco Island, Florida, for example, where The Times company also owns the local weekly newspaper.)

What Times regulars often do not know is that news articles from The Times and all of the regular columnists are distributed to more than 300 newspapers by the New York Times News Service. James Reston, Russell Baker, Tom Wicker, Anthony Lewis, Red Smith and

165

other Times columnists appear (though not every column) in the Miami News, Anchorage News, West Palm Beach Post and other newspapers. Of the over 300 clients in the U.S. and Canada, there are about a dozen college newspapers (Baker, Lewis and Wicker are the favorites) and even one weekly, the Laurens Advertiser in South Carolina.

The New York Times Special Features distributes specially commissioned material, most of which does not appear in The Times, nor are they available through The New York Times News Service. Columns and features are sold individually, including such widely distributed columns as Dr. Michael Halberstam and others which do not appear in The Times itself.

The three-times-a-week columns of Mary McGrory, the highly respected Pulitzer Prize winning columnist of The Washington Star, still are distributed by the Washington Star Syndicate, and also are available to customers of The New York Times News Service. A similar arrangement exists daily with Bernie Harrison, the long-time TV reviewer of The Washington Star.

Special Features newcomers include clothing consultant John T. Molloy and Steve Kahn, who edits SuperScene, an array of entertainment news, photos, puzzles and other items for 8- to 16-year-olds.

Special Features does select from The Times, particularly the op-ed page, Magazine, Arts & Leisure, Travel, and News of the Week in Review section, and also distributes the crossword puzzles, chess column and other features which are similar to those offered by various general syndicates.

Under the management of Ross Roy Buckingham, Special Features has picked up many major subscribers all over the world, particularly in Latin America, where distribution is in Spanish, and in Europe and Africa, via an office in Paris.

Comics, which are a major source of income of many syndicates, recently have become, for some, a loss operation. The Times does not print any comic strips. Special Features distributes one cartoon strip, "Don Q," the bewildered hero of David Gantz.

The combined operation of the News Service and Special Features is sizable, and the importance of James Reston and other Times columnists, particularly on other journalists, as well as government officials and the general public is monumental.

The regular political columnists of The Times are James Reston, William Safire and Russell Baker in Washington, Tom Wicker in New York, and Anthony Lewis, who is a roving correspondent. The New York Times is one of the few newspapers which does not publish any columns by non-staffers. However, The Times subscribes to 15 news services, including AP, UPI and Reuters. The simple, overwhelming fact is that The Times has the largest staff of any newspaper and it is

166

unable to publish all of the material produced by its own writers. For example, the New York Times Special Features distributes several columns which do not appear in The Times. Among them is a delightful three times a week essay on grammar, of all things, which appears in the Philadelphia Bulletin and a few other major newspapers. Titled "Bernstein on Words," the column is written by Ted Bernstein, whose word-watching predilections are well known to Times staffers who receive "Winners & Sinners," a bulletin which analyzes Times prose.

The first columnist at The Times was Arthur Krock. From 1933 to 1966, Washington politicians started their day by reading Walter Lippmann and Arthur Krock.

Born in 1886 in Glasgow, Kentucky, Arthur Bernard Krock started as a reporter in 1907 on the Louisville Courier-Journal. William Howard Taft was the first of many presidents who were confidants of Mr. Krock and who not only supplied him with news but also sought his advice, an unusual relationship which few other journalists have achieved.

Mr. Krock worked for several newspapers, including the New York World, and joined The New York Times in 1927. He became chief of the Washington bureau in 1932, succeeding Richard V. Oulahan who had supervised the bureau for 20 years.

Mr. Krock had been raised in a small Southern town in the home of his grandparents after his father, a bookkeeper, deserted his mother. In 1904, he studied at Princeton but transferred after a year, due to lack of money, to the Lewis Institute in Chicago. His writings reflected a frugal Southern conservative attitude. He became strongly anti-New Deal after Franklin D. Roosevelt's first term, and in 1944 opposed FDR's reelection, in contrast to the editorial endorsement of The Times. Though Jewish, his opinions about Zionism and other issues also generally were conservative. Actually Krock's father, Joseph, was Jewish, but Arthur was raised as a Christian, under the influence of his mother, Caroline Morris. His maternal grandparents provided the efunds for his freshman year at Princeton. At the Lewis Institute, where he received a Bachelor of Associated Arts degree, he paid for his tuition by running the school newspaper. His first job, as a cub reporter, paid $15 a week, a fact which Mr. Krock sometimes reiterated to his employees when they pressed for raises.

The 700-word column, "In The Nation," was not syndicated separately and his salaried income was about $300,000 at its peak. He lived extremely graciously, however, as if he were a millionaire, with vacations in Palm Beach, Fla., Hot Springs, Va., and other society resorts, and maintained an apartment in Washington and a 170-acre Virginia farm, called Limestone, about 55 miles from Washington.

The column appeared three times a week on column five of the editorial page and on Sundays in the News of the Week in Review section. Its position was to the right of the editorials, and indeed Mr. Krock often was more conservative than the newspaper's official position. For example, Mr. Krock supported Eisenhower and frequently was critical of Kennedy and of the Supreme Court decisions on civil rights.

He was called a Typewriter Statesman and the Tallyrand of The Times. His keen, deliberate focus, as he gazed at an interview subject through his glasses, made many powerful people quiver. Franklin D. Roosevelt offered Cordell Hull the post of Secretary of Commerce in 1932, but Mr. Krock astutely advised Hull to hold out for Secretary of State. He also counseled fellow Kentuckian Alben Barkley and countless other veeps, presidents, cabinet officials and statesmen from all over the world.

The column was polite, as was the author in person, and not like Pegler, Sokolsky and others whom Mr. Krock considered boors. However, Mr. Krock always let his readers know his stance and his column often was filled with irony, snipes, clever criticisms and oblique attacks.

"There's a barb or a hook at the end of everything l'il Arthur writes," FDR once said. Roosevelt called Arthur Krock the Cassandra of the press, but Mr. Krock was credited with knowing more about FDR than any other journalist.

Mr. Krock was highly respected by his staff—he was quiet, formal, courtly and *always* referred to as *Mister* Krock—and he developed The Times bureau on K Street into a journalistic fiefdom. He received two Pulitzer Prizes, in 1935 an 1938, and many awards, including an honorary degree from Princeton. In 1951, Mr. Krock received a Pulitzer special commendation for his exclusive interview with Harry Truman in which the President voiced his unshaken hope of peace, foresaw "man's better nature bringing peace to an ill world," but said that "normal dealing with the Soviet is hopeless."

In 1953, pipe smoker James Reston succeeded cigar smoker Arthur Krock as Times bureau chief. Mr. Krock continued as a columnist until he retired in 1966, at the age of 78. In 1968, he wrote an autobiography, "Memoirs; Sixty Years on the Firing Line," which included a few personal glimpses. He had a son, Thomas, from his first wife, Margaret Polleys, who died in 1938, after 27 years of marriage. In 1939, he married Martha Granger Blair, a society columnist for the Washington Times-Herald.

In her February 15, 1939, column, Martha Blair had written a profile of Arthur Krock, one of the Washington Glamour Boys, who "thinks he has a deceptive charm, but hasn't." Six months later, they married. Though Mr. Krock thereafter never ruled his home the way he did his office, he did convince his wife to drop her column.

As for Arthur Krock's relationship with Walter Lippmann, the man who was his prime competitor, the two giants did not get along in spite of similar views on many social and political subjects. At the New York World, Mr. Krock first reported to publisher Ralph Pulitzer but then reported to Lippmann, who was editor. In 1927, Mr. Krock moved to The Times as editorial writer and political reporter. It irked Mr. Krock that Lippmann's syndication gave him a considerably larger readership but Mr. Krock finally caught up in recent years when The Times started its own news service.

Additional reflections are detailed in Mr. Krock's 1971 book, "The Consent of the Governed and Other Deceits," in which he noted that he had known more presidents than any other reporter and, during more than 60 years as a newspaper writer, had never "broken a confidence," but "that can be said by most members of the Washington press."

When he turned over the bureau chores to Reston, Mr. Krock discussed the importance of the reportorial function. "The reporter is the *sine qua non* of a newspaper. If the reporters are good, the newspaper is good."

Arthur Krock did not graduate from a four-year college, and developed his erudition, authoritative tone, and ability to report in a careful documented manner, as a result of several decades in a variety of newspaper positions. In 1920, for example, he was editor-in-chief of the Louisville Times. During his exclusive interviews with FDR in 1937 and Truman in 1950, Mr. Krock took no notes, so as to not interfere with the conversation.

On March 27, 1972, readers of The Times op-ed page may have been startled to see the Krock byline. President Nixon's trip to China and the Soviet Union prompted Mr. Krock to note the parallels with the negotiations between FDR and the Soviet Union in 1933.

Mr. Krock died in 1974.

Another Times legendary columnist was C.L. Sulzberger, who died in late 1977.

Tall, white haired, imposing looking and often seen in an old trench coat, Cyrus Leo Sulzberger looked like a foreign correspondent, or at least what a lot of romantics think a foreign correspondent should look like.

The son of Leo Sulzberger, brother of The New York Times publisher Arthur Hays Sulzberger, C.L. Sulzberger for many years possessed the unique title of Times' "chief foreign correspondent." A 1934 Harvard magna cum laude graduate, Sulzberger worked for the Pittsburgh Press and United Press in Washington, before joining The Times in 1939. He covered the Second World War from the London bureau and traveled extensively so that in the post war years he came to know most of the European political leaders.

Anne O'Hare McCormick had joined The Times in 1937 as its first woman columnist. When she died in 1954, Sulzberger started his tri-weekly column.

In 1951, Sulzberger received a Pulitzer special citation for an exclusive interview with the leading Roman Catholic of Yugoslavia, Aloysius Stepinatz, known to Westerners as Archbishop Stepinac.

The Sulzberger tri-weekly column "Foreign Affairs," was serious, somber and sometimes was considered too heavy by some Times readers. The ludicrous nature of world events occasionally caused even C.L. Sulzberger to crack up. On January 9, 1972, an article, datelined Paris, described Operation Lemming, a diabolic plan to divert the migration of the lemmings eastward to Russia. The details were conveyed to the author "through the good offices of Baron C.L. Munchausen." The author was not Art Buchwald, but, rather, C.L. Sulzberger.

Sulzberger wrote his first book, "Sit-Down with John L. Lewis," in 1938 at the age of 26, and did not resume book writing until the late fifties, when he wrote "The Big Thaw" and "What's Wrong with U.S. Foreign Policy." In 1969, Sulzberger collected two decades of memoirs and diaries in a book of over 1000 pages which was a magnificent, personalized history of 1934 to 1954. Indispendable reading for European historians, "A Long Row of Candles," provided many personal glimpses into the life of a columnist. His only fiction book, published in 1973, was a surprise. Titled "The Tooth Merchant," the novel of intrigue in the Middle East was a sexy satire.

Sulzberger played golf, bridge or chess with Eisenhower, Nixon and countless other statesmen whom he knew intimately, including many Russian and Chinese friends. The man he most admired was Churchill, who "had the qualities of a poet and a pirate; I can ask no better mixture," though "in some ways de Gaulle was the most consistently interesting man of them all to talk to."

"The greatest lesson I have learned," wrote Sulzberger, "is that, despite Marxist worship of events and trends, it is men who influence history by their will; and Churchill, de Gaulle and Tito have confirmed this view."

Of these giants, Sulzberger had a special fondness for Tito, for whom he once conveyed a secret request for alliance with Greece. The Balkan area has a particular appeal—"it is a region I loved and love for its vigor, poetry and charm, the valor of its people and the persistence of its beauty." (It was in Athens, in 1941, that Sulzberger met his wife, Marina Tatiana Lada, who died in 1976.)

"When young men ask me for advice on how to become a foreign correspondent," stated Sulzberger in the book's preface, "I tell them today: 'Don't! It is like becoming a blacksmith in 1919—still an honorable and skilled profession; but the horse is doomed.' "

170

C.L. Sulzberger, the man who organized and ran The New York Times' Foreign Service, was overly modest, for he was a modern, exciting inspiration to neophyte journalists. He once said that his first book took him ten days to write and was "perhaps the worst book ever printed."

In those days, his nickname was Sulzy and he worked for $30 a week at the United Press, where Harrison Salisbury (of The Times), was his boss.

C.L. Sulzberger may have gotten his job at The Times because of his name, but he kept it because of his ability, and his column actually improved through the years.

The dean of The Times columnists today is James Reston.

"Who does Scotty Reston think he is, telling me how to run the country!" snapped Dwight Eisenhower.

John F. Kennedy, on reading a Reston column about the steel strike, allegedly shouted, "Doesn't he know I need his help with this?"

The target of these presidential explosions is a polite, pleasant looking, slight man who was born in Scotland in 1909 as part of a poor Presbyterian family in a small Scottish town. This background not only resulted in his nickname, "Scotty," but also is reflected in his writing, which generally is idealistic, moralistic, optimistic, logical, and precise.

The Reston family emigrated to the United States in 1920 and James Barrett Reston grew up in Dayton, Ohio. Scotty had been brought over once before, when he was an infant, but James Reston Sr., a machinist, didn't fare well in America and the family returned to Scotland.

As a teenager in Dayton, Reston answered the phone, taking down scores in the sports department of the Daily News. An accomplished golf player, Reston considered becoming a pro, and instead, worked his way through the University of Illinois, where his courses included one in sports writing, for which he received an A. He worked his way through college, graduated in 1932, and became a sports writer for the Springfield Daily News for $10 a week. He then worked as a sports publicist for Ohio State University and the Cincinnati Reds baseball team. (Other prominent columnists who started as sports writers included Heywood Broun, Bob Considine, Westbrook Pegler and Ed Sullivan.)

Reston then moved to New York where he worked for the Associated Press as drama critic, and assorted other assignments, including a column called "A New Yorker at Large," which competed with fellow Buckeye O.O. McIntyre.

In 1937, the AP sent him to London and two years later he joined The New York Times. His first book, published in 1942, was titled "Prelude to Victory" and included this characteristic Restonian philosophy: "We must look forward to the future with faith in each other and in the rightness of the American dream."

Reston joined The Times Washington bureau in 1941 and, in 1953, was appointed chief correspondent, succeeding the imposing Arthur Krock, who had built the bureau into a fiefdom. During the next decade, Reston recruited columnists Russell Baker and Tom Wicker, who, like several other Reston proteges, were Southern newspapermen. "He calls himself a Calvinist," says Baker, "and he does represent that ethic. He believes in hard work, in thrift, honor your parents, woman's place is in the home, play by the rules, and live clean. He is basically Tom Mix: Be a square shooter, good fellows always win. Scotty belives that to his marrow."

Reston has been idolized by his staff and the emotional drama concerning his successors (Tom Wicker in 1964 and Max Frankel in 1968) was chronicled in detail by Gay Talese.

On the afternoon of November 22, 1963, Reston, in Washington, received Tom Wicker's report of the assassination in Dallas and wrote "Somehow the worst in the nation had prevailed over the best."

A pipe smoker (and Scotch drinker) who looks much younger than his age, Reston is a popular college lecturer. Reston's serious simplicity occasionally shows a change of pace with whimsey and gentle humor. He often relates that he wasn't a particularly good student but he managed to marry a Phi Beta Kappa, Sally Fulton, who had been a classmate.

In 1971, Reston was one of the first American journalists admitted to China and his interviews with Mao and others made world headlines, though perhaps the greatest conversation was generated by his emergency appendectomy, which included acupuncture and other Chinese medical techniques. When Max Frankel returned from covering President Nixon's visit to China in 1972, he wrote in the house organ of The Times, "Scotty Reston's appendix is still the most permanent American relic on the mainland."

Reston was accompanied on the trip to China by his wife. "He believes his marriage helped him," says former Timesman David Halberstam (also a Reston recruit), "and that wives should help husbands and husbands help wives and they should hold hands while jointly going into the sunset. He believes the values he preaches, even though they may be values that are under enormous assault right now."

Gay Talese calls Reston the essence of "apple pie America." Says Talese: "He stands for a belief in virtue and religion, a respect for the system and the divine deity."

James Reston has won the Pulitzer Prize twice, in 1945 for his reports on the 1944 Dunbarton Oaks conference which preceded the formation of the United Nations, and in 1957, for outstanding national reporting.

The lead sentences of these two articles demonstrate the variety in Reston's writing style, which is always lucid regardless of the sentence length or subject complexity. The first Pulitzer Prize was awarded for a series which began with a 63-word sentence, "The attempt of the American, British, Russian and Chinese delegates at Dunbarton Oaks to draft recommendations for an international organization to keep the peace has raised again the constitutional question of the right of the Senate to enter into treaties which may obligate us to wage war when the Constitution specifically says that, the whole Congress shall have the power to declare war."

The 1957 Prize for national reporting was for an article which started with this 11-word change of pace, "President Eisenhower said 'no' to the Russians in 1200 polite words."

At a 1949 lecture at the University of Minnesota, Reston stated, "In the past, we in the newspaper business have been satisfied too often with reporting the literal truth instead of the essential truth . . . We have no right, therefore, to twist the mass of facts into forms which are exciting but misleading; to take out of it that portion which conforms to our prejudices, to preserve the shocking or amusing, and to leave out the dreary but important qualifications which are necessary to essential truth."

Reston has had this philosophy put to the test during several incidents of critical historical importance. During the Eisenhower administration, he knew about the fights by American U-2 planes over the Soviet Union, but didn't write about it until Francis Gary Powers' plane was shot down. During the Kennedy administration, he further patriotically attempted to protect American security by toning down a story about the impending Bay of Pigs invasion of Cuba. In 1971, however, Reston was one of the key people who strongly urged The Times to publish the Pentagon Papers.

Reston has been columning for 20 years and there's a tendency for some critics to describe him as stale, dull, predictable, old fashioned. None of these words is apt. Reston remains one of the country's most respected and influential political commentators precisely because he is incisive, dedicated, eloquent and contemporary.

As befits a top executive of The Times, Reston's office does not resemble the typical city room cubicle. The Washington bureau, the largest in the Capital, is on the eighth floor of a small building on the corner of 20th and L Streets. Reston has a large, comfortable office. "It's untidy," he says, "and it's full of history books and reference books and books of quotations. I have a strong feeling that a newspaper office should be an open-door joint where everyone can come in and shout about the latest stupidity in Washington and talk it over. If the doors are closed, it takes a lot of fun out of newspapering, which I've always thought should be a kind of mutual aid society." He also has an office in New York.

Another Times columnist in New York is Tom Wicker.

Born in North Carolina in 1926, Thomas Grey Wicker is one of several Southern newspapermen who became editors at The New York Times. He has held several positions, including bureau chief, in the Washington bureau of The Times since 1960, and currently has the title of associate editor and columnist. Though not as well known as fellow columnist James Reston, Wicker has developed a large number of fans who enjoy and highly respect his sensitive essays, perceptive critiques, and news reports. He is an extremely fine writer, and has authored several novels.

When George Jackson was killed at San Quentin, Wicker wrote an emotional column in which he praised the convict as "a talented writer, a sensitive man, a potential leader and political thinker of great persuasiveness . . . For once, this predominantly white society ought not passively to accept the usual assumption that authority is blameless and truthful, and those who defy it are fools or depraved, especially if black."

An editorial in The Times and quite a few readers disagreed with Wicker, but the major result of the column was that it prompted the Attica prisoners to invite Wicker as one of the observers during their rebellion in September, 1971. Tom Wicker's columns about this tragedy were exquisite examples of his journalistic skill and integrity, combining a restrained sober objectivity with a strong indication of his personal emotionalism.

Only once before had Wicker been a witness to a shocking moment in history—he was in Dallas when John F. Kennedy was shot. As the only Timesman covering the President on November 22, 1963, Wicker's dispatches literally became history. He vividly described the drama a few weeks later in Times Talk, the house organ of The Times. "Even now, however, I know no reporter who was there who has a clear and orderly picture of that surrealistic afternoon; it is still a matter of bits and pieces thrown hastily into something like a whole."

Wicker has had occasion to recall the shooting many times. In May, 1972, he cried out:

"Never mind what George Wallace stands for. The attempt to assassinate him was a foul and terrible act, incomprehensible in its motivation unless—as may be—the attempted assassin was deranged.

"Never mind the political consequences of this senseless deed. The only thing men of reason and decency can hope for is that Mr. Wallace recovers, as speedily as possible.

"They must also ask how often this wracked and contorted nation can go through such traumatic moments. How often can it? If Alabama's Governor should die, there would be no difference—in terms of our common humanity—from the murders of John and Robert Kennedy and Martin Luther King. The bell tolls for us all, and most particularly so when man has turned to wanton violence against his fellow man."

Born in a small North Carolina town, Hamlet, Thomas G. Wicker studied journalism at the University of North Carolina. After graduating in 1948, he worked for several newspapers in North Carolina, including nine years at the Winston-Salem Journal. He then worked for the Nashville Tennessean and joined the Washington bureau of The New York Times in 1960.

Wicker's columns often are quite personal. His father was a railroad freight conductor, and he nostalgically refers to railroads. He once was sports editor of the Winston-Salem Journal and uses sports metaphors. Readers often feel a warmness and rapport with Wicker which is lacking with other political columnists. Not that everyone loves Tom Wicker. He was on Nixon's enemy's list. When Wicker inherited Arthur Krock's column, David Broder resigned in protest as The Times national political correspondent.

In recent years, Wicker has shaved his beard, raised his sideburns and become stockier. His writing has remained brilliant.

Tom Wicker has written six novels, including three mysteries under the name of Paul Connolly. Sales of the fiction books were modest and none are memorable. Tom Wicker, the newspaper writer, is in the same league as John Steinbeck, Heywood Broun, and John Dos Passos.

Another brilliant writer in The Times Washington bureau is Russell Baker, a gentle humorist who is in the tradition of Finley Peter Dunne, Will Rogers and other writers who were able to make readers laugh at the ironies, perversities and foolishness of routine living. He is not a cynic, nor is he a comedian.

Among contemporary writers, the two top satiric columnists are Buchwald and Baker. Buchwald has been doing a column longer, appears in more newspapers including The Washington Post. Baker does not have a Washington outlet, though his column in The New York Times outranks Buchwald's column in the New York Post. Perhaps a major difference between the two columnists is that Baker is a former news reporter and his essays often reflect his journalistic background.

Baker's humor now is known to millions of readers outside of New York as a result of The Times News Service. His delightful style includes family characters, professors with ridiculous names, and other "experts" (such as Senator Merle Survive) who converse about political trends and various aspects of our lives. "It's just nonsense," says Baker, but it's really much more.

In Baker's world, people often talk like television commercials, or

175

meticulously follow the advice of authorities, and, in general, act inanely, as in real life, only more so. Baker occasionally interrupts his jabs with walloping criticism. His report of the Democratic Party convention in Chicago in 1968 was "written in the style of Hemingway" according to the Business Week review (Jan. 22, 1972) of Baker's book, "Poor Russell's Almanac."

The biographical note on the jacket of the Doubleday book includes this description of the author: "Russell Baker was born in 1853 aboard a schooner in the Malay Straits, served as a bag man for the railroad during the administration of Ulysses S. Grant, and graduated eight years later from the University of Heidelberg."

Commenting on the Almanac, which was his fifth collection of columns to appear in a book, Russell Baker told Publishers Weekly (Jan. 24, 1972) that he tries to vary the pace of the Tuesday-Thursday-Sunday columns "sometimes to be me in high dudgeon, sometimes to carry on a casual, convivial conversation with my reader . . . Those who say humor is dying are talking about the old humor of gaiety, a limited humor, when the country was more isolated than it is today. Now we have a sophisticated humor, a worldly humor that comes out of an awareness that ours is a country with global responsibilities," said Baker.

Russell Baker's own favorite humor writers are (in alphabetical order) Woody Allen, Roger Angell, Donald Barthelme, Art Buchwald, Art Hoppe and S.J. Perelman. Actually, it is not necessary to list these writers in alphabetical order, as Baker is not competitive with them, including the two columnists (Buchwald and Hoppe) and Baker is highly admired by journalists, readers, and even by his political targets.

Baker and Buchwald often lunch together, at the Sans Souci restaurant in Washington.

Unlike Buchwald, Baker frequently travels (preferably by train) to observe political figures on a first-hand basis. As he told Thomas Chastain of Publishers Weekly:

"I am basically a guy with a yearning for the past. A time when things were better. Life was better when there were trains. It's probably a sign of the hardening of the mental arteries, this yearning for boyhood, the kind of thing I dislike when I hear it from other people. When my own boys were younger, I took them on cross-country train trips. I felt it was important for them to get the feel of the country in their bones in a way that never happens in an airplane but does on a train," says Baker.

Born in Virginia in 1925, Russell Baker graduated from Johns Hopkins University and worked for the Baltimore Sun for seven years before joining the Washington bureau of The New York Times in 1954. His column has appeared three times a week on the op-ed page of

The Times since 1962, in the space that had been occupied for about 50 years by "Topics of the Times," informal essays anonymously written by Simeon Strunsky and various Timesmen.

"I didn't set out in life to be a humorist," Baker told fellow Timesman Israel Shenker. "I set out to be a novelist, and I look like a novelist."

Baker, who is six feet two, has also described himself as "a little like the young Gary Cooper, shy and charming."

Russell Baker is not a one-line jokester and it's not fair to his artistry to extract quips or epigrams from his essays, but having made that apologia, here are a few sample "Bakergrams:"

"In the year 1894 there was absolutely no progress whatsoever any place on earth, in spite of what a lot of people thought at the time . . .

"Eventually America will run smack into the problem problem. What are we going to do when the problems run out? . . .

"There are no liberals behind steering wheels."

And on a final serious note:

"In general I'm against presidents. I've been in Washington through Eisenhower, Kennedy, Johnson and now Nixon and I've been against them all. It's nothing personal, because I've liked all of them personally. But I just don't like what happens to men when they become President of the United States. I think the office is much too powerful and it's alarming. It is the last totalitarian office in the world that is still elective. The President is the last elected dictator. I don't like people with that much power. I'm afraid of them."

Outside of Washington are two Times roving political columnists, Tom Wicker in New York, and Anthony Lewis, now living in Boston.

Born in New York in 1927, Anthony Lewis graduated from Horace Mann, a prestigious private school, and Harvard (1948). He is charming, erudite, sophisticated, and has almost acquired a British accent, as a result of ten years as chief of the London bureau.

Lewis has received two Pulitzer prizes. The first, awarded in 1955 when he was 28 years old and a reporter on the Washington Daily News, was for a series on the Federal loyalty-security program. The second, in 1963, was for his New York Times coverage of the Supreme Court which included this lyrical lead, "Like the death of Kings, a change in the membership of the Supreme Court of the United States dramatizes the continuity of the Institution."

Times readers in the early sixties often thought Lewis was a lawyer as he became the Times expert on the Supreme Court and Justice Department. He did study law as a Nieman fellow at Harvard. Commenting on Lewis, Justice Felix Frankfurter stated, "There are not two members of the Court itself who could get the gist of each decision so accurately in so few words."

Lewis' coverage of the Court's landmark decision on civil rights and other matters in the early sixties has been quoted in many textbooks. One of these cases was the basis for "Gideon's Trumpet," a highly praised 1964 book by Lewis.

Lewis was a protégé of James Reston and was a contender to succeed Reston as the Washington bureau chief. The other contenders were Tom Wicker, who got the job, and Max Frankel, who succeeded Wicker.

In early 1972, Anthony Lewis wrote two columns, titled "To Grow and To Die," about the staggering implications of ecological doomsday. Here's a small part of what surely will become a journalistic classic:

"In the memory of the race, man has always struggled to overcome the limits imposed by nature. His success has been spectacular, especially in this last century of accelerating technology: Today he sees that he has the means to fight pestilence and disease, to unlock even the binding energy of the material world.

"When he is told now that the growth of population and production threatens his existence—that growth is approaching its earthly limits—his inevitable reaction is to regard that warning as one more challenge to be overcome. Surely the technology that has enabled human society to grow so rapidly will find a way to break through the limits."

A few months later, Lewis returned to the United States (his column was retitled "Abroad At Home"), a stranger, at 45, taking a fresh look at his country. One exquisite piece of prose stemmed from his attendance at a memorial ceremony at the Supreme Court for Hugo Black. The column opened nostalgically:

"The beauty of spring in Washington is even more intense than remembered. The sudden heat, the blossoms, the parks set out with flowers, the acres of marble and granite gleaming in the sun: It all suggests, as it was intended to, the freshness and promise of a new country."

Lewis then examined the incongruity of the phyical setting and the awry cynicism of the self-interested politicians, and sadly concluded:

"Not so many years ahead, we are likely to look back at this time as we do now at the arid years of Harding and Coolidge. If we can. The trouble is that in the world of 1972 the hollow men are so much more destructive and dangerous."

In May, 1972, after two years of persistent requests to the North Vietnamese officials in Paris, Anthony Lewis was granted a two-week visa. His Hanoi-datelined dispatches, front-paged by The Times, evoked strong disagreement from the White House and Pentagon. Lewis replied that: "the difficulty of forming accurate judgments about North Vietnam is not just a newspaper problem; it has been at the heart of the whole American entanglement in this war for seven years," and meditated, in his column of May 19, "Writing from North Vietnam is a strange experience. A reporter seldom goes to a country with which his own is actively at war. But it is not only the emotions that are confusing. There is the problem of facts."

In the 1972 election, all of The Times political columnists supported George McGovern, with the solitary exception of C.L. Sulzberger. Anthony Lewis and Tom Wicker approached hysteria in their condemnation of President Nixon's policies, and even James Reston became much more partisan than in previous campaigns. In 1973, The Times added balance by hiring William L. Safire to write a semi-weekly column. A former public relations executive, Bill Safire had worked for General Dwight Eisenhower, Florida Governor Claude Kirk and other Republicans, and had been a speech writer and special assistant to President Nixon.

In 1955, when he was only 25, Safire produced the Tex and Jinx radio program on WNBC in New York, and then went to work for Tex McCrary in a public relations firm where, at one time, the president was gossip columnist Igor Cassini. In the late sixties and early seventies, Safire wrote several articles for The Times op-ed page, under his own name and for Spiro Agnew, for whom he coined various colorful alliterative phrases, such as "nattering nabobs of negativism." He has written several books, including "The New Language of Politics" and has had many other successes in his multi-faceted career, but perhaps his most famous exploit was the 1959 Moscow kitchen debate between Nixon and Khrushchev. Safire is a facile, clever writer and he adds much more to the Times roster than his Republicanism.

Bill Safire's office in The Times' Washington bureau formerly was occupied by Tom Wicker. "Liberal ghosts in every corner," says Safire, who does most of his writing in his 20-room home in Chevy Chase, Md., where he lives with his wife, Helene, and two children.

Times columnists are not limited to politics.

In 1927, John Kieran started "Sports of the Times." The column was rare among sports columns—well written, honest, unbiased, intellectual, critical commentary rather than anecdotal gossip potpourri.

Kieran erudition and love of nature and the outdoors, as well as sports, became well known as a result of his column, and also his appearances, with Clifton Fadiman and Oscar Levant, on the "Information Please" network radio program.

Kieran's successor in 1942 was Arthur John Daley, a New Yorker who had joined The Times upon graduation from Fordham University in 1926, when he was 22.

It took a while for Daley to establish himself, particularly since he had colorful competition from Red Smith at the New York Tribune, Jimmy Cannon at the Journal, Grantland Rice at the Sun, and quite a few others.

Recognition came in 1956 when Daley became the only sports columnist to receive a Pulitzer Prize. The category was local reporting and the only other Timesman to be so honored was J. Anthony Lukas in 1968. Daley died in 1974. Among the other Times sports columnists, the best known is Walter Wellesley Smith, better known as Red Smith.

"In his attitude, a nice blend of enthusiasm, skepticism and wit, he is in the line of descent of such clear-eyed sports writers as Damon Runyon, and the first and greatest of the debunkers, Ring Lardner," said the Saturday Evening Post about Red Smith, whose prizes include the Grantland Rice and George Polk Memorial Awards, Newspaper Guild Page One Award, and many others.

Born in Green Bay, Wisconsin, in 1905, Red Smith graduated from Notre Dame and returned to Wisconsin as a reporter for the Milwaukee Sentinel. His first sports reporting was on the Star in St. Louis. He then moved to the Philadelphia Record and joined the New York Herald Tribune in 1945. Sports editor Stanley Woodward had recruited one of the most literate staffs in the country and, for the next 21 years, Red Smith was one of the delights of the Trib. His fans included devotees who loved his honesty, nostalgia, humor, and exciting style, including many readers who otherwise were not sports followers. Woodward called Smith "the best newspaper writer in the country," which may have been sports writer's hyperbole, but Smith unquestionably has long ranked with America's top newspaper writers, on or off the sports pages.

"Anybody who has been a working newspaperman must respect Smith," wrote Scripps-Howard sports writer Tom Meany. "He turns out his columns on the spot and under the gun. Red goes to no sports event with a preconceived idea of what he is to write, nor armed with frozen similes or oft-told tales to weave into his column. He lets the action itself write his column."

Red Smith indeed is a facile writer, but though the column may be produced quickly, it is the artful result of considerable preparation and experience. A delightful example is one he wrote in Janaury, 1960, titled "Leave Us Defense Against Solecisms," in which Smith resolved to avoid the "linguistic garbage" often turned out by sports writers. He rarely has deviated from that New Year's resolution.

Just the titles of his columns give an idea of his delightful style and viewpoint.

"What Has Football to Do With College." (1956)
"No Crusades for Campanella." (1958)
"Debauchery and Tennis." (1960)
"North Disneyland: The Winter Olympics." (1960)
"Man Who Neither Gabs Nor Coos—Don Dunphy." (1961)
"Sam Snead Runs Afoul P.G.A. Panjandrums." (1961)
"How The Russians Invented Beizbol." (1962)

Following the demise of the Herald Tribune in 1966, Smith's "Views of Sport" column was distributed five times a week to the Long Island Press and about 70 other clients of Publishers-Hall. However, Smith lacked a Manhattan outlet until late 1971 when Robert Lipsyte suddenly resigned from The New York Times. Red Smith was quickly recruited to do three columns a week.

What hair Red Smith has is white now, but otherwise he has changed very little and millions of readers now are developing a renewed respect and affection for him.

Not an athlete—he once referred to himself as "a seedy amateur with watery eyes behind glittering glasses" Smith is an expert on the history and current action in almost all sports, but somehow baseball, once the great American pastime, seems to evoke the greatest nostalgia and most beautiful writing.

One of Red Smith's best known columns was the obituary he wrote on August 18, 1966, on the death of the 131-year-old New York Herald Tribune. Following are excerpts:

"When you have lived with a woman for 21 years, parting comes hard, no matter what the cause. When you know she has been kicked to death, there is blind anger along with grief . . .

"Usually this space is reserved for fun and games, but there is no heart today for writing about base hits or left hooks or the safety blitz. Whenever any newspaper dies, everybody loses."

REGISTER AND TRIBUNE

Most of the major syndicates are affiliated with newspapers in New York, Chicago, Los Angeles or Washington, D.C., and most of the independent syndicates also are headquartered in these cities.

An outstanding exception is The Register and Tribune Syndicate, which is affiliated with the newspaper which cover Iowa, The Des Moines Register and The Des Moines Tribune. The RTS was founded in the 1920s by the Cowles family, which still has substantial holdings in the Des Moines newspapers. The RTS functions as an independent corporation, separate from the newspapers, headed by Dennis R. Allen.

A strength of the RTS is its comprehensive lineup of features for the Family Living and Style sections of the nation's newspapers. Among them are "Why Grow Old?" by Josephine Lowman; "Sew Simple" by Eunice Farmer; "Know Your Antiques" by Ralph and Terry Kovel; "The Mother Earth News" by magazine publisher John Shuttleworth; Better Homes and Gardens Step-By-Step Cooking column; "Makin' Things," a leading crafts column by Ed and Stevie Baldwin; "The Average American" by Lowell Smith; "Freebies" by Brian Weiss; "After Divorce" by Joanne Grant and Dr. Melvyn Berke; and "Buy Right" by Arthur Darack.

Although its heritage is in the Midwest, the RTS has a balanced lineup of features and services that are international in scope. It produces The Christian Science Monitor News and Photo Service, and carries columns by Daniel Schorr, consumer advocate Ralph Nader, Pulitzer Prize winner Lauren Soth on Food and Agriculture Affairs, Roy Wilkins of the National Association for the Advancement of Colored People, and Stanley Karnow. The RTS distributes the editorial cartoons of C.P. Houston of The Houston Chronicle and

Ed Gamble of The Nashville Tennessean.

The RTS also carries several humor columns, including "The Country Parson" by Frank A. Clark. It contains gentle homilies, a typical example being: "Funny how a dollar can look so big when you take it to church, and so small when you take it to the store." The syndicate in early 1974 obtained rights to recreate the columns the famed humorist Will Rogers wrote during the 1920s and 1930s. The new "Will Rogers Says . . . " small-space feature is selected and edited by Rogers' buff Bryan Sterling.

The number one cartoon panel, "The Family Circus" by Bil Keane, appears in more than 600 newspapers. Other cartoon panels include: "Amy" by Jack Tippit, "The Better Half" by Ruth Barnes, Dave Gerard's "Citizen Smith," "Off the Record" by Ed Reed, and "Elwyn" by Mehlman/Brenner.

Since 1972, RTS has distributed all staff produced material in The Christian Science Monitor to about 200 subscribers. The Monitor is one of the world's most respected publications and is particularly known for its Washington and foreign news coverage.

Prominent members of the staff include Godfrey Sperling Jr., Joseph C. Harsch and Richard L. Strout. In addition to his Monitor work, Strout also is the author of The New Republic's "TRB" column, an incisive commentary he has written for over 45 years.

In addition to its newspaper feature business, the syndicate is active in comic characters' licensing, preparation of television specials, book publishing, direct mail and related enterprises.

THE CHRONICLE

Many Americans, particularly New Yorkers and other big city dwellers, regard San Francisco with considerable envy. The city has a reputation of being beautiful, sophisticated, clean, and possessing various other attributes. Most Americans have never been to San Francisco or have visited only once or twice, and a large part of the reputation is due to the cluster of syndicated columnists headquartered at the San Francisco Chronicle. Among these, the number one columnist, Herb Caen, has become known as "Mr. San Francisco." The author of many books about San Francisco, he lives in, loves and promotes the Bay area with skill, humor and devotion. His six columns a week are a potpourri of anecdotes and news, and three of them, which are deemed to be of interest beyond the local area, are syndicated by Chronicle Features.

Born in 1916 in Sacramento, Caen dropped out of high school to work at the Sacramento Union, where, at the age of 20, he was a police reporter and part-time radio columnist. He moved to the Chronicle in 1936 as a radio columnist, started "It's News to Me" in 1938 and quickly became a lively source of conversation among San Franciscans. Caen deserted the Chronicle in 1949 and went to the Examiner for a little over eight years, returning to the Chronicle in 1958. For a while, he did a weekly radio program for a beer sponsor, called "What's Brewing in San Francisco."

Caen's allegiances have varied. He once said, "I hope I'm never so poor that I have to work for Hearst," and then when he worked for Hearst's Examiner, he chortled, "Now I'm eating my words—with caviar." With regard to marital allegiances, he's had three of them. One devotion that has remained unswerving is his love affair with San Francisco.

185

Caen's first book, "Baghdad-By-the-Bay," was written just after his return from World War II army service. "Don't Call it Frisco," published in 1953, furthered his identification with the Bay area. "Isn't it nice that the kind of people who prefer Los Angeles to San Francisco live there?" wrote Caen. "I wouldn't say we're sorry. It's more like the humble pride of natural superiority."

Others in the series include "Caen's Guide to San Francisco" (1957) and "Only in San Francisco" (1960).

Readers are familiar with Caen's cants, particularly his lampoons of Ronald Reagan, S.I. Hayakawa, Richard Nixon, U.S. Steel and other owners of San Francisco skyscrapers, Shirley Temple Black and pigeons.

A chain cigarette smoker, Caen works hard at his beat and, like many California columnists, is on the phone early every morning in order to talk to New Yorkers and others in later time zones.

Caen is not a brilliant writer, but he is bright, amusing and often writes with a verve. He is not malicious and frequently runs corrections and explanations under the title, "Writing the Wrongs." And, most important, he's still "fresh," after over 40 years as a columnist. His first column, in 1931, was titled "Corridor Gossip." It appeared in the Sacramento High School newspaper and the byline was Raisin Caen.

The San Francisco version of Will Rogers is Stanton Hill Delaplane, who was born in Chicago in 1907 but has been a Californian since his high school days. In 1936, he became a reporter at the San Francisco Chronicle, he received a Pulitzer Prize for general reporting in 1942, and after a variety of assignments, developed the first humorous travel column, which is supplemented by a once-a-week question-and-answer column, "Around the World with Delaplane."

When not traveling, Delaplane generally can be found at home in Tiburon, California, or at various restaurants and clubs in the Bay area. Delaplane's Postcards include satiric interviews with talking dogs and perpetual motion inventors, but he's also a skilled reporter and commentator, and he's had a great influence on travel. Perhaps his greatest contribution was that he virtually introduced Irish coffee to Americans.

The Pulitzer Prize was for a series he wrote about the attempt by five cities in northern California and southern Oregon to form a new state. Perhaps Delaplane should come East to chronicle the efforts of New York City to become the 51st state.

Perhaps the most urbane and eclectic of the Chronicle columnists is Charles McCabe, a transplanted New Yorker who has been a publicist, police reporter and foreign correspondent. McCabe's respect for journalism is indicated in his book, "Damned Old Crank," a biography of E.W. Scripps, and in his columns which express strong opinions in carefully sculpted prose.

In 1970, McCabe, and other columnists at the two daily newspapers, the Chronicle and the Examiner, joined in protesting against U.S. Steel and other builders of skyscraper buildings in the Bay front area. The protests may have stemmed the tide, not for the controversial project, which was built, but probably with regard to future projects.

In one of his columns on this subject, McCabe concluded:

"The steel project, since it is on city land, can be prevented by civic action of a vigorous kind. Because it is dramatic, and dramatically bad, it can remind us of the other phallic horrors we have allowed the city to build on private property. We might even get the idea that it's time to stop.

"There's an old saying that you can't hurry the crops. Farmers are wiser than city folks. If only because they are compelled to live with blights and frosts and lack of rain, they develop a great patience. We have been impatient long enough in developing this city. Let's leave it alone for a while, and look to other and more inventive solutions for our problems than tall office buildings. There's a time to go, and a time to stop."

A collection of McCabe's most entertaining columns appear in a 1970 book, "The Fearless Spectator," which is the title of his weekly column.

Arthur Hoppe (pronounced Hoppy) is a good-looking, articulate satirist whose syndicated commentary, "The Innocent Bystander," appears three times a week, though Chronicle readers are treated to Our Man Hoppe more frequently.

Born in Hawaii in 1925, Art Hoppe went East for his college education (he graduated from Harvard in 1949) and then settled in San Francisco. He started as a copy boy at the Chronicle and soon became a local celebrity. In 1968, he authored "The Perfect Solution to Absolutely Everything," a book which reproduced many of his most popular columns, including one about total birth control as a final cure-all.

Of course, Hoppe was kidding. He married his childhood girlfriend in 1946 and they have four Hoppes.

Hoppe, whose specialty is parables, occasionally uses a character, Joe Sikspak, a beer-drinking blue-collar worker who discusses politics in a neighborhood bar, in the tradition of "Mr. Dooley." He once said,

"Columns should express outrageous opinions to be of any value. The more outrageous, the more they tend to make people think. I don't want to tell people things. I don't know anything. I want to stir people up so they'll do their own thinking."

Art Hoppe sometimes is called the Art Buchwald of the West. Hoppe's fans resent this comparison and claim that, among other skills, Hoppe is a better tennis player.

San Francisco always has been loaded with columnists, local and syndicated. As a Chronicle columnist, Lucius Beebe set the standard for style and sophistication. The humor orientation is carried over to "The Wonderful World of Animals," the nation's top column about pets. The author is Dr. Frank Miller, a veterinarian.

The Chronicle Features lineup has other columnists, including Terrence O'Flaherty, the long-time TV critic of the Chronicle. Recent additions to the roster are butcher Merle Ellis, medical reporter Leonore Feinstein, consumerist Kate MacQueen and sewing specialist Sandra Betzina. Several of these columnists, notably Merle Ellis, The Butcher, are quite popular, but Caen, Delaplane, McCabe, Hoppe and Dr. Miller are the stars, and their columns enhance the glory of San Francisco.

McNAUGHT

O.O. McIntyre, Will Rogers and Irvin S. Cobb were McNaught Syndicate columnists. This trio alone would establish McNaught's importance among syndicates, but the added significance of the company is indicated by the following names.

William Jennings Bryan covered the 1912 political conventions. He got 75% of the gross income, which he used to buy property in Coral Gables.

Walter Winchell columned for McNaught before and after he worked for King Features, and "Dear Abby" started at McNaught. Eleanor Roosevelt's first columns were edited by McNaught's Charles B. Driscoll, the former editor of the Wichita Eagle who vainly attempted to correct the grammar of the First Lady.

Alexander de Seversky, Albert Einstein, Alfred E. Smith, Bob Hope, Dale Carnegie, Mary Pickford, Milton Berle and Wendell Wilkie wrote series.

Byron Nelson, Tony Lema, Babe Didrickson, and Ben Hogan were McNaught sports stars, as were Paul Gallico, Burns Mantle, Whitney Bolton, humorists Sam Blythe, Homer Croy and others.

Just as Samuel McClure published McClure's Magazine, Mc-Naught published "An Independent, Informal Review." The January, 1925, issue of McNaught's magazine featured several of the syndicate's columnists, including Chester T. Crowell, Robert L. Duffus, and Stuart P. Sherman whose article was titled "Rebirth at Forty." A long-time McNaught column, by Bob Peterson, was titled "Life Begins at Forty." In 1975, when Peterson retired, Joanne Farris took over the column, but it didn't click, and was dropped.

Neal O'Hara of the Boston Herald-Traveler wrote "Pull Up A Chair" for many years, and when he died, the column was continued for a few years by Frank Jay Markey. There's something about McNaught which encourages longevity. Markey worked on the Baltimore Sun, operated his own syndicate, and worked at McNaught while in his eighties.

Frank Markey, who started a syndicate in 1936 which was acquired by McNaught, died in 1978, at the age of 84. Markey, who started as a cub reporter at the Baltimore Sun in 1912, was a friend of H.L. Mencken and syndicated his columns.

Started in 1922, McNaught is owned mostly by Charles V. McAdam, chairman of the board, and his son, Charles McAdam Jr., president. McAdam Sr., who was born in 1892, started the syndicate (together with Cleveland newspaperman Virgil McNitt), and his son has been with the company for more than 20 years.

Annual sales are about $1 million. The number one feature is the daily astrology column by Carroll Righter and biggest sales are from comic strips including "Yogi Bear," "The Flintstones," "The Jackson Twins," "Joe Palooka," "Mutt & Jeff" and "Heathcliff."

Text columns include moneyman Louis Rukeyser, conservative Holmes Alexander, humorist John Keasler, forecaster Criswell, psychic Uri Geller, Dr. Peter J. Steincrohn, who has been writing "Stop Killing Yourself" for over 30 years, "The Christophers," one of the longest-running inspirational columns, Rev. Lester Kinsolving, the controversial author of "Potomac Ethics" and "Inside Religion," Andrew Tully, long-time author of "Capital Fare" and Dr. A.J. Palmaccio Jr., a newcomer who writes about sports medicine.

COLUMBIA

Formed in 1950 by Joseph M. Boychuk, Columbia Features has outlasted many other independent syndicates. Its success formula relates to a select list of quality features, a tight budget operation and perseverance.

Sunday School Lesson, for example, was started in the early part of the century by Earl L. Douglass. It has been continued by his son, Elisha Douglass, and is one of the country's most popular inspirational columns, together with Strength for the Day, which also is written by Rev. Douglass.

Other Columbia winners are written by Dorothy Hammond, Joey Adams, Lydel Sims and Kurt Lassen.

The staff includes executive editor Chris Riley and associate editor Helen M. Staunton (formerly managing editor of Publishers-Hall).

UNIVERSAL

In March, 1970, John P. McMeel and James F. Andrews incorporated Universal Press Syndicate, a small company that had sold exclusively to Catholic publications. Within a year they had achieved phenomenal success with a varied assortment of new features that were bought by more than 500 newspapers. Clients range all the way from the New York News, Chicago Tribune, Washington Post, and Baltimore Sun to the Arkansas Banner News in Magnolia, Arkansas, and the Whitehorse Yukon in Alaska.

The syndicate's first roster included two of the hottest new columns in the business, Nancy Stahl's "Once Over Lightly" and Garry Wills' "The Outrider." The syndicate added, in 1974, a column by J.F. terHorst, former press secretary to President Ford. Other successes followed, notably the youth-oriented comic strips "Ziggy," by Tom Wilson, "Doonesbury" by Garry Trudeau, "Herman" by Jim Unger and "Wordsmith" by Tim Menees.

John McMeel, president, formerly was national sales director of Publishers-Hall Syndicate. James Andrews, executive vice president and editor, formerly was managing editor of the National Catholic Reporter.

UPS has collected a group of irreverent byliners including Andrew Greeley, William A. Rusher, Charlie Shedd, Philip Nobile, who does a weekly interview column, and Steve Harvey, who debunks football polls with his popular "The Bottom Ten."

Universal Press Syndicate is an amazingly successful independent syndicate which is thriving on diverse talent.

Bob Walton, formerly a syndicate salesman, retired to California to write "A Time to Live." Mike Wendland writes the country's biggest CB column, Niki Scott is "Working Woman," Dr. Walt Menninger provides psychiatric Insights, Dr. Aaron Rutledge counsels families and Mickey Herskowitz and Steve Perkins write "Sports Hot Line" and Sandra Kelly writes "Sew What's New."

Universal newcomers include commentator Jonathan Power, consumerist Carolyn Nolte-Watts, do-it-yourselfer Norman Stark, and Jim Reitz, who succeeded Charlotte Slater as author of "Things Your Mother Never Taught You."

In 1977, Universal took over the distribution of The Mini Page, the weekly four-page tabloid created by Betty Debnam. In 1977 and 1978, Universal launched several comic strips, including "Cathy," the creation of Cathy Guisewite, a Detroit advertising agency executive.

Universal has had the greatest growth of any new syndicate and now is one of the "majors." One of its comics, Doonesbury, has become part of our culture, with such accolades as a Pulitzer Prize and this statement by President Gerald R. Ford:

"There are only three major vehicles to keep us informed as to what is going on: the electronic media, the print media, and Doonesbury, not necessarily in that order."

MAJOR COLUMNISTS

About the Listings

Columnists are listed alphabetically within each category.

The title of the column is included only where it is other than the name of the columnist.

The syndicate is not listed for those columnists who distribute their own columns.

The telephone number is not included in a few cases in which the columnist has requested this omission or where the address is a mailing address.

ADVICE

Jean Adams   Teen Forum   United
United Feature Syndicate, 200 Park Ave., N.Y. 10017

George Alderson   Crutches-Cane-Wheelchair   Alderson
Enterprises
Box 295, Altoona, Pa. 16603

Melvyn Berke, Ph.D. and
Joanne Grant   After Divorce   Register
Register and Tribune Syndicate, Des Moines, Iowa 50304

Helen & Sue Bottel   King
2060 56th Ave., Sacramento, Ca. 95822, (916) 421-5832

Joyce Brothers, Ph.D.   King
1530 Palisade Ave., Fort Lee, N.J. 07024

Polly Cramer   Polly's Pointers   NEA
NEA, 200 Park Ave., N.Y. 10017, (212) 679-3600

Susan Deitz   Single File   LAT
Los Angeles Times Syndicate, L.A. 90053

Heloise   Hints From Heloise   King
King Features, 235 E. 45th St., N.Y. 10017

Joyce Lain Kennedy   Career Corner   Universal
1160 Rockville Pike, Rockville, Md. 20852, (301) 340-0992

Virginia Knauer   Dear Consumer   Copley
9601 Milnor St., Philadelphia, Pa. 19111

Miriam Landau, Ph.D.   LAT
2212 Via Cerritos, Palos Verdes Estates, Ca. 90274
(213) 375-3845

Ann Landers   Field
Chicago Sun-Times, Chic. 60611, (312) 321-3000

Mike Musick   Heartline   Field
114 E. Dayton St., W. Alexandria, Ohio 45381

Dorothy Ricker   Teen Age Mail
2521 Waltrous Ave., Tampa, Fla. 33609, (813) 257-0241

Madge Saksena   Ask Aunt Madge
3757 Macbeth Dr., San Jose, Ca. 95127, (408) 258-7125

Charlie Shedd   Strictly for Dads   Universal
Universal Press, 6700 Squibb Rd., Mission, Kans. 66202

Ruth Carter Stapleton   Universal
Universal Press Syndicate, 6700 Squibb Rd., Mission, Kans. 66202

Abigail Van Buren   Dear Abby   CTNYNS
132 Lasky Dr., S. Beverly Hills, Ca. 90212

Robert Wallace Jr., Ph.D. Tween 12 & 20   Copley
Copley News Service, Box 190, San Diego, Ca. 92112

Val Winsey   Susie Mac   United
United Feature Syndicate, 200 Park Ave., N.Y. 10017

Beth Winship   Ask Beth   LAT
Boston Globe, Boston 02107, (617) 288-8000

AUTOMOTIVE

Harry Anderson   Your Wheels   LAT
Los Angeles Times, Los Angeles 90053, (213) 625-2345

Bilko   Car Crazy   B.P. Singer
3164 W. Tyler Ave., Anaheim, Ca. 92801, (714) 527-5650

Robert A. Cutter   The Steering Column
340 Old Battery Rd., Bridgeport, Conn. 06605, (203) 335-6405

Al Fleming   Detroit Update   Wash. Star
Car Biz, 24500 Southfield Rd., Southfield, Mich. 48075
(313) 557-1013

Ida Fried   Automotive
108 E. 66th St., N.Y. 10021, (212) 988-5190

Doyle K. Getter   Your Auto and You
Automotive Features, 814 E. Manor Circle, Milwaukee, Wis. 53217,
(414) 352-7359

Ray Hill   Caring for Your Car   LAT
Popular Science, 380 Madison Ave., N.Y. 10017, (212) 687-3000

Ray Hite   Let's Talk About Your Car
Editor's Copy Syndicate, 419 Green St., Orangeburg, S.C. 29115,
(803) 534-1110

Edward Janicki   Auto Topics
Trans-World News Service, 767 Ntl. Press Bldg., Wash., D.C. 20045

Fred W. Kline   Motor Talk
Capital News Service, 1127 11th St., Sacramento, Ca. 95814
(916) 445-6336

Michael Lamm   On Wheels
Box 7607, Stockton, Ca. 95207, (209) 931-1056

Don O'Reilly   Dateline: Detroit (and others)
Auto News Syndicate, Box 2085, Daytona Beach, Fla. 32015,
(904) 439-2634

Brent Russell   Auto World
11816 Riders Lane, Reston, Va. 22091

Jane Sherrod   Teenage Driving Tips
BP Singer Features, 3164 W. Tyler Ave., Anaheim, Ca. 92801,
(714) 527-5650

Ray Stapley   Your Car
Toronto Star, 1 Younge St., Toronto, Ont. M5E 1E6, Canada
(416) 421-3039

Charles Yarbrough   Wheels
Washington Star, 225 Virginia Ave., S.E., Wash., D.C. 20061,
(202) 484-5000
(The Wheels package also includes columns by Charles Ewing, Ev
Gardner and Kent Goforth. All are at the Washington Star.)

BEAUTY AND FASHION

April Anastasi   Beauty Hints
Ascher Syndicate, 214 Boston Ave., Mays Landing, N.J. 08330

Jennifer Anderson   Ask Jennifer   LAT
Los Angeles Times Syndicate, L.A. 90053

Amelia Bassin
Bassinova, 18 E. 41st St., N.Y. 10017, (212) 679-4733

Peggy Bendel   Behind the Seams   NEA
Box 175, Ridgefield Park, N.J. 07660, (201) 343-3613

Sandra Betzina   Sew With Flair   Chronicle
2395 21st Ave., S.F. 94117, (415) 552-1426

Lucille Bouchard   Beauty
37 E. 64th St., N.Y. 10021, (212) 744-0200

Harriet Carlson   Charm
1943 Lake Ave., Wilmette, Ill. 60091, (312) 251-2653

Richard Carreno   Suit Yourself   Clearinghouse
                        (men's fashions)
Box 118, Fabyan, Conn. 06245, (203) 923-9925

Marian Christy   After A Fashion   United
Boston Globe, 135 Morrissey Blvd., Boston, Mass. 02107,
(617) 288-8000

Dina Dellale
108 E. 66th St., N.Y. 10021, (212) 988-5190

Florence de Santis   Fashion, Face & Figure   United
United Feature, 200 Park Ave., N.Y. 10017, (212) 557-2333 and
61-32 228th St., Queens, N.Y. 11364, (212) 321-1356

Eunice Farmer   Sew Simple   Register
Register and Tribune Syndicate, Des Moines, Iowa 50304

Ellie Grossman   Beauty and Fashion   NEA
NEA, 200 Park Ave., N.Y. 10017, (212) 557-5870

200

Paul Hamlin   What Next?   Spadea
                         (also Style for Men)
Spadea Syndicate, 2 Bridge St., Milford, N.J. 08848, (201) 995-2201

Rosette Hargrove   Paris Scene   NEA
Newspaper Enterprise Assn., 200 Park Ave., N.Y. 10017

Charles Hix   (men's fashions)   NEA
301 E. 22nd St., N.Y. 10010

Sandra Kelly   Sew What's New   Universal
Universal Press Syndicate, Mission, Kans. 66202

Eleanor Lambert   She   Field
32 E. 57th St., N.Y. 10022, (212) 688-2130

Lydia Lane   Beauty
Box 1417, Burbank, Ca. 91507, (213) 848-0615

Eleanor Lee   Sewing Sense   Columbia
Columbia Features, 36 W. 44th St., N.Y. 10036

Gloria Lintermans   Looking Great   Inter-Continental
Box 991, Glendale, Ca. 91209

Shirley Lord (Mrs. David Anderson)   Field
Helena Rubinstein, 300 Park Ave., N.Y. 10022

Judy Love   Knitting   NEA
NEA, 200 Park Ave., N.Y. 10017

Gene Loyd   Now!   Register
Register and Tribune Syndicate, Des Moines, Iowa 50304

Marylou Luther   Clothesline   LAT
Los Angeles Times, Times-Mirror Sq., L.A. 90053, (213) 625-2345

Julia McCombs   Sew Business
Cole Associates, 28 E. 22nd St., N.Y. 10010, (212) 254-8370

Mary Sue Miller   A Lovelier You   Field
440 E. 79th St., N.Y. 10021, (212) 535-1340

John Molloy   Making It
Dress For Success, Inc., Box 526, N.Y. 10033, (212) 781-4729

Lila Nadell   Fashion Sense
Spring Lake Rd., Sherman, Conn. 06784, (203) 355-1848

Joan O'Sullivan   Women's Way   King
("Jeanne D'Arcy")
King Features, 235 E. 45th St., N.Y. 10017, (212) 682-5600

Paige Palmer   Fashion 'N Figure
Box 255, Bath, Ohio 44210, (216) 659-6231

Lucille Rivers   Sewing   Field
Field Newspaper Syndicate, 30 E. 42nd St., N.Y. 10017

Joanne Schreiber   Patterns, Sewing   NEA
200 NEA, 200 Park Ave., N.Y. 10017

Eugenia Sheppard   Inside Fashion   Field
Field Syndicate, 30 E. 42nd St., N.Y. 10017, (212) 682-6502

Mrs. Hugo Sims   Fashions   Editor's Copy
Editor's Copy Syndicate, Box 532, Orangeburg, S.C. 29115,
(803) 534-1110

Pat Trexler   Pat's Pointers (needlepoint)   Field
699 Iver Place, N. Myrtle Beach, S.C. 29582

Besty von Furstenberg   Beauty   Universal
230 Central Park W., N.Y. 10024

Emily Wilkins   A New You   King
Delmonico Hotel, Park Ave. and 59th St., N.Y. 10022,
(212) 355-2500

Charlotte Wilkinson   Your Fashion Image
30 W. 54th St., N.Y. 10019, (212) 247-7300

Erica Wilson   Needleplay   CTNYNS
717 Madison Ave., N.Y. 10021, (212) 832-7290

BOOKS

John Austin   Books-of-the-Week
Box 49957, L.A. 90049, (213) 826-9602

Gary P. Baranik   Authors & Books
1648 10th Ave., Brooklyn, N.Y. 11215, (212) 965-4433

Arthur Brickman   Readers World
14524 W. Dixie Hwy., N. Miami, Fla. 33181, (305) 944-0179

Carroll Ann Brooks   Book Look   News World
The News World, 401 Fifth Ave., N.Y. 10016, (212) 532-8300

Alan Caruba   Book Views
Box 40, Maplewood, N.J. 07040, (201) 763-6392

Marc Drogin
74 Court St., Exeter, N.H. 03833, (603) 772-3221

Carol Felsenthal   About Books   NEA
American Library Assn., 50 E. Huron St., Chicago 60611,
(312) 944-6780

Ralph Hollenbeck   Parade of Books   King
King Features, 235 E. 45 St., N.Y. 10017, (212) 682-5600

David Horowitz   Book Reviews
World Union Press, 507 5th Ave., N.Y. 10017, (212) 688-7557

Martin Levin   Paperback Guide   AP
333 W. 56th St., N.Y. 10019

Bruce McCabe   Lit'ry Life   CTNYNS
Boston Globe, Boston, Mass. 02107, (617) 929-2000

Robert Emmett McLeod
Feature News Service, 2330 S. Brentwood Blvd., St. Louis, Mo.
63144, (314) 961-9826

William McPherson   Book World   Wash. Post
Washington Post, 1150 15th St., N.W., Wash., D.C. 20071,
(202) 334-6000

Mildred Paulus   Book Marks   Mid-Continent
Box 1662, Pittsburgh, Pa. 15230, (412) 562-4067

John Pinkerman   Today's Books   News Associates
Drawer J, Idylwild, Ca. 92349, (714) 659-2329

Robert S. Righetti   Book Mart   Danney Ball
Ball Productions, 147 N. Franklin Ave., Hemet, Ca. 92343

Philippa Roth   Bout Books   World News
Box 449, Hollywood, Ca. 90028

David Vaughan   Book Reviews
277 West End Ave., N.Y. 10023

Victor Wilson   Newhouse
Newhouse News Service, 1750 Pennsylvania, N.W., Wash., D.C.
20006, (202) 393-7130

Caution: Several columnists, particularly those at small syndicates
or the self-syndicators, have very limited distribution, or are
interested only in specific types of books.

BRIDGE

B.J. Becker   King
144-37 70 Ave., Queens, N.Y. (212) 544-6091

Carl Brett
c/o Theodore M. Ginsburg, 1209 W. Wynnewood Rd., Wynnewood,
Pa. 19096, (215) 647-0666

Ira G. Corn, Jr.   The Aces   United
Southland Center, Dallas, Tex. 75215, (214) 748-8388

Charles Goren and Omar Sharif   CTNYNS
5767 Alton Rd., Miami Beach, Fla. 33140, (305) 865-0381
(Also Backgammon)

Oswald Jacoby
and Alan Sontag   Win at Bridge   NEA
4246 Woodfin Dr., Dallas, Tex. 75220

Fred L. Karpin   CTNYNS
Washington Post, 1515 L. St., N.W., Wash., D.C. 20005

Richard A. Miller   Better Bridge
141 E. Philadelphia St., York, Pa. 17403, (717) 854-2715

Robert Rosenblum   Better Bridge   Copley
Box 190, San Diego, Ca. 92041

Alfred Sheinwold   LAT
1300 Midvale Ave., L.A. 90024 (Also Backgammon)

Alan Truscott   NYT
New York Times, 229 W. 43 St., N.Y. 10036

BUSINESS
(Including Consumer Advice and Labor)

Sally and Jim Adams   Get Your $ Worth   McNaught
c/o Roseanne Gordon, McNaught Syndicate, 60 E. 42 St., N.Y.
10017

Babson's Reports
(edited by John Willison, also titled "How's Business")
Publishers Financial Bureau, 370 Washington St., Wellesley Hills,
Mass. 02181, (617) 235-0900

Herman Baum   The House Doctor   Register
Register and Tribune Syndicate, Des Moines, Iowa 50304

Hal Betancourt   Advertising Basics
7324 Convoy Court, San Diego, Ca. 92111, (714) 565-2635

Dorothea Brooks   Business Today   UPI
United Press, 220 E. 42nd St., N.Y. 10017, (212) 682-0400

Robert J. Bruss   Real Estate Mailbag
Real Estate Feature, 711 Commercial St., S.F. 94108,
(415) 344-2600

Jerome Cahill   Knight-Ridder
N.Y. News, 1272 Ntl. Press Bldg., Wash., D.C. 20045,
(202) 628-5058

Don G. Campbell   Daily Investor   United
(Mr. Campbell also writes "About Real Estate" for The Register
Syndicate.)
Box 2693, Phoenix, Ariz. 85002, (602) 943-1329

Howard Cohen   Today's Consumer
17 Pine Grove St., Woodstock, N.Y. 12498, (914) 679-2645

Bob Cooke
16115 S.W. 101st Ave., Miami, Fla. 33157, (305) 233-4816

Hank and Sylvia Cronin   Tip Off . . . The Rip Off
8418 S.W. 103rd Ave., Miami, Fla. 33173, (305) 595-6050

Margaret Dana   Before You Buy   United
216 King Rd., Chalfont, Pa. 18914

Arthur Darack   Buy Right   Register
Consumers Digest, 6316 N. Lincoln Ave., Chic. 60659,
(312) 588-3020

Edwin Darby
Chicago Sun-Times, Chic. 60611, (312) 321-2571

Sam Dix   Energy Report   Publishers Syndicate
Energy Education Publishers, Box 6488, Grand Rapids, Mich. 49506
(616) 454-8264

Dan Dorfman   Esquire
Esquire Magazine, 488 Madison Ave., N.Y. 10022, (212) 644-5656

Merle Dowd   Managing Your Family's Money   Register
11800 Sunrise Valley Dr., Reston, Va. 22070, (206) 232-2171
also
7438 S.E. 40th St., Mercer Island, Wash. 98040

William A. Doyle   Investor's Guide   King
The Star-Ledger, Newark, N.J. 07101, (201) 877-4141

John Dvorak   Small Business Tips
Tagumi Features, Box 275, El Cerrito, Ca. 94530, (415) 527-7730

Samuel Fishlyn   Home Repairs
Box 62, 10 Madoc St., North Centre, Mass. 02159

Paul Fortney Jr.   Labor
138 S. Virginia Ave., Falls Church, Va. 22046

Jordan Goodman   Info. . . . a world of $ense
Tudor City Plaza, N.Y. 10017, (212) 986-1826

Dave Goodwin   Insurance (Also: Money Matters)
Box 54-6661, Surfside, Fla. 33154, (305) 531-0071

Arthur S. Green
485 S. Robertson Blvd., Beverly Hills, Ca. 90211, (213) 274-1283

G. Douglas Hafely Jr.   Consumer Finance   Trans-World
2232 Arrowhead Ave., Brooksville, Fla. 33512, (904) 683-0210

Eliot Janeway
15 E. 80 St., N.Y. 10021, (212) 249-8833

207

Myron Kandel and Phil Greer   EF
200 W. 57th St., N.Y. 10019, (212) 245-3700

Llewellyn King   Energy
Energy Daily, 300 Ntl. Press Bldg., Wash., D.C. 20045

Virginia Knauer   Dear Consumer   Copley
9601 Milnor St., Philadelphia 19114

Edith Lank   House Calls
240 Hemingway Drive, Rochester, N.Y. 14620, (716) 271-6230

George Lazarus   Marketing   Knight-Ridder
Chicago Tribune, 435 N. Michigan Ave., Chic. 60611,
(312) 222-3232

Mike LeFan   More For Your Money
1802 S. 13th St., Temple, Tex. 76501, (817) 773-4768

Samuel P. Levine   Consumer's Dilemma
Box 174, Canoga Park, Ca. 91305, (213) 343-0550

Joseph A. Livingston   Business Outlook   Field
Phil. Inquirer, Phil. 19101, (215) 854-2077

G.L. Ludcke   A Woman and Her Money
Belmont Associates, 37 Oakley Rd., Belmont, Mass. 02178,
(617) 484-4169

Kate MacQueen   Common Cents   Chronicle
Chronicle Features, 870 Market St., S.F. 94102

Sidney Margolius   For the Consumer   United
74 Davis Rd., Port Washington, N.Y. 11050, (516) 767-4607

Carol Mathews   Money Watch   LAT
N.Y. Post, 210 South St., N.Y. 10002, (212) 349-5000

Jack McArthur   Finance
Toronto Star, 1 Yonge St., Toronto, Ont. M5E 1E6, Canada,
(416) 367-2000

Bernard C. Meltzer   Real Estate   Field
Station WOR, 1440 Broadway, N.Y. 10018

John Meyer   Canadian Business Report
Toronto Star Syndicate, 1 Yonge St., Toronto, Ont. M5E 1E6,
Canada, (416) 367-2461

Milton Moskowitz   LAT
32 Vista Linda Dr., Mill Valley, Ca. 94941, (415) 388-1508

Bess Myerson   Ask Bess   CTNYNS
3 E. 71st St., N.Y. 10021

Ralph Nader   In the Public Interest   Register
Box 19367, Wash., D.C. 20036, (204) 833-3400

Peter S. Nagan   The Economy   Newhouse
Newhouse News Service, 1750 Pennsylvania Ave., N.W., Wash.,
D.C. 20006

George Nobbe   Real World (careers)   King
King Features, 235 E. 45th St., N.Y. 10017

Carolyn Nolte-Watts   Watch This Space   Universal
St. Petersburg Times, Box 1121, St. Petersburg, Fla. 33731,
(813) 893-8111

Sylvia Porter   Your Money's Worth   Field
30 E. 42nd St., N.Y. 10017, (212) 682-6504

Mrs. Jane Bryant Quinn   Wash. Post
7 Berrybrook Circle, Chappaqua, N.Y. 10514

Carter Randall   Miami Herald Syndicate
Royal Trust Bank, 627 S.W. 27 Ave., Miami, Fla. 33135

Victor Riesel   Inside Labor   Field
30 E. 42nd St., N.Y. 10017, (212) 682-3337

John A. Ritter   Legal Briefs
3641 Main Hwy., Miami, Fla. 33133, (305) 444-7187

Merrill Rose   Help-Mate
Consumer News, 813 Ntl. Press Bldg., Wash., D.C. 20045,
(212) 737-1190

Robert Rosefsky   Speaking Dollarwise   LAT
5521 E. Exeter Blvd., Phoenix, Ariz. 85018

Martin J. Ross
Law Education Institute, 50 N. Terrace Pla., Valley Stream, N.Y.
11580, (516) 561-1483

Hobart Rowen   Economic Impact   Wash. Post
Washington Post, 1150 15th St., N.W., Wash., D.C. 20071,
(202) 334-6000

Arthur E. Rowse   Consumer Contact
813 Ntl. Press Bldg., Wash., D.C. 20045, (202) 737-1190

Louis Rukeyser   Money   McNaught
Money, 1271 Ave. of the Americas, N.Y. 10020

Merryle S. Rukeyser   Everybody's Money
c/o B.H. Simon, 20 Old Mamaroneck Rd., White Plains, N.Y. 10605

Sidney Rutberg   Money Matters   Fairchild
Women's Wear Daily, 7 E. 12 St., N.Y. 10003, (212) 741-4360

David R. Sargent   Successful Investing   LAT
United Business and Investment Service, 16 Babson Park Ave.,
Babson Park, Wellesley Hills, Mass. 02181, (617) 235-0900

Lou Schneider   Trade Winds   NANA
J-4 West Ridge, W. Orange, N.J. 07052, (201) 736-3266

David G. Schuchat   Your Real Estate
1511 K St., N.W., Wash., D.C. 20005, (202) 737-4911

Dr. Whitt N. Schultz   How To Be Successful
Knowledge News, Box 100, Kenilworth, Ill. 60043, (312) 256-0059

Howard Shonting   World of Real Estate
Real Estate Research Institute, 353 Willett Ave., Port Chester, N.Y.
10573, (914) 937-3500

George W. Smith   Easy Tax Tips   Inter-Continental
Box 991, Glendale, Calif. 91209

Earl Snyder   Realty Investing
14909 Kalmia Dr., Laurel, Md. 20810

David Stanford   Homing In (real estate Q. and A.)
Box 26622, S.F. 94126

Herbert Stein, Ph.D.   The Economy Today   United
9342 Harvey Rd., Silver Spring, Md. 20910

Mark Stevens   Small Business
Box 487, Chappaqua, N.Y. 10514, (914) 238-3569

Richard Suter   Suter's Perspective   Investor's Features
Bardwell and Abbott, 534 Stratford Place, Chic. 60657

Ben Tarris   More For Your Money
Danney Ball Productions, 147 N. Franklin Ave., Hemet, Ca. 92343

Peter Weaver   Mind Your Money   King
5102 Cammack Dr., Wash., D.C. 20016, (301) 320-5101

Brian Weiss   Freebies   Register & Tribune
Register and Tribune Syndicate, Des Moines, Iowa 50304

Chris White   Real Estate   Danney Ball
Ball Productions, 147 N. Franklin Ave., Hemet, Ca. 92343

Betty Yarmon   Family Finance   United
35 Sutton Pl., N.Y. 10022, (212) 755-3487

DECORATING
(Including Antiques)

Carolyn Anderson   Carolyn's Collections
American Way Features, 100 River Rd., Pigeon Forge, Tenn. 37863, (615) 453-6111

Thomas A. Bateson   Collector's Corner   United
United Feature, 200 Park Ave., N.Y. 10017

Barbara Taylor Bradford Designing Woman   LAT
135 E. 83rd St., N.Y. 10028

Ann Frances Dolan   Save Time and Money   NEA
Box 1025, Pensacola, Fla. 32507, (904) 453-5739

Genevieve Fernandez   Interior Decorating   United
United Feature, 200 Park Ave., N.Y. 10017

Anne S. Gilbert   Antiques & Stuff   United
United Features, 200 Park Ave., N.Y. 10017

Arthur S. Green
485 S. Robertson Blvd., Beverly Hills, Ca. 90211, (213) 274-1283

Dorothy Hammond   Antique Wise   Columbia
Columbia Features, 36 W. 44th St., N.Y. 10036

Lillian Hughes   About Your Home   Editor's Copy
Syndicate
Box 532, Orangeburg, S.C. 29115, (803) 534-1110

Ralph and Terry Kovel   Know Your Antiques   Register
Register and Tribune Syndicate, Des Moines, Iowa 50304

Emily Malino   Design For People   United
1054 31st St., N.W., Wash., D.C. 20007, (202) 333-0126

Roberta Mathews   Home Line   LAT
Los Angeles Times, L.A. 90053, (213) 972-5000

Donna Meilach   Creative Crafts
3991 Crown Point Dr., San Diego, Ca. 92109, (714) 270-5784

Carolyn S. Murray   Your Home   LAT
Los Angeles Times, L.A. 90053, (213) 625-2345

Joseph K. Ott   Antiques in America
Providence Journal, Providence, R.I., 02902, (401) 277-7463

Jan S. Paul   Around the House
Box 6488, Bakersfield, Ca. 93306, (805) 871-8569

Jean-Paul St. Michel   Deco Plans   LAT
Los Angeles Times Syndicate, L.A. 90053

Jennifer Tahtinen   Apartment Decorating   NEA
9014 Brook Ford Rd., Burke, Va. 22015

Carleton Varney   Your Family Decorator   Field
60 E. 56th St., N.Y. 10022, (212) 758-2810

ECOLOGY AND ANIMALS

David Berkowitz   Landscape
4307 Underwood St., University Park, Md. 20782, (301) 927-5811

Doug & Jean Borgstedt   The Pet Set
Box 298, Paoli, Pa. 19301, (215) 644-3211

Dr. Michael Fox   Ask Your Vet   CTNYNS
Washington Univ. of St. Louis, St. Louis, Mo. 63130

Peter Horton   Wild Animals
News Associates, Drawer J, Idyllwild, Ca. 93249, (714) 659-2329

Dr. Frank Miller   Wonderful World of Animals   Chronicle
269 S. Van Ness Ave., S.F. 94103, (415) 861-7354

William Patterson   The Pet Parade
4354 Clybourn Ave., Burbank, Ca. 91505, (213) 849-5077

John Shuttleworth   Mother Earth News   Register
Box 70, Hendersonville, N.C. 28739

EDUCATION

Howard Hurwitz, Ed.D.   Hurwitz on Education   Columbia
Columbia Features, 36 W. 44th St., N.Y. 10036

Patricia McCormack   UPI
United Press, 220 E. 42nd St., N.Y. 10017, (212) 682-0400

Richard Meisler   This Learning World
1203 Gardner, Ann Arbor, Mich. 48104, (313) 769-0124

David Nydick
22 Lesly Dr., Syosset, N.Y. 11791, (516) 681-4161

Dr. Max Rafferty   LAT
Troy State Univ., Troy, Ala. 36081

ENTERTAINMENT
(Including Movies)

Joey Adams   Strictly For Laughs   Columbia
160 W. 46th St., N.Y. 10036

Russell B. Adams   At The Movies
6515 Sunset Blvd., Hollywood, Ca. 90028, (213) 654-7575

John Austin   Hollywood Inside
Box 49957, L.A. 90049, (213) 826-9602

James Bacon   Hollywood Hotline   NANA
Los Angeles Herald-Examiner, L.A. 90054, (213) 748-1212

Marilyn Beck   Hollywood   United
Box 655, Beverly Hills, Ca. 90213, (213) 273-8116

Byron Belt   Critic-At-Large   Newhouse
50 W. 67th St., N.Y. 10023, (212) 799-1806

Jay Brown   Mini-Movie Reviews   Cineman
7 Charles Court, Middletown, N.Y. 10940, (914) 692-4572

Wally Burke   Hollywood Connection
Box 872, Santa Monica, Ca. 90406, (213) 451-4312

Dave Campbell   Reel Facts
Le-Pac Feature Syndicate, 65 Cresta Vista Dr., S.F. 94127,
(415) 586-4802

Igor Cassini and   Cassini Carousel   Columbia
Diane Judge
c/o Diane Judge, 38 E. 38th St., N.Y. 10016

Colin Dangaard   Hollywood Cover
6254 Seadrift Cove, Malibu, Ca. 90265, (213) 457-2996

Angela de T. Gingris   Women's News Service
316 N. Carolina Ave., S.E., Wash., D.C. 20061, (202) 543-1109

Shirley Eder   Hollywood   Knight-Ridder
Detroit Free Press, Detroit, Mich. 48231, (313) 222-6400

Ted Green   Main Street
Backstage, 165 W. 46th St., N.Y. 10036, (212) 581-1080

Joseph A. Kaliff   Broadway
Amusement Features, 218 W. 47th St., N.Y. 10036, (212) 586-4358

Dick Kleiner   Showbeat   NEA
1665 N. Beverly Dr., Beverly Hills, Ca. 90210, (213) 271-0150

Bill and Nancy Lane   Hollywood Beat
World News Syndicate, Box 449, Hollywood, Ca. 90028,
(213) 467-7024

Dan Lewis   TV Time Previews   United
The Record, Hackensack, N.J. 07602, (201) 646-4000,
(212) 279-8484

Damon Loy and   Entertainment World   TransWorld
Dart Anthony
Box 2801, Wash., D.C. 20013, (202) 638-5568

Mary Byrne McDonnell   Hearst
Hearst Newspapers, 959 Eighth Ave., N.Y. 10019, (212) 262-7795

Tichi W. Miles   Hollywood Reporter
6715 Sunset Blvd., Hollywood, Ca. 90028, (213) 464-7411

Dick Miller   New York, N.Y.
Garrett Enterprises, 1560 Broadway, N.Y. 10036, (212) 223-6600

Norman Nadel   Theatrical   Scripps-Howard
234 College Ave., Staten Island, N.Y. 10314

Rex Reed   CTNYNS
1 W. 72nd St., N.Y. 10023

Rolling Stone   King
745 Fifth Ave., N.Y. 10022

Joey Sasso   McNaught
65 W. 55th St., N.Y. 10019, (212) 541-7230

Vernon Scott   UPI
United Press, Box 2231, L.A. 90053, (213) 620-1230

Liz Smith   CTNYNS
160 E. 38th St., N.Y. 10016, (212) 689-2639

Anita Summer   New York
619 Oakwood Ct., Westbury, N.Y. 11590, (516) 333-4822

Dorothy Treloar   Hollywood   King
Suite 209, 205 S. Beverly Dr., Beverly Hills, Ca. 90212,
(213) 271-4222

Earl Wilson   It Happened Last Night   Field
340 W. 57th St., N.Y. 10019, (212) 586-6669

Ray Wilson   New York Today
78-11 Kew Forest Lane, Queens, N.Y. 11375, (212) 544-1254

FOOD AND WINE

Robert Balzer   Wine Connoisseur   LAT
Los Angeles Times, L.A. 90053, (213) 625-2345

Rosemary Bascome   Along the Food Trail
62 Cobbetts Lane, Shelter Island, N.Y. 11964, (516) 749-0111

Harold Bearak   Wine
108-11 Queens Blvd., Queens, N.Y. 11375, (212) 268-9104

James Beard   Beard on Food   Wash. Star
119 W. 10th St., N.Y. 10011, (212) 675-4984

Johna Blinn   Celebrity Cookbook   LAT
Los Angeles Times Syndicate, L.A. 90053

Susan Broersma   Happy Cooker   Danney Ball
Box 2174, Idyllwild, Ca. 92349

Cecily Brownstone   Food   AP
81 Jane St., N.Y. 10014

Marcia Burg   Chef Marcia   United
Women's News Service, 200 Park Ave., N.Y. 10017, (212) 557-2321

Ruth Ellen Church   All About Wine
9247 S. Winchester Ave., Chic. 66620, (312) 222-3232

William Clifford   Wine on the Table
Box 392, Morris, Conn. 06763, (203) 567-5336

Philomena Corradeno   Nutrition Cookbook   King
330 8th Ave., N.Y. 10001, (212) 675-1376

Jamie Crane   Nutrition   Inter-Continental
Box 991, Glendale, Ca. 91209

Bob Dana   Tips on Tables
New York Today, 78-11 Kew Forest Lane, Queens, N.Y. 11375
(Mr. Dana, the former N.Y. World-Telegram restaurant columnist,
also writes a wine column.)

Susan Dart   Natural Food   LAT
Los Angeles Times Syndicate, L.A. 90053

Roy Andries de Groot   One Great Dish   CTNYNS
463 West St., N.Y. 10014

"Susan Delight"   Cooking Corner   Copley
(Opal Crandall)
San Diego Union, 350 Camino de la Reina, San Diego, Ca. 92108,
(714) 299-3131
Home: 6141 La Pintura Dr., La Jolla, Ca. 92037,
(714) 454-5527

Mary Durkin   Nature's Kitchen   United
United Feature, 200 Park Ave., N.Y. 10017

Merle Ellis   The Butcher   Chronicle
337 Karen Way, Tiburon, Ca. 94920, (415) 383-6585

Sandal & Pritch English Gourmet on a Budget
129 S. Irving, Tucson, Ariz. 85711, (602) 793-2857
Also: Box 26807, Tucson 85726, (602) 294-4433

Barbara Gibbons   Slim Gourmet   United
15 Wayland Drive, Verona, N.J. 07044, (201) 857-0934

Paul Gillette   Enjoying Wine
1750 Washington St., S.F. 94109, (415) 885-2392

John Knoblock and   Wine   Miami Herald Syndicate
Bob Housman
University of Miami, Coral Gables, Fla. 33146

Carl Larsen   Frying Pan Follies   American
84 Susquehanna Ave., Lock Haven, Pa. 17745, (717) 748-5351

Jeanne Lesem   Cooking   UPI
United Press, 220 E. 42nd St., N.Y. 10017, (212) 682-0400

Mary Lester   Wine Taster
Box 1183, Cupertino, Ca. 95014, (408) 257-9567

Joy Louras and   Cooking Good   McNaught
Roseanne Gordon
McNaught Syndicate, 60 E. 42nd St., N.Y. 10017, (212) 682-8787

Gaynor Maddox   Food   NEA
179 E. 79th St., N.Y. 10021, (212) 861-0638

220

Susan Duff Mastro   Calorie Countdown   McNaught
McNaught, 60 E. 42nd St., N.Y. 10017

Carol McGarvey   Let's Ask the Cook   Register
5717 Kingman Ave., Des Moines, Iowa 50311

Mike McGrady   Your Husband's Cookbook
c/o Robin Elliser, 55 W. Fort Salonga Rd., Northport, N.Y. 11768

Jane Mengenhauser   Kitchen Sampler
8905 Camfield Dr., Alexandria, Va. 22308, (703) 360-5062

Robert J. Misch   Wine   United
251 W. 71st St., N.Y. 10023, (212) 597-4086

Jean Nidetch   Thinking Slim   NEA
Weight Watchers Intl., 800 Community Drive, Manhasset, N.Y.
11030, (516) 627-9200

Joan O'Sullivan   Food for Thought   King
King Features, 235 E. 45th St., N.Y. 10017

Michael Pakinham   Wine   Knight-Ridder
Phil. Inquirer, Phila., Pa. 19101

Jan S. Paul   Around the House
Box 6488, Bakersfield, Ca. 93306, (805) 871-8569

Joyce Pollack   Culinary Corner
141 Sherman Ave., Rockville Centre, N.Y. 11570, (516) 776-4795

Mark Pugner   Wine Primer   Tagumi
Box 275, El Cerrito, Ca. 94530, (415) 527-7730

June Roth   Special Diets
1057 Oakland Court, Teaneck, N.J. 07666, (201) 836-2218

Sheila Sandy   The Mini-Gourmet   NEA
3550 N. Lakeshore Dr., No. 819, Chicago 60657

Lauren Soth   Food and Agriculture Affairs   Register
Register and Tribune Syndicate, Des Moines, Iowa 50304

"Aileen Claire" Snoddy   Food, Wine   NEA
NEA, 200 Park Ave., N.Y. 10017, (212) 551-5870

William Sonstein   On Wines
Box 11278, 624 Stetson Rd., Elkins Park, Pa. 19117, (215) 635-0876

GARDENING AND FARMING

George Abraham   The Green Thumb
Ingleside Rd., Naples, N.Y. 14512, (315) 374-5400

Jane Adler   Indoor Gardening   Field
Field Newspaper Syndicate, 401 N. Wabash Ave., Chic. 60611

Jud Arnold   Green Talk
Canada Wide Feature Service, 231 rue St. Jacques, Montreal,
Quebec H2Y 1M6, Canada, (514) 282-2441

Mike Beaudoin   Gardening
1112 S. Magnolia Dr., Tallahassee, Fla. 32301, (904) 224-2364

John Bradshaw   On Gardening
Toronto Sun, 322 King St., W., Toronto, Ont., Canada,
(416) 366-9141

Dennis Cleary   Your Green Thumb   Trans-World
1845 Old Freehold Rd., Toms River, N.J. 08753, (201) 240-4108

George Creed   It's Your Landscape   Field
Field Newspaper Syndicate, 401 N. Wabash Ave., Chic. 60611

Mary Furey Crymes   Jolly Green Thumb   NEA
Rt. 1, Lot O, Perdido Key, Pensacola, Fla. 32507,
(904) 453-5739

Patrick Denton   The Backyard Gardener   Copley
Box 190, San Diego, Ca. 92112

Joan Lee Faust   Around the Garden   NYT
The New York Times, 229 W. 43rd St., N.Y. 10036

J. Finletter   Miracle Gardening   B.P. Singer
3164 W. Tyler Ave., Anaheim, Ca. 92801, (714) 527-5650

Terri Gabriel   Homegrown   LAT
Los Angeles Times Syndicate, L.A. 90053

Sonja Hillgren   On the Farm Front   UPI
United Press, 315 Ntl. Press Bldg., Wash., D.C. 20045,
(202) 393-3430

Roderick Mann   Inside Plants   LAT
View, Los Angeles Times, L.A. 90053

Walter Masson   Down to Earth
Box 66, 45 Plymouth Rd., Needham, Mass. 02192, (617) 444-1913

Elvin McDonald   Plants in the Home   King
House Beautiful, 717 Fifth Ave., N.Y. 10022, (212) 935-5900

David Merkowitz   Landscape
4307 Underwood St., University Park, Md. 20782, (301) 927-5811

Henry Mitchell   Earthman
Washington Post, Wash., D.C. 20071, (202) 223-6000

James B. Nelson   The Part Time Gardener   Flagler & Nelson
Buffalo Courier-Express, Buffalo, N.Y. 14240

Jan S. Paul   Around the House
Box 6488, Bakersfield, Ca. 93306, (805) 871-8569

Kenneth Scheibel   Washington Farm Beat
1325 18th St., N.W., Wash., D.C. 20036, (202) 223-1569

Eve Schroeder
Eagle Bend, Minn. 56446

Tom Stevenson   Garden Counselor   LTWP
Washington Post, 1150 15th St., N.W., Wash., D.C. 20071,
(202) 223-6000

Allan A. Swenson   Outdoor Gardening   NEA
Windrows Farm, Box 94, Kennebunk, Maine 04043, (207) 985-3161

GENERAL
(incl. astrology and miscellaneous subjects)

Steve Allen   Inter-Continental
15201 Burbank Blvd., Van Nuys, Ca. 91401

Barbara Allison   This N That   NEA
148 Riverview Ave., Yardley, Pa. 19067, (609) 396-3232

Cleveland Amory   Amory's People   LAT
140 W. 57th St., N.Y. 10019, (212) 757-3425

Ellen Appel   Make It Yours   Copley
Box 249, Balboa Island, Calif. 92662

Sid Ascher
214 Boston Ave., Mays Landing, N.J. 08330, (609) 927-1842

Paul T. Aunger   Free for the Asking U.S.A.
12 Muirkirk Rd., Willodale, Ont., Canada M2R 1W3

Bert Bacharach   Now See Here   King
200 E. 57th St., N.Y. 10022

Letitia Baldrige   Contemporary Living   LAT
909 Third Ave., N.Y. 10022, (212) 697-4430

Phyllis Battelle   Assignment America   King
King Features, 235 E. 45th St., N.Y. 10017, (212) 682-5600

Theodore Bernstein   Words   NYT
New York Times, 229 W. 43rd St., N.Y. 10036, (212) 556-1234

Jim Bishop   King
Golden Isles, Hallandale, Fla. 33009

Monte F. Bourjaily   Editorials
Globe Syndicate, 2209 Prospect Ave., Spring Lake, N.J. 07762,
(201) 449-7127

L.M. Boyd
Crown Syndicate, 5 Crown Rd., Weatherford, Tex. 76086,
(817) 594-5125

James Brady   Class Act   Murdoch
New York Post, 210 South St., N.Y. 10002, (212) 349-5000   **225**

Jimmy Breslin   CTNYNS
N.Y. News, 220 E. 42nd St., N.Y. 10017

Terry Brickley   Handicapsules
Manson Western Syndicate, 12031 Wilshire Blvd., L.A. 90025,
(213) 478-2061

Tony Brown   Tony Brown's Journal   News World
Tony Brown Productions, Inc., 1501 Broadway, N.Y. 10036,
(212) 575-0878

Art Buchwald   LAT
1750 Pennsylvania Ave., N.W., Wash., D.C. 20006, (202) 298-7990

Herb Caen   It's News To Me   Chronicle
San Francisco Chronicle, S.F. 94119, (415) 777-1111

Thurlow Cannon   Nostalgia Notes
58 E. Main St., Canton, N.Y. 13617, (315) 386-8859

Dan Carlinsky   Tip of My Tongue   NEA
301 E. 78th St., N.Y. 10021, (212) 861-2526

John Chamberlain   These Days   King
King Features, 235 E. 45th St., N.Y. 10017, (212) 682-5600

Maxine Cheshire   V.I.P.   LAT
Wash. Post, Wash., D.C. 20071, (202) 334-6000

John Clift   City Editor's Tip Service   LAT
1200 West Bond, Denison, Texas 75020

Nomnee Coan   Small Fry Diary
2828 Bammel Lane, Houston, Tex. 77098

Matthew Conroy   The Pepper Mill   News World
c/o The News World, 401 Fifth Avenue, N.Y. 10016

Betty Debnan   The Mini Page   Universal
Charlotte Observer, Charlotte, N.C. 28201

Nina Diamond   All About Town
2820 E. Brigstock Rd., Midlothian, Va. 23113, (804) 794-7790

226

Jeane Dixon Astrology LAT
1144 18th St., N.W., Wash., D.C. 20510

Farnham Dudgeon, Community and Suburban Press Service
100 E. Main St., Frankfort, Ky. 40601, (502) 223-1621

James H. Dygert Eye on the Media American
American Syndicate, 120 W. 2nd St., Dayton, Ohio 45402,
(513) 228-2473

Ear (Diana McClellan) (gossip) CTNYNS
Washington Star, Wash., D.C. 20061, (202) 484-5000

Lou Edman
390 Woodstock Ave., Putnam, Conn. 06260, (203) 928-3500

Dick Edwards People's Voice News World
The News World, 401 Fifth Ave., N.Y. 10016, (212) 532-8300

Eye (gossip) Fairchild
Women's Wear Daily, 7 E. 12th St., N.Y. 10003, (212) 741-4360

Facing South (profiles of Southerners) Inst. for Southern Studies
Box 230, Chapel Hill, N.C. 27514

Tom Fesperman Otherwise EF
NEA, 200 Park Ave., N.Y. 10017, (212) 557-5870

Jim Fitzgerald If It Fitz LAT
Detroit Free Press, Detroit, Mich. 48231, (313) 222-6583

Susan Fogg Social Issues
Newhouse News Service, 1750 Pennsylvania Ave., N.W., Wash.,
D.C. 20006, (202) 298-7080

Jim Foley
4938 S.W. 2nd Ave., Cape Coral, Fla. 33904

Hy & Marilyn Gardner Glad You Asked That Field
1111 Brickell Ave., Miami, Fla. 33131, (305) 377-0811

Uri Geller McNaught
357 E. 57th St., N.Y. 10022, (212) 751-8866

Aaron Gold The Tower Ticker Knight-Ridder
Chicago Tribune, Chic. 60611, (312) 222-3232

Ellen Goodman   At Large   Wash. Post
Boston Globe, Boston, Mass. 02107

Andrew Greeley   People and Values   Universal
Universal Press Syndicate, 6700 Squibb Rd., Mission, Kans. 66202

Bob Greene
Chicago Tribune, Chic. 60611

Pete Hamill   CTNYNS
N.Y. News, 220 E. 42nd St., N.Y. 10017, (212) 949-1234

Sidney J. Harris   Strictly Personal   Field
Chicago Sun-Times, Chic. 60611, (312) 321-2587

Smith Hempstone   Our Times
7611 Fairfax Rd., Bethesda, Md. 20014, (301) 657-2918

Arthur Hoppe   The Innocent Bystander   Chronicle
San Francisco Chronicle, S.F. 94119, (415) 777-1111

Harry Humphreys   Ideas, Issues & Insights
Box 2524, N. Hollywood, Ca. 91602

Reed J. Irvine   Accuracy in Media   AIM
777 14th St., N.W., Wash., D.C. 20005, (202) 783-4406

John Keasler   McNaught
Miami News, Miami, Fla. 33101

Mrs. Irene Corbally Kuhn It's My Opinion   Columbia
45 Christopher St., N.Y. 10014, (212) 242-4541

Irv Kupcinet
Chicago Sun-Times, Chic. 60611, (312) 321-2587

Bryan Langton   Limey at Large   News World
The News World, 401 Fifth Ave., N.Y. 10016, (212) 532-8300

Max Lerner   LAT
N.Y. Post, 210 South St., N.Y. 10002, (212) 349-5000

Martin Levin   Ask Anybody Anything   United
333 W. 56th St., N.Y. 10019

228

Paul J. Levine   Law   Copley
Morgan, Lewis & Bockius, 1 Biscayne Tower, Miami, Fla. 33131,
(305) 371-2200

Rae Lindsay   First Person Singular   AP
Associated Press Newsfeatures, 50 Rockefeller Pl., N.Y. 10020,
(201) 567-8986

Judith Martin   Miss Manners   United
Washington Post, Wash., D.C. 20071, (202) 223-6000

Charles McCabe   Fearless Spectator   Chronicle
San Francisco Chronicle, S.F. 94119, (415) 777-1111

Hank Messick   Crime File   American
American Syndicate, 120 W. 2nd St., Dayton, Ohio 45402,
(513) 228-2473

Norton Mockridge
Beach Lane, Wainscott, N.Y. 11975

Larry Moffitt   For the People   News World
The News World, 401 Fifth Ave., N.Y. 10016, (212) 532-8300

Gerald Nachman   Double Take   CTNYNS
New York News, 220 E. 42nd St., N.Y. 10017

Philip Nobile   Uncommon Conversations   Universal
30 Park Terrace E., N.Y. 10034, (212) 569-0899

Jack O'Brian   King
Station WOR, 1440 Broadway, N.Y. 10018, (212) 764-7000

Jane O'Reilly   Social Commentary   EF
333 Central Park W., N.Y. 10025

Ed Orloff   Your Immediate Future   Crown
San Francisco Chronicle, S.F. 94109, (415) 777-1111

Bernice Bede Osol   Astrograph   NEA
NEA, 200 Park Ave., N.Y. 10017

Virginia Payette   United
United Feature Syndicate, 200 Park Ave., N.Y. 10017

Karen Peterson   Features and News Service
4307A Ann Fitzhugh Dr., Annandale, Va. 22003, (703) 978-2976

Neil Pierce
610 G St., S.W., Wash., D.C. 20024, (202) 857-1417

Elizabeth Post   Etiquette   CTNYNS
120 E. 36th St., N.Y. 10016, (212) 689-0175

Sue Reed   Samantha Reads Your Stars   NEA
16921 New Hampshire Ave., Silver Spring, Md. 20904

Charles Rehns   Isn't It the Truth
457 W. 57th St., N.Y. 10019, (212) 246-6335

Carroll Righter   Astrology   McNaught
1757 N. Vista, L.A. 90046

Milton Rockmore   The View From the Top
The Rockmore Co., Box 84, Glenville, Conn. 06830, (203) 661-1143

Mike Royko
Chicago Sun-Times, Chic. 60611, (312) 321-2587

Donald Saltz   Trivia Quiz
4007 Conn. Ave., N.W., Wash., D.C. 20008, (202) 966-0025

Miv Schaaf   Things
686 W. California Blvd., Pasadena, Ca. 91105, (213) 681-5353

Mrs. Phyllis Schlafly P.S. To The News   Copley
Staton WBBM, Chic. 60611

Whitt N. Schultz, Ph.D. (self-help)
Knowledge News and Features, Box 100, Kennilworth, Ill. 60691,
(312) 256-0059

Charles B. Seib   The News Business   Wash. Post
Washington Post, 1150 15th St., N.W., Wash., D.C. 20071

John Shuttleworth   Mother Earth News   Register
Box 70, Hendersonville, N.C. 28739, (704) 692-4256

Lydel Sims   Watch Your Language   Columbia
Columbia Features, 36 W. 44th St., N.Y. 10036
230

John Sinor   (humor)   Copley
San Diego Tribune, San Diego, Ca. 92108, (714) 229-3131

"Robin Adams Sloan"   King
King Features, 235 E. 45th St., N.Y. 10017

Liz Smith   People   CTNYNS
160 E. 38th St., N.Y. 10016, (212) MU 9-2639

Lowell Smith   The Average American   Register
Register and Tribune Syndicate, Des Moines, Iowa 50304

Jimmy (The Greek) Snyder   Field
Box 976, N. Miami Beach, Fla. 33160, (305) 445-3702

"Senator Soaper"   United
Sanford Teller, 964 Third Ave., N.Y. 10022

Suzy (Aileen Mehle)   CTNYNS
Milton Fenster Associates, 540 Madison Ave., N.Y. 10022

Tom Teepen   American
Dayton Daily News, Dayton, Ohio 45401, (513) 223-2112

Y.L. Tiacliff   Have You Met ——?
News Portraits Syndicate, Box 564, Hackensack, N.J. 07602,
(201) 342-2985

Lindsy Van Gelder   United
Ms., 370 Lexington Ave., N.Y. 10017, (212) 725-2666

David Vaughan
277 West End Ave., N.Y. 10023

Robert Wallace Jr.   'Tween 12 and 20   Copley
Box 190, San Diego, Ca. 92112

Brian Weiss   Freebies   Register
Register and Tribune Syndicate, Des Moines, Iowa 50304

Dick West   Lighter Side   UPI
315 Ntl. Press Bldg., Wash., D.C. 20045, (202) 393-3430

Tom Williams   Career Corner   Columbia
Columbia Features, 36 W. 44th St., N.Y. 10036

Jim Wilson   Sorry to Bother You
Box 42, Casper, Wyo. 82602

John Wykert   Insight   United
25 W. 68th St., N.Y. 10023

Robert Yoakum   Another Look
Reservoir Rd., Lakeville, Conn. 06039, (203) 435-2549

HOBBIES
(Including Photography, Do-It-Yourself, Stamps, Coins, Chess)

Ron and Clarice Anders Coin Notes   Arcadia
Box 5263, Chic. 60680, (312) 276-0715

Ed and Stevie Baldwin   Makin' Things   Register
Box 52000, Tulsa, Okla. 74101

Bill Baughman   Photo Info
1190 Yellowstone Rd., Cleveland, Ohio 44121, (216) 382-7192

Ford & Angela Bothwell   Camping Family Style   NEA
148 Riverview Ave., Yardley, Pa. 19067, (609) 396-3232

Irving A. Brace   Let's Take Pictures   Miller
Miller Services, 45 Charles St. East, Toronto, Ontario M4Y 1S6,
Canada, (416) 925-4323

Ellen Brooks   Ask Andy   LAT
San Francisco Chronicle, S.F. 94119, (415) 777-1111

Bill Burmester   CBing   Flagler & Nelson
1640 Statler Hilton, Buffalo, N.Y. 14202

Robert T. Byrne   Chess   NYT
The New York Times, 229 W. 43 St., N.Y. 10036

Al Carrell   Super Handyman   King
King Features, 235 E. 45th St., N.Y. 10017

Ben Corey   Let's Make
Harvard Features, 21 B Hews St., Cambridge, Mass. 02139,
(617) 491-2637

William E. Cote   CB   Booth
Booth News Service, 1501 Bank of Lansing Bldg., Lansing, Mich.
48933, (517) 487-8888

Dick Cowan   Tech Talk   King
14 Vanderventer Ave., Port Washington, N.Y. 11050, (516) 883-6200

Polly Cramer   Polly's Pointers   NEA
NEA, 200 Park Ave., N.Y. 10017

Norman M. Davis   The Coin Box
1263 W. Pratt Blvd., Chic. 60626, (312) 973-1060

Lawrence Day   Canadian Chess
Toronto Star, 1 Yonge St., Toronto, Ont., M5A 3X5, Canada

Al De Ciccio   You Can Do It   CTNYNS
4 Falls Rd., Larchmont, N.Y. 10538, (914) 834-4390

Gustav Detjen, Jr.   Philatelic News
Box 150, Clinton Corners, N.Y. 12514, (914) 266-3150

Larry Eisinger   Home Workshop File   CTNYNS
233 Spring St., N.Y. 10012, (212) 255-5380

Steve Ellingson   Do-It-Yourself
U-B Newspaper Syndicate, 15233 Stagg St., Van Nuys, Ca. 91409,
(213) 785-6368

Larry Evans   Evans on Chess
Chess Tours, Box 1182, Reno, Nev. 89504, (702) 786-3178

Phyllis Fiarotta   The Leisure Craftsman   King
King Features, 235 E. 45th St., N.Y. 10007

"Gene Gary"   Here's How (home repair)   Copley
Clyde and Helen Smith, 419 Minot Ave., Chula Vista, Ca. 92010,
(714) 422-4850

Bernard Gladstone   NYT
N.Y. Times, 229 W. 43rd St., N.Y. 10036, (212) 556-1234

Fred Gregg, Jr.   CB   NEA
CB Times, 1005 Murfreesboro Rd., Nashville, Tenn. 37217,
(615) 259-4050

A.J. Hand   A Hand Around the House   LAT
Popular Science, 380 Madison Ave., N.Y. 10017, (212) 687-3000

R. Winston Harris   Coinversations
Box 622E, Franklin, Mich. 48025, (313) 626-8132

D.J. Herda   Ski, Photo
Brooks Publishing, 4701 Crescent Rd., Madison, Wis. 53711,
(608) 271-7436

Randolph Karch   Do-It-Yourself
2713 Sand Hollow Court, Clearwater, Fla. 33519

Mark A. Kellner   The Stamp Scene   News-World
Box 131, Rego Park, N.Y. 11374, (212) 830-0333

George Koltanowski   Chess-Master   Golden Gate
1200 Gough St., S.F. 94109, (415) 776-6942

Andy Lang   Home Repairs   AP
Associated Press, 50 Rockefeller Plaza, N.Y. 10020, (212) 262-4000

Jeffrey Lee   Adventure Postpaid
2 Holly Dr., New Rochelle, N.Y. 10801, (914) 235-2347

Joseph A. Livingston   Chess   Spadea
2110 Delancy Pl., Philadelphia, Pa. 19103, (215) 732-3221

Shelby Lyman   Chess & Checkers   Basic Chess Features
Box 630, Freeport, N.Y. 11520, (516) 546-9194

Michael J. McCormack   CB Sender   Copley
CBer's News, 104 Clinkscales Rd., Columbia, Mo. 65201,
(314) 445-1682

Dona Meilach   Creative Crafts
3991 Crown Point Dr., San Diego, Ca. 92109, (714) 270-5784

Albert Moldvay   Your Photos   LAT
443 19th St., Santa Monica, Ca. 90402

Gary Palmer   Coin Box
Box 190, San Diego, Ca. 92112, (714) 299-7000

William & Carol Patterson Pet Parade
4354 Clybourn Ave., Burbank, Ca. 91505, (213) 849-5077

Edward C. Rochette   Coins   LAT
Box 2366, Colorado Springs, Co. 80901, (303) 473-9142

Sidney A. Silberman   Chess
Canada Wide Feature Service, 231 Rue St. Jacques, Montreal,
Quebec H2Y 1M6, Canada

235

Charlotte Slater and   Things Your Mother   Universal
Jim Reitz   Never Taught You
Detroit News, Detroit, Mich. 48231

Frank G. Spadone   Coins
226 Linden Ave., Irvington, N.J. 07111, (201) 375-5499

Margaret Strong and   How
Lois Libien
75 Prospect Park W., Brooklyn, N.Y. 11215, (212) 965-3205

William Taylor   Why Be Bored?
321 E. 43rd St., N.Y. 10017, (212) 986-1177

Julius Weiss   Stamps-Coins
16000 Terrace Rd., Cleveland, Ohio 44112, (216) 451-3331

Mike Wendland   CB Break   Universal
Detroit News, Detroit, Mich. 48231

Barbara White   Coins
Numismatic Information Service, Rossway Rd., Pleasant Valley,
N.Y. 12569, (914) 635-2361

Roger Whitman   First Aid For The Ailing House   United
United Feature Syndicate, 200 Park Ave., N.Y. 10017

Ross Williams   Chess Points   Copley
Box 190, San Diego, Ca. 92112

Joe Zollman   Stamping Grounds
25 E. Penn St., Long Beach, N.Y. 11561, (516) 431-6697

MEDICAL AND SCIENCE

Ruth Nathan Anderson   VIP Medical Grapevine
161 Nasa Circle, Round Lake, Ill. 60073, (312) 546-6557

Karen Blaker, Ph.D.   Choices   NEA
NEA, 200 Park Ave., N.Y. 10017

F.J.L. Blasingame, M.D. Let's Stay Well   United
United Features, 200 Park Ave., N.Y. 10017

John Brennan   Rex Medica   LAT
Los Angeles Times Syndicate, L.A. 90053

Joyce Brothers, Ph.D.   Ask Dr. Brothers   King
1530 Palisade Ave., Fort Lee, N.J. 07024

Bob Brown   Science For You   LAT
Los Angeles Times Syndicate, L.A. 90053

Lester Coleman, M.D.   Speaking of Your Health   King
162 E. 80th St., N.Y. 10021, (212) 737-4420

George W. Crane,
M.D., Ph.D.   Dr. Crane's Quiz   Hopkins Syndicate
Hopkins Bldg., Mellott, Ind. 47958, (317) 295-2253

Leo M. Croghan, Ph.D.   Mind Matter   Flagler & Nelson
Albemarle Mental Health Center, Elizabeth City, N.C. 27909

Salvatore Didato   Behavior & Living   News-World
Didato Associates, 280 Madison Ave., N.Y. 10016, (212) 725-9224

Edward Edelson   Knight-Ridder
New York News, 220 E. 42nd St., N.Y. 10017, (212) 949-1234

Dr. Frank Falkner   Young and Healthy   LAT
Fels Research Institute, Yellow Springs, Ohio 45387

Leonore Feinstein   Medical Frontiers   Chronicle Features
Chronicle Features, 870 Market St., S.F. 94102

George S. Fichter   Gannett
Box 1368, Homestead, Fla. 33030

Kendrick Frazier   Science Service
1719 N St., N.W., Wash., D.C. 20036, (202) 785-2255

William J. Goldwag, M.D.   Copley
7433 Cerritos Ave., Stanton, Ca. 90680, (714) 827-5180

Joe Graedon   The People's Pharmacy   King
School of Nursing, Duke University, Durham, N.C. 27706

Michael J. Halbèrstam,
M.D.   Modern Medicine   NYT
2520 L St., N.W., Wash., D.C. 20037, (202) 965-3703

Clarke Hankey, M.D.   Staying Healthy   Mid-Continent
Box 1662, Pittsburgh, Pa. 15230

William Hines   Field
Chicago Sun-Times, 1901 Pennsylvania Ave., N.W., Wash., D.C.
20006, (202) 785-8200

Norma Hols   International Medical Tribune
Suite 410, 600 New Hampshire Ave., N.W., Wash., D.C. 20037,
(202) 338-8866

G.Timothy Johnson, M.D. House Call   CTNYNS
Dept. of Continuing Education, Harvard Medical School, Cambridge,
Mass. 02115

Saul Kapel, Ph.D.   Psychology   CTNYNS
27 Cayuga Rd., Scarsdale, N.Y. 10583, (914) 723-6306

Dolly Katz   Knight-Ridder
Detroit Free Press, 321 W. Lafayette Blvd., Detroit 48231,
(313) 222-6400

Bob Kleinmann   Feelin' Great   American
Box 190, Dayton, Ohio 45402

Ronald Kotulak   Knight-Ridder
Chicago Tribune, 435 N. Michigan Ave., Chic. 60611, (312) 222-3232

Lawrence E. Lamb, M.D.   NEA
Box 326, San Antonio, Tex. 78292

Miriam F. Landau, Ph.D.   LAT
2212 Via Cerritos, Palos Verdes Estates, Ca. 90274, (213) 375-3845

Robert Long, M.D.   Sex   Princeton
Dept. of Human Sexuality, Univ. of Louisville School of Medicine,
Louisville, Ky. 40208

M.W. Martin   Medicalia
Box 15518, Columbus, Ohio 43215, (614) 228-2437

Allen W. Mathies Jr., M.D.   Inter-Continental
University of Southern California School of Medicine, L.A. 90007

Jean Mayer, M.D.
and Johanna Dwyer   Food for Thought   CTNYNS
Tufts University, Medford, Mass. 02155

Robert Mendelsohn, M.D. People's Doctor   CTNYNS
Suite 600, 664 N. Michigan Ave., Chic. 60611, (312) 642-7472

Walter Menninger, M.D.   In-Sights   Universal
Box 829, Topeka, Kansas 66601

Ida Nettleton   A Problem Today   Singer
BP Singer, 3164 W. Tyler Ave., Anaheim, Ca. 92801

Robert C. Newman, M.D. For Women Only   United
United Feature Syndicate, 200 Park Ave., N.Y. 10017

Ed Orloff   Medical Digest   Crown
S.F. Chronicle, S.F. 94103, (415) 777-1111

Michael A. Petti, M.D.
and Jud Hurd   Health Capsules   United
1611 S. Green Rd., Cleveland, Ohio 44121, (216) 381-8109

Irwin J. Polk, M.D.   Man and Medicine
19 Page Dr., Red Bank, N.J. 07701, (201) 741-8900

Alvin Poussaint, M.D.
& James P. Comer, M.D. Getting Along   Summit Press
25 Shattuck St., Boston, Mass. 02115 (Dr. Poussaint also writes
"Minority Human Relations" for Black Press Syndicate.)

Lawrence Power, M.D.   Food & Fitness   LAT
Wayne State Univ. College of Medicine, 540 Canfield St., E., Detroit
48201, also Box 1501, Ann Arbor 48106

James G. Price, M.D.   Your Family Physician   NEA
Family Practice Center, 39th St. and Rainbow Blvd., Kansas City,
Kans. 66103

Judith Randal   Knight-Ridder
818 3rd St., S.W., Wash., D.C. 20024, (202) 467-6670

Charles Rehns   Live Longer
457 W. 57th St., N.Y. 10019, (212) 246-6335

Joann Ellison Rodgers   Hearst
Baltimore News American, Baltimore, Md. 21202

Al Rossiter Jr.   Science Today   UPI
United Press, 315 Ntl. Press Bldg., Wash.; D.C. 20045,
(202) 393-3430

Paul Ruble, M.D.   To Your Good Health   Field
Field Newspaper Syndicate, 401 N. Wabash, Chic. 60611

Aaron L. Rutledge, Ph.D. Of Men and Women   Universal
Grosse Pointe Psychological Center, 377 Fisher Rd., Grosse Pointe,
Mich. 48230

Lee Salk, Ph.D.   Parent and Child   Field
941 Park Ave., N.Y. 10028, (212) 861-4448

Laura Schlessinger, M.D. Closer Encounters   Copley
Univ. of Southern California, L.A. 90007

Neil Solomon, M.D., Ph.D.   LAT
Dept. of Psychiatry, Johns Hopkins Hospital, 301 W. Preston St.,
Baltimore, Md. 21201

Frederick Stare, M.D., and
Elizabeth Whelan, Ph.D. Food and Your Health   Field
Harvard Medical School, 665 Huntington Ave., Boston 02115

Peter J. Steincrohn, M.D. Stop Killing Yourself   McNaught
1430 Ancona Ave., Coral Gables, Fla. 33146

MUSIC

Buddy Basch   Music Whirl
771 West End Ave., N.Y. 10025, (212) 666-2300

Byron Belt   Newhouse
Newhouse News Service, 1750 Pennsylvania Ave., N.W., Wash.,
D.C. 20006, (202) 298-7080

Dianne Bennett   Sound Track
Hollywood Reporter, 6715 Sunset Blvd., Hollywood, Ca. 90028,
(213) 464-7411

Robert E. Curtis   The Scene
Garden State Media, Box 104, Oradell, N.J. 07649, (201) 385-2000

Leonard Feather   LTWP
13833 Riverside Dr., Sherman Oaks, Ca. 91423

Harold Fuller   Spin Off   News World
The News World, 401 Fifth Ave., N.Y. 10016, (212) 532-8300

Jeanne Harrison   Platter Patter   Columbia
c/o Kurt Lassen, 200 E. 36th St., N.Y. 10016

Jack Hurst   Country Music   CTNYNS
Chicago Tribune—N.Y. News, 220 E. 42nd St., N.Y. 10017

Joe Kaliff   DISCussion
Amusement Features Syndicate, 218 W. 47th St., N.Y. 10036,
(212) 586-4358

Dick Kelliher   Record Reviews
Box 2191, Denver, Co. 80201

William D. Laffler   Popular and Classical Records   UPI
United Press, 220 E. 42nd St., N.Y. 10017, (212) 682-0400

Barbara Lewis   Pop Scene Service   United
The Record, 150 River St., Hackensack, N.J. 07602,
(201) 646-4000, (212) 279-8484

James Riordan   Rock/Pop Times
Box 1233, Kankakee, Ill. 60901, (815) 932-5789

242

Lisa Robinson   Rock Talk   Field
Field Newspaper Syndicate, 401 N. Wabash Ave., Chic. 60611

Robin Welles   The World of Music   Copley
San Deigo Tribune, San Diego 92108, (714) 299-3131

Irwin Stambler   Pop, Rock & Soul   News World
205 S. Beverly Drive, Beverly Hills, Ca. 90210

POLITICAL

Sen. George D. Aiken   Inter-Continental
Senate Office Bldg., Wash., D.C. 20510

Holmes Alexander   McNaught
922 25th St., N.W., Wash., D.C. 20037, (202) 628-1511

Robert S. Allen   Field
1292 Ntl. Press Bldg., Wash., D.C. 20045, (202) 628-2091

Jack Anderson and Les Whitten   United
1401 16th St., N.W., Wash., D.C. 20036, (202) 483-1442

Martha Angle and Robert Walters   NEA
777 14th St., N.W., Wash., D.C. 20005, (202) 347-4461

Russell Baker   NYT
N.Y. Times, 229 W. 43rd St., N.Y. 10036

Charles Bartlett and Cord Mayer   Field
1901 Pennsylvania Ave., N.W., Wash., D.C. 20006, (202) 785-8205

Betty Beale   Washington   Field
2926 Garfield St., N.W., Wash., D.C. 20008, (202) 232-3525

William Beecher   NANA
Boston Globe, 1750 Pennsylvania Ave., N.W., Wash., D.C. 20006,
(202) 298-9169

Miles Benson   Congress   Newhouse
Newhouse News Service, 1750 Pennsylvania Ave., N.W., Wash.,
D.C..20006, (202) 393-7130

Julian Bond   Black Press Service
361 Westview Dr., S.W., Atlanta, Ga. 30310

Robert Boyd   Knight-Ridder
1195 Ntl. Press Bldg., Wash., D.C. 20045, (202) 637-3600

Tom W. Braden   LAT
101 E. Melrose St., Chevy Chase, Md. 20015, (301) 652-2312

David W. Broder   Wash. Post
Washington Post, 1150 15th St., N.W., Wash., D.C. 20071,
(202) 334-6000

Patrick J. Buchanan   The Dividing Line   CTNYNS
St. Louis Globe-Democrat, 1750 Pennsylvania Ave., N.W., Wash.,
D.C. 20006, (202) 298-7080

Art Buchwald   LAT
1750 Pennsylvania Ave., N.W., Wash., D.C. 20006, (202) 298-7990

William Buckley   King
National Review, 150 E. 35th St., N.Y. 10016, (212) 697-7330

Mike Causey   Federal Diary   LTWP
Washington Post, 1150 15th St., N.W., Wash., D.C. 20071,
(202) 334-6000

Marquis Childs   United
1701 Pennsylvania Ave., N.W., Wash., D.C. 20006, (202) 298-6880

Joseph Cloherty
and Bob Owens   The Investigators   LAT
991 Ntl. Press Bldg., Wash., D.C. 20045, (202) 347-6685

Norman Cousins   LAT
Saturday Review, 1290 Ave. of Americas, N.Y. 10019,
(212) 246-9700

Joe Crump   Congressional Record
0-4491 Leonard, N.W., Rt. 1, Coopersville, Mich. 49404,
(616) 677-3158

Ernest Cuneo   Ntl. Whirligig   United
1511 K St., N.W., Wash., D.C. 20045, (202) 783-7900

Ralph de Toledano   Copley
398 Ntl. Press Bldg., Wash., D.C. 20045, (202) 638-1037

Roscoe Drummond   LAT
3900 Cathedral Ave., N.W., Wash., D.C. 20016, (202) 333-0714

Lt. Gen. Ira C. Eaker   LAT
USAF Retired Officers Office, 1612 K St., N.W., Wash., D.C. 20006,
(202) 331-1280

Ted Edwards   Dateline Washington
Trans-World News Service, 767 Ntl. Press Bldg., Wash., D.C. 20045,
(202) 638-5568

Alan S. Emory   NANA
1273 Ntl. Press Bldg., Wash., D.C. 20045, (202) 638-4642

Robert Estill   Assignment Illinois   Copley
1100 Ntl. Press Bldg., Wash., D.C. 20045, (202) 737-6960

M. Stanton Evans   LAT
Indianapolis News, Indianapolis, Ind. 46206, (317) 633-1240

Rowland Evans Jr. and
Robert D. Navak   Inside Report   Field
1750 Pennsylvania Ave., N.W., Wash., D.C. 20006, (202) 393-4340

Jim Fiebig   United
United Features, 200 Park Ave., N.Y. 10017

Clayton Fritchey   LAT
3337 P St., N.W., Wash., D.C. 20007, (202) 965-3369

William Frye   United Nations
2 Tudor City Place, N.Y. 10017, (212) 421-0319

Ernest B. Furguson   By No Means Neutral   LAT
Baltimore Sun, 1214 Ntl. Press Bldg., Wash., D.C. 20045,
(202) 347-8250

Jack Germond and Jules Witcover   CTNYNS
Washington Star, 225 Virginia Ave., S.E., Wash., D.C. 20061,
(202) 484-4369

Georgie Anne Geyer   LAT
1006 The Plaza, 800 25th St., N.W., Wash., D.C. 20037,
(202) 333-9176

Vera Glaser   Knight-Ridder
1195 Ntl. Press Bldg., Wash., D.C. 20045, (202) 637-3600

Louis Halasz   Dateline: UN   United
301 Press Section, United Nations, N.Y. 10017, (212) 754-1234

Paul Harvey   LAT
American Broadcasting Co., 190 N. State St., Chicago 60601,
(312) 782-2002

Col. Robt. Debs Heinl Jr. Of Arms and Men   NANA
2400 California St., N.W., Wash., D.C. 20008, (202) 628-4567

Ron Hendren   In America   LAT
1 Pettit Court, Potomac, Md. 20854, (301) 840-1342

John Herling   Report on Labor   Ntl. Newspaper
1411 K St., N.W., Wash., D.C. 20005, (202) 737-2511

John L. Hess   United
United Features Syndicate, 200 Park Ave., N.Y. 10017

David Horowitz   United Nations
World Union Press, 507 Fifth Ave., N.Y. 10017, (212) 688-7557

Henry Huglin   Affairs of Nations
1427 Greenworth Pl., Santa Barbara, Ca. 93108, (805) 969-1341

Reed J. Irvine   Accuracy in Media
777 14th St., N.W., Wash., D.C. 20005, (202) 783-4407

Rev. Jesse Jackson   Universal
Smith Hempstone, 7611 Fairfax Rd., Bethesda, Md. 20014,
(301) 657-2918

Howard Jarvis   At the Grass Roots   Inter-Continental
Apartment Assn. of L.A. County, 551 S. Oxford Ave., L.A. 90020,
(213) 384-4131

Jenkin Lloyd Jones   LAT
Tulsa World, Tulsa, Okla. 74102

Stanley Karnow   Register
1220 Ntl. Press Bldg., Wash., D.C. 20045, (202) 483-4554

James J. Kilpatrick   Wash. Star
White Walnut Hill, Woodville, Va. 22749, (703) 987-8289

Bodgan Kipling   Canadian-American   Toronto Star
Toronto Star, 715 Ntl. Press Bldg., Wash., D.C. 20045,
(202) 628-5167

Ted Knapp   Scripps-Howard
777 14th St., N.W., Wash., D.C. 20005, (202) 347-7750

Louis Kohlmeier   CTNYNS
932 Ntl. Press Bldg., Wash., D.C. 20045, (202) 638-3499

Joseph Kraft   Washington Insight   Field
3314 P St., N.W., Wash., D.C. 20007, (202) 965-2871

Jack Landau   The Law   Newhouse
Newhouse News Service, 1750 Pennsylvania Ave., N.W., Wash.,
D.C. 20006, (202) 393-7130

Roger Langley   Hispanic Beat   Wash. Writers
Washington Writers' Syndicate, 758 Ntl. Press Bldg.,
Wash., D.C. 20045, (202) 638-6971

Victor Lasky   Say It Straight   NANA
700 New Hampshire Ave., N.W., Wash., D.C. 20037, (202) 337-0178

Anthony Lewis   NYT
New York Times, 50 Commonwealth Ave., Boston, Mass. 02116,
(617) 492-7170

John Lofton   United
7603 Erica Lane, Laurel, Md. 20810, (301) 497-0105

George Mair   A Liberal View   LAT
Box 4972, L.A. 90049

Dorothy Marks   Washington Women   United
2833 McGill Terrace, N.W., Wash., D.C. 20008, (202) 232-2229

Colman McCarthy   Wash. Post
Washington Post, Wash., D.C. 20071, (202) 334-6000

Eugene McCarthy   Wash. Star
3053 Q St., N.W., Wash., D.C. 20007

Sarah McClendon   NANA
2933 28th St., N.W., Wash., D.C. 20008, (202) 483-3791

Mary McGrory   NYT
2710 Macomb St., N.W., Wash., D.C. 20008, (202) 484-4240

248

John F. McManus   The Birch Log
John Birch Society Features, Belmont, Mass. 02178, (617) 489-0600

Michael J. McManus   The Northeast Perspective
85 Halliwell Drive, Stamford, Conn. 06902

Marianne Means   King
1621 31st St., N.W., Wash., D.C. 20067, (202) 298-6920

Jesse H. Merrill   Washington Letter
1500 Massachusetts Ave., N.W., Wash., D.C. 20005, (202) 659-8280

Edward J. Michelson
1032 Ntl. Press Bldg., Wash., D.C. 20045, (202) 638-4523

Clark R. Mollenhoff
806 Ntl. Press Bldg., Wash., D.C. 20045, (202) 347-5829

Ralph Nader   In the Public Interest   Register
Box 19367, Wash., D.C. 20036, (202) 833-3400

Edward Neilan   Asia Memo   Copley
Box 1044, Alexandria, Va. 22313, (703) 548-2881

Martin F. Nolan   United
Boston Globe, 1750 Pennsylvania Ave., N.W., Wash., D.C. 20004,
(202) 298-9169

Michael Novak   Illusions and Realities   Wash. Star
5 Snug Cove, Bayville, N.Y. 11709, (516) 628-8825
Also: 1150 17 St., N.W., Wash., D.C. 20036, (202) 862-5838

Robert D. Novak   Evans-Novak Column   Wash. Star
1750 Pennsylvania Ave., N.W., Wash., D.C. 20006, (202) 393-4340

Don Oakley   Scripps-Howard
Scripps-Howard News Service, 777-14 St., N.W., Wash., D.C. 20005

Neal Peirce   Wash. Post
National Journal, 1730 M St., N.W., Wash., D.C. 20036,
(202) 857-1200. Also: 610 G St., S.W., Wash., D.C. 20024,
(202) 554-8191

Kevin P. Phillips   King
4720 Montgomery Ave., Bethesda, Md. 20014, (202) 654-4990

Susan Preston   The Public Concern   Newhouse
Newhouse News Service, 1750 Pennsylvania Ave., N.W., Wash., D.C.
20006, (202) 393-7130

Robert & Bella Queen
Press Wire Services, 144-45 35th Ave., Queens, N.Y. 11354,
(212) 539-6427

William Raspberry   Wash. Post
Washington Post, 1150 15th St., N.W., Wash., D.C. 20071,
(202) 334-6000

Ronald Reagan   ·King
1669 San Onofre Drive, Pacific Palisades, Ca. 90272

Dean Reed   The Reed Report   Field
Newhouse News Service, 1750 Pennsylvania Ave., N.W., Wash.,
D.C. 20006, (202) 393-7130

James Reston   NYT
N.Y. Times, 1717 K St., N.W., Wash., D.C. 20036, (202) 862-0300

Dr. John P. Roche   A Word Edgewise   King
Brandeis Univ., Waltham, Mass. 02154

Edith Kermit Roosevelt   Between the Lines
1661 Crescent Place, N.W., Wash., D.C. 20009, (202) 387-3957

Carl T. Rowan   Field
1220 19th St., N.W., Wash., D.C. 20036, (202) 659-2636

William A. Rusher   The Conservative Advocate   Universal
National Review, 150 E. 35th St., N.Y. 10016, (212) 679-7330

Mark Russell   humor   LAT
2828 Wisconsin Ave., N.W., Wash., D.C. 20007

William F. Ryan   United
United Features, 200 Park Ave., N.Y. 10017

Morrie Ryskind   Wash. Star
Washington Star, Wash., D.C. 20061, (202) 484-5000

William L. Safire
N.Y. Times, 1717 K St., N.W., Wash., D.C. 20036, (202) 862-0300
250

Daniel Schorr   Register
3113 Woodley Rd., Wash., D.C. 20008

Isabelle Shelton   Mirror of Washington   United
4519 43rd St., N.W., Wash., D.C. 20016

Benjamin Shore   Pennsylvania Avenue   Copley
1100 Ntl. Press Bldg., Wash., D.C. 20045, (202) 737-6960

Edward H. Sims   Washington
Editor's Copy Syndicate, 419 Green St., Orangeburg, S.C. 29115,
(803) 534-1110

J.J. Smith and
Walter Riley   Dateline Washington   Trans-World
Trans-World News, Ntl. Press Bldg., Wash., D.C. 20045

John Kingsbury Smith   King
1701 Pennsylvania Ave., N.W., Wash., D.C. 20006, (202) 298-6920

Philip Smith   The Presidency   Newhouse
Newhouse News Service, 1750 Pennsylvania Ave., N.W., Wash.,
D.C. 20006, (202) 393-7130

Godfrey Sperling, Jr.   Monitor
Christian Science Monitor, 910 16th St., N.W., Wash., D.C. 20006,
(202) 785-4400

James Steele and Donald Bartlett   Knight-Ridder
Philadelphia Inquirer, Philadelphia 19101, (215) 854-2000

William Steif   The U.S. and You   NEA
Scripps-Howard News Service, 777-14th St., N.W., Wash., D.C.
20005

Malvina Stephenson   United
2111 Jefferson Davis Hwy., Arlington, Va. 22202, (703) 979-1357

Richard L. Strout ("TRB")   New Republic
1220 19th St., N.W., Wash., D.C. 20036, (202) 331-7494

Henry J. Taylor   United
150 E. 69th St., N.Y. 10021

Jerry ter Horst   Universal
Detroit News, 511 Ntl. Press Bldg., Wash., D.C. 20045,
(202) 628-4566

Karol C. Thaler   Europe   NANA
United Feature Syndicate, 200 Park Ave., N.Y. 10017

Nick Thimmesch   LAT
6301 Broadbranch Rd., Chevy Chase, Md. 20015, (303) 652-1588

Tom Tiede   NEA
Newspaper Enterprise Assn., 200 Park Ave., N.Y. 10017,
(212) 271-0150

Andrew Tully   Capitol Fare   McNaught
2104 48th St., N.W., Wash., D.C. 20007, (202) 333-7241

Duane Turner   In Washington
Box 173, Route 6, Frederick, Md. 21701, (301) 662-2791

Gus Tyler   United
AFL-CIO, 815 16th St., N.W., Wash., D.C. 20006, (202) 293-5000

Frank van der Linden   United
110 D St., N.E., Wash., D.C. 20003, (202) 544-5200

Harriet Van Horne   LAT
11 E. 68th St., N.Y. 10021

Nicholas von Hoffman   Poster   King
Washington Post, 1150 15th St., N.W., Wash., D.C. 20071,
(202) 334-6000

Robert J. Wagman   United
8806 First Ave., Silver Spring, Md. 20910, (301) 585-6444

Philip Wagner
Box 38, Riderwood, Md. 21139, (301) 823-4624

George C. Wallace   Editor's Copy
1142 S. Perry St., Montgomery, Ala. 36104

Robert Walters and Martha Angle   NEA
NEA, 777 14th St., N.W., Wash., D.C. 20005

Peter Ward   Canadian Comment   NEA
Ntl. Press Gallery, Ottawa, Ont., Canada

Tom Wicker   NYT
N.Y. Times, 229 W. 43rd St., N.Y. 10036

Alice Widener   U.S.A.
530 E. 72nd St., N.Y. 10021, (212) 535-4830

James Wieghert   Knight-Ridder
New York News, 1272 Ntl. Press Bldg., Wash., D.C. 20045,
(202) 628-5058

Roy Wilkins   Register
NAACP, 1790 Broadway, N.Y. 10036, (212) 245-2100

George F. Will   Wash. Post
6683 32nd Pl., N.W., Wash., D.C. 20015, (202) 362-3907

Garry Wills   The Outrider   Universal
106 Upnor Rd., Baltimore, Md. 21212, (301) 323-8756

Richard L. Wilson   Register
952 Ntl. Press Bldg., Wash., D.C. 20045, (202) 347-9111

Elmo R. Zumwalt Jr.
(and Worth H. Bagley) The Informed View   LAT
Tulare, Ca. 93274

POLLS

Gallup Poll   Field
American Institute of Public Opinion, 53 Bank St., Princeton, N.J.
08540, (609) 924-9600

Hoyt Gimlin   Editorial Research Reports
Congressional Quarterly, 1414 22nd St., N.W., Wash., D.C. 20037,
(202) 296-6800

Louis Harris   The Harris Survey   CTNYNS
Louis Harris & Associates, 1270 Ave. of the Americas, N.Y. 10020,
(212) 245-7414

Lester Rand   Youth
Youth Research Institute, 404 E. 55th St., N.Y. 10022,
(212) 752-3489

Roper Poll   LAT
Roper Organization, 1 Park Ave., N.Y. 10016, (212) 679-3523

Albert Sindlinger   Phillips-Sindlinger Survey   King
Harvard and Yale Ave., Swarthmore, Pa. 19081, (215) 544-8260

WomenPoll
2200 Benjamin Franklin Pky., Philadelphia, Pa. 19130,
(215) 567-7556

RELIGION
(Including Inspirational)

Dr. Carlyle Adams   Our Religions   Register
Register and Tribune Syndicate, Des Moines, Iowa 50304

David E. Anderson   Religion in America   UPI
United Press, 315 Ntl. Press Bldg., Wash., D.C. 20045,
(202) 393-3430

Richard Armstrong   Three Minutes A Day   McNaught
The Christophers, 12 E. 48th St., N.Y. 10017, (212) 759-4050

Rev. A. Purnell Bailey   Our Daily Bread   LAT
3900 Wisconsin Ave., N.W., Wash., D.C. 20016

George Cornell   AP
Associated Press, 50 Rockefeller Plaza, N.Y. 10020, (212) 262-4000

Fred Dodge   Candle and Mirror
Minute Messages, 1702 St. Mary's St., Raleigh, N.C. 27608,
(919) 829-0587

Elisha P. Douglass   Sunday School Lesson   Columbia
41 Armour Rd., Princeton, N.J. 08540

Dr. Billy Graham   My Answer   CTNYNS
1300 Harmon Pl., Minneapolis, Minn. 55403

Andrew Greeley   People and Values   Universal
820 N. Michigan Ave., Chic. 60611

Rita Harper   Lifestyle
2017 Marker Ave., Dayton, Ohio 45414, (513) 274-2793

Rev. Lester Kinsolving   Inside Religion   McNaught
                         (also Potomac Ethics)
1517 Beulah Rd., Vienna, Va. 22180, (202) 281-2808

Jesse H. Merrell   Religion and the Times
Merrell Enterprises, 1500 Massachusetts Ave., N.W., Wash., D.C.,
(202) 659-8280

Phyllis Mitchell   Happier Living
126 Melcalfe St., E., Strathroy, Ont., Canada N7G 1P3,
(519) 245-2931

Phil E. Pierce   Pungent Prayer
404 E. Elm St., W. Frankfort, Ill. 62896, (618) 937-2898

Rev. Robert H. Schuller   It's Possible   NEA
Garden Grove Community Church, Garden Grove, Ca. 92640
also c/o Chicki Kleiner, 204 Beverly Dr., Beverly Hills, Ca. 90212

Boris Smolar   Between You and Me
Jewish Telegraphic Agency, 165 W. 46th St., N.Y. 10036
(212) 575-9370

James Lee Young   News and Features
Baptist Press, 460 James Robertson Pkwy., Nashville, Tenn. 37219,
(615) 244-2355

RETIREMENT

Harold Blumenfeld   Retirement   NEA
(with Lou Cottin)
137 Golden Isles Dr., Hallandale, Fla. 33009, (305) 454-0066

Cy Brickfield   Prime Time   NRTA-AARP
Amer. Assn. of Retired Persons, 1909 K St., N.W., Wash., D.C.
20049, (202) 872-4700

Beulah Collins   Golden Years   LAT
15 S. Lake Shore Dr., Chapel Hill, N.C. 27514
(Also writes Senior Forum and Today's Chuckle)

Wendell Coltin
Boston Herald American, 300 Harrison Ave., Boston, Mass. 02106,
(617) 426-3000

Lou Cottin and
Harold Blumenfeld   Growing Older   NEA
619 Dartmouth St., Westbury, N.Y. 11590, (516) 333-1367

Ghita Levine   Years Ahead   United
United Features, 200 Park Ave., N.Y. 10017

Eugene Miller   Your Medicare
376 Sunrise Circle, Glencoe, Ill. 60022, (312) 835-5063

Muriel Oberleder, Ph.D. Living With Aging
Jack Posner, 220 Madison Ave., N.Y. 10016, (212) 686-2332

Jack Smith   Time of Your Life   United
11085 Tom Shaw Dr., El Paso, Tex. 79936

W. Robert Walton   A Time to Live   Universal
29642 Preston Drive, Laguna Niguel, Ca. 92677

John T. Watts   Mainly For Seniors   Copley
Box 190, San Diego, Ca. 92041

SPORTS

David Anderson   NYT
New York Times, N.Y. 10036, (212) 556-1234

Hank Andrews   Outdoor Tips
Wilson Features, Box 369, Marysville, Ohio 43040

David Bachman, M.D.   Dr. Jock   CTNYNS
Chicago Tribune-New York News Syndicate, 220 E. 42nd St., N.Y.
10017

Robert G. Black   Boating
343 Flaxhill Rd., S. Norwalk, Conn. 06854

Don Blazer   Of Course, A Horse   Copley
Box 190, San Diego, Ca. 92112, (714) 299-3131

Dave Bowring   Outdoors   Enterprise News
Sports Afield, 250 W. 55th St., N.Y. 10019, (212) 262-5700

Tom Callahan
Combined News Service, Box 25518, Phoenix, Ariz. 85202

Dick Dunkel
94 Ormond Pky., Ormond Beach, Fla. 32074, (904) 677-6100

Milt Dunnell
Toronto Star, Toronto M5E 1E6, Ont., Canada (416) 367-2000

Melvin Durslag   King
Los Angeles Herald-Examiner, L.A. 90054, (213) 748-1212

Bud Furillo   Sports   Inter-Continental
Box 991, Glendale, Ca. 91209

Darnell Gary
2745 Ketchum Rd., Memphis, Tenn. 38114, (901) 743-0497

Curt Gowdy   Fish and Game Tips   King
ABC-TV, 1330 Ave. of Americas, N.Y. 10019

Jo Haring   Baseball   Enterprise News
Enterprise News, 220 E. 42nd St., N.Y. 10017, (212) 682-2754

258

Dick Harris
247 S. 800 East, Logan, Utah 84321, (801) 753-3587

Steven Harvey   Bottom Ten   Universal
Los Angeles Times, L.A. 90053

Mickey Herskowitz and
Steve Perkins   Sports Hot Line   Universal
Universal Press Syndicate, Mission, Kansas 66202

Joe Marcus   Soccer
Soccer Communications, 166 Madison Ave., N.Y. 10016,
(212) 686-6850

Norman C. Meyers I Didn't Know That
Box 5321, N.Y. 10017; (212) 369-6516

Irma Ganz Miller Sports & Recreation
Soccer Associates, 2 Holly Dr., New Rochelle, N.Y. 10801,
(914) 235-2347

Jim Murray   LAT
Los Angeles Times, L.A. 90053, (213) 625-2345

Bob Nesoff   Camping All Year McNaught
Box 104, Oradell, N.J. 07649, (201) 385-2000

Christopher Nyerges Hiking & Biking Inter-Continental
Inter-Continental, Box 991, Glendale, Ca. 91209, (213) 241-4141

V. Lee Oertle   The RV Trail   Inter-Continental
Inter-Continental, Box 991, Glendale, Ca. 91209, (213) 241-4141

Murray Olderman All You Got To Do Is Ask NEA
Box 6346, Incline Village, Nev. 89450

Mort Olshan
9255 Sunset Blvd., L.A. 90069, (213) 274-1913

Le Pacini   One-Lining Sports
Le-Pac Features, 65 Cresta Vista Dr., San Francisco 94127

Maureen Reardon Women Sports
Summit Press Syndicate, 4037 Prospect St., Milwaukee, Wis. 53211,
(414) 963-9055

John Robinson   Football   Inter-Continental
Univ. of Southern California, L.A. 90007

Joan Ryan   Wash. Post Writers Group
Athletic Dept., Yale Univ., New Haven, Conn. 06520

John H. Shropshire   Horses
Sharpless Rd., Landenberg, Pa. 19350, (215) 274-8416

Howard Siner   NEA
NEA, 200 Park Ave., N.Y. 10017

Sam Skinner   Black Sports
Black Press Service, 166 Madison Ave., N.Y. 10016, (212) 686-6850

Red Smith   NYT
New York Times, N.Y. 10036, (212) 556-1234

Dick Young   Young Ideas   CTNYNS
N.Y. News, 220 E. 42nd St., N.Y. 10017, (212) 682-1234

Note: Columns by Billy Casper, Rod Laver, Jack Nicklaus, Arnold Palmer, Gary Player and other athletes are not listed as these rarely offer publicity opportunities and generally are ghost written.

TELEVISION AND RADIO

Jerry Buck   Tube Talk   AP
Associated Press, 1111 S. Hill, L.A. 90015

Hal Butts   TV Listings   NEA
1819 Peachtree Rd., N.E., Atlanta, Ga. 30309

John and Nancy Castle   TV Time
Castle Communications, 121 Industrial Dr., DeKalb, Ill. 60115

Bente Christensen   TV commentary   Editor's Copy
Box 523, Orangeburg, S.C. 29115

Joan Crosby   TV Scout   NEA
5036 Strohm Ave., Toluca Lake, Ca. 91601, (213) 396-6000

Gary Deeb   CTNYNS
Chicago Tribune, 435 N. Michigan Ave., Chicago 60611,
(312) 222-3232 ·

Don Freeman   Point of View   Copley
San Diego Union, San Diego 92108, (714) 299-3131
Home: 3119 Ibsen, San Diego 92106

Kay Gardella   TV   Knight-Ridder
New York News, 220 E. 42nd St., N.Y. 10017, (212) 949-1234

Joan Hanauer   Television in Review   UPI
United Press, 220 E. 42nd St., N.Y. 10017, (212) 682-0400

Bernard Harrison   TV Today   NYT
Washington Star, 225 Virginia Ave., S.E., Wash., D.C. 20061,
(202) 484-5000

Paul Henniger   Shows to Watch   LAT
Los Angeles Times, L.A. 90053, (213) 625-2345

Lynda Hirsch   Daytime Dial   Field
Field Syndicate, 401 N. Wabash Ave., Chic. 60611

Bruce Joffe
(with Vicki Murphy)   Soap Opera   NEA
10813 Violet Ct., Manassas, Va. 22101

Tom Jory   TV Talk   AP
Associated Press, 50 Rockefeller Pl., N.Y 10020, (212) 262-4000

Marvin Kitman   LAT
Newsday, Garden City, N.Y. 11530

Dick Kleiner   TV   NEA
1665 N. Beverly Dr., Beverly Hills, Ca. 90210, (213) 271-0150

Frances M. Knox   Today's TV Programs
Dickinson Newspaper Services, 271 Madison Ave., N.Y. 10016,
(212) 532-0170

Marcia Michaels   TV From a Woman's Viewpoint
Amusement Features Syndicate, 218 W. 47th St., N.Y. 10036,
(212) 586-4358

Vicki Murphy   Soap Opera   NEA
1130 James Madison Circle, Falmouth, Va. 22401

Pepper O'Brien   NEA
NEA, 200 Park Ave., N.Y. 10017, (212) 557-5870

Terrence O'Flaherty   Assignment: Television   Chronicle
San Francisco Chronicle, S.F. 94119, (415) 421-1111

Jon-Michael Reed   Tune In Tomorrow   EF
Daily TV Serials, 180 Madison Ave., N.Y. 10016, (212) 689-2830

Joey Sasso   Inside TV   McNaught
65 W. 55th St., N.Y. 10019, (212) 541-7230

Steven H. Scheuer   King
TV Key, 25 W. 43rd St., N.Y. 10036, (212) 575-1722
(In addition to the TV Key package service, Steve Scheuer and his
staff also write Soap Opera Scene, a weekly column.)

Vernon Scott   Television in Review   UPI
UPI, Box 2231, L.A. 90053, (213) 620-1230

Jay Sharbutt   Radio-TV   AP
Associated Press, 1111 S. Hill, L.A. 90015, (213) 746-1200

Richard K. Shull   Shull's Mailbag   Inter-Continental
Indianapolis News, Indianapolis, Ind. 46206, (317) 633-1240

Cecil Smith   LAT
Los Angeles Times, L.A. 90053, (213) 625-2345

Lee Winfrey   TV   Knight-Ridder
Philadelphia Inquirer, Philadelphia, Pa. 19101, (215) 854-19101

TRAVEL

Joseph Adler
Box 128, St. John, New Brunswick, Canada E2L 3X8,
(506) 657-8671

Sid Ascher   Around the World
214 Boston Ave., Mays Landing, N.J. 08330, (609) 927-1842

Norman Austin   Freighter Travel
Hollywood Inside Syndicate, Box 49957, L.A. 90049,
(213) 826-9602

Stephen Birnbaum   CTNYNS
Diversion, 60 E. 42nd St., N.Y. 10017, (212) 682-3710

Murray Brown   UPI
United Press, 220 E. 42nd St., N.Y. 10017, (212) 682-0400

Ron Butler   Passport to Everywhere   Columbia
20 W. 86th St., N.Y. 10023, (212) 787-0950

Rosellen Callahan   Tips for Trips   Editor Enterprises
                         (and other columns)
25 Sutton Pl., South, N.Y. 10022, (212) 753-1862

Kay Cassill   Travel Addict   Trans-World News
Box 2801, Wash., D.C. 20013, (202) 638-5568

Mary Comara   Where in the World
Box 26E, L.A. 90026, (213) 613-0935

Stan Delaplane   Postcards   Chronicle
San Francisco Chronicle, S.F. 94103, (415) 777-1111
home: 6 Tennyson Dr., Mill Valley, Ca. 94941

Landt & Lisl Dennis   Travel Facts
Photo Features Intl., 135 E. 39th St., N.Y. 10016, (212) 532-8226

Paul Friedlander   Traveler's World
113 Magnolia Lane, East Hills, N.Y. 11577, (516) 621-2494

William Frye   Footloose with Frye
2 Tudor City Pl., N.Y. 10017, (212) 421-0219

Sally George
12 Washington Ave., Lawrence, N.Y. 11559

Gerry Hall & G. Bryant
Toronto Star, Toronto M5E 1E6, Ont., Canada, (416) 367-2000

Robin and Patricia Harris
Hearst Service, 959 Eighth Ave., N.Y. 10019, (212) 987-8807

Jerry Hulse   LTWP
Los Angeles Times, L.A. 90053, (213) 625-2345

Marie Mattson   Trip Tips
1250 Vallejo St., S.F. 94109, (415) 885-5064

Peter Menkin   Travel Case
1563 Lincoln Ave., San Rafael, Ca. 94901

Randy Mink   Youth On The Go
9429 Bay Colony Dr., Des Plaines, Ill. 60016, (312) 824-2133

Neil Morgan   Copley
Box 191, San Diego, Ca. 92112, (714) 299-3131

Jane Morse   Penny-Wise Traveler   King
2853 Ontario Rd., Wash., D.C. 22009, (202) 462-7713

Robert Nesoff   Travel & Leisure   Garden State Media
Box 104, Oradell, N.J. 07649, (201) 385-2000

Paige Palmer
Box 225, Bath, Ohio 44210, (216) 659-6231

Martin Pine   Generally Speaking
1073 Gerritsen Ave., Brooklyn, N.Y. 11229, (212) 339-1417

John Pinkerman   Travel   Copley
Drawer J, Idyllwild, Ca. 92349, (714) 659-2329

Dan Schlossberg   Travel & Sports   Enterprise Newsfeatures
Suite 2814, 220 E. 42nd St., N.Y. 10017, (212) 682-2754

Joel Sleed   In Travel Circles   Field
Star Ledger, Newark, N.J. 07101

Robert Sloane   Going Our Way   Star Service
Box 15610, Fort Lauderdale, Fla. 33318, (305) 472-8794

Horace Sutton   Field
Saturday Review, 1290 Ave. of Americas, N.Y. 10019
(212) 246-9700

William Wolf   movies and travel   Trans-World
155 W. 68th St., N.Y. 10023, (212) 787-7020

WOMEN'S AND FAMILY

Erma Bombeck   At Wit's End   Field
Field Syndicate, 401 N. Wabash Ave., Chic. 60611

June Bringham   One Woman's Voice   Princeton
Princeton Features, 280 Nassau St., Princeton, N.J. 08540
(609) 921-1018

William D. Brown   Families Under Stress
Suite 217, 1025 Connecticut Ave., N.W., Wash., D.C. 20036,
(202) 833-8792

Edith Carter   News World
Box 86, North Egremont, Mass. 01252

Kathy Clark   Family
Box 105, Kintnersville, Pa. 18930

Mary Ellen Corbett   Feminist Q. & A.
46 Colrain St., Greenfield, Mass. 01301

David J. Lavin   The Teen-Age Corner
70-540 Gardenia Court, Rancho Mirage, Ca. 92270, (714) 324-3744

Muriel Lederer   Memo to a Working Woman   Register
800 Prospect Ave., Winnetka, Ill. 60093, (312) 446-0317

Josephine Lowman   Why Grow Old   Register
Register & Tribune, Des Moines, Iowa 50304

Dorothy Marks   Washington Women   Women's News
2833 McGill Terrace, N.W., Wash., D.C. 20008, (202) 232-2229

Carolyn Murray   Home Lines   LAT
Los Angeles Times, L.A. 90053, (213) 625-2345

George Nobbe   Real World   King
King Features, 235 E. 45th St., N.Y. 10017

David Nydick   You, Your Child and School
22 Lesley Drive, Syosset, N.Y. 11791, (516) 681-4161

John Pinkerman   News Associates
Drawer J, Idyllwild, Ca. 92349, (714) 659-2329

Thomas F. Ris   Neat Stuff (for 6-13 yr. old)
Education/Research Systems, 2121 Fifth Ave., Seattle, Wash.
98121, (206) 623-2103

Niki Scott   Working Woman   Universal
Universal Press Syndicate, Mission, Kansas 66202

Nancy Stahl   Once Over Lightly   Universal
Calgary Herald, Calgary, Alberta, Canada

BIBLIOGRAPHY

Adler, Ruth, The Working Press, New York: G.P. Putnam's, 1966

Alsop, Joseph and Stewart, The Reporter's Trade, New York: Reynal, 1958

Amory, Cleveland, Celebrity Register, New York: Harper & Row, 1963

Bagdikian, Ben H., articles in Columbia Journalism Review, New York, 1964-1967

Best, Silas, Ballyhoo, The Voice of the Press, New York: Boni and Liveright, 1927

Blackwell, Earl, Celebrity Register, New York: Simon and Schuster, 1975

Bombeck, Erma, At Wit's End, New York: Fawcett, 1978

Buchwald, Art, Counting Sheep, New York: G.P. Putnam's, 1970

Buckley, William F., Quotations From Chairman Bill, New Rochelle: Arlington House, 1970

Cassini, Igor, and Molli, Jeane, I'd Do It All Over Again, New York: Putnam's, 1977

Cheshire, Maxine and Greenya, John, Maxine Cheshire, Reporter, Boston: Houghton Mifflin, 1978

Cohen, Lester, The New York Graphic, Philadelphia, Chilton, 1964

Considine, Bob, It's All News to Me, New York: Meredith, 1967

Davis, Hallam Walker, The Column, New York: Knopf, 1926

Dixon, George, Leaning On A Column, Philadelphia: Lippincott, 1961

Drewry, John E., Post Biographies of Famous Journalists, Athens: University of Georgia Press, 1942

Driscoll, Charles B., The Life of O.O. McIntyre, New York: Greystone Press, 1938

Edson, C.L., The Gentle Art of Columning, New York: Brentano's, 1920

Eells, George, Hedda and Louella, New York: G.P. Putnam's Sons, 1972

Emery, Edwin, The Press and America, Englewood Cliffs, N.J.: Prentice-Hall, 1962

Evans, Rowland and Novak, Robert, Lyndon B. Johnson: The Exercise of Political Power, New York: New American Library, 1967

Fisher, Charles, The Columnists, New York: Howell, Soskin, 1944

Gardner, Hy, Champagne Before Breakfast, New York: Holt, 1954

Gauvreau, Emile, My Last Million Readers, New York: E.P. Dutton, 1941

Greene, Ward, Star Reporters And 34 Of Their Stories, New York: Random House, 1948

Gross, Gerald, The Responsibility of the Press, New York: Fleet, 1966

Halberstam, David, The Best and the Brightest, New York: Random House, 1972

Jones, Robert W., Journalism in the United States, New York: E.P. Dutton, 1947

Keogh, James, President Nixon and the Press, New York: Funk & Wagnalls, 1972

Klurfeld, Herman, Winchell: His Life and Times, New York: Praeger, 1976

Koenigsberg, M., King News, Philadelphia, F.A. Stokes, 1941

Krock, Arthur, The Consent of the Governed and Other Deceits, Boston: Little, Brown, 1971

Krock, Arthur, Memoirs, New York: Funk & Wagnalls, 1968

Landers, Ann, Truth Is Stranger, Englewood Cliffs: Prentice-Hall, 1968

Landers, Ann, Ann Landers Speaks Out, New York: Fawcett, 1978

Lash, Joseph P., Eleanor and Franklin, New York: W.W. Norton, 1971

Luskin, John, Lippmann, Liberty and the Press, University: University of Alabama Press, 1972

Lyon, Peter, Success Story, The Life and Times of S.S. McClure, New York, Scribner's, 1963

Marbat, F.B., News from the Capital, Carbondale: Southern Illinois University Press, 1971

Markham, Charles Lam, The Buckley's: A Family Examined, New York: Morrow, 1973

McGrady Jr., Patrick M., The Love Doctors, New York: Macmillan, 1972

McKelway, St. Clair, Gossip: The Life and Times of Walter Winchell, New York, Viking, 1940

McLendon, Winzola and Smith, Scottie, Don't Quote Me!, New York: E.P. Dutton, 1970

Montgomery, Ruth, A Gift of Prophecy, New York: Morrow, 1965

Mott, Frank Luther, American Journalism, New York: Macmillan, 1962

Mott, George Fox, New Survey of Journalism, New York: Barnes & Noble, 1958

Pilat, Oliver, Pegler: Angry Man of the Press, Boston: Beacon Press, 1963

Porter, Sylvia, Sylvia Porter's Money Book, New York: Doubleday, 1975

Reed, Rex, Do You Sleep in the Nude?, New York: New American Library, 1968

Rivers, Wm. L., The Opinion Makers, Boston: Beacon Press, 1965

Royko, Mike, I May Be Wrong, But I Doubt It, Chicago: Regnery, 1968

Shepard, Elaine, Forgive Us Our Press Passes, Englewood Cliffs: Prentice-Hall, 1962

Smith, Walter, The Best of Red Smith, New York: Franklin Watts, 1963

Sulzberger, E.L., A Long Row of Candles, New York: Macmillan, 1969

Swanberg, W.A., Citizen Hearst, New York: Scribner's, 1961

Talese, Gay, The Kingdom and the Power, New York: World, 1969

Thomas, Bob, Winchell, Garden City: Doubleday, 1971

Thomas, William H., The Road to Syndication, New York: Talent Information Press, 1967 (Reissued by Fleet in 1977)

Thompson, Dorothy, Refugees: Anarchy or Organization, New York: Random House, 1938

Watson, Elmo Scott, A History of Newspaper Syndicates in the United States, Chicago: Publisher's Auxiliary, 1936

Weiner, Ed, The Damon Runyon Story, New York: Longmans, Green, 1948

Weiner, Ed, Let's Go to Press, New York: G.P. Putnam's Sons, 1955

Wheeler, John, I've Got News For You, New York: E.P. Dutton, 1961

Wicker, Tom, On Press, New York: Viking, 1978

Wills, Garry, Nixon Agonistes, Boston: Houghton Mifflin, 1970

Wills, Garry, Inventing America, Jefferson's Declaration of Independence, New York: Doubleday, 1978

Wilson, Earl, The Show Business Nobody Knows, Chicago: Cowles, 1972

INDEX

Berke, Melvyn, 115, 183, 196
Berkeley Barb, 126
Berkowitz, David, 214
Berle, Milton, 189
Bernstein, Ted, 167, 225
Berry, Jim, 150
Betancourt, Hal, 206
Better Homes and Gardens, 83
Betzina, Sandra, 188, 200
Big Thaw, The, 170
Bigman, Rose, 13
Birnbaum, Stephen, 26, 155, 264
Bishop, Jim, 3, 22, 51, 71, 133, 142,
    145, 225
Black Press Service, 239, 260
Black, Robert G., 258
Black, Shirley Temple, 186
Blackwell, Earl, 26
Blasingame, F.J.L., 149, 237
Blazer, Don, 238, 258
Blinn, Johna, 92, 94, 158, 219
Block, Herbert L., 162
Bloodgood, John, 145
Blumenfeld, Harold, 257
Blythe, Sam, 189
Boggs, Peter, 105
Bok, Edward W., 41
Bolton, Whitney, 34, 189
Bombeck, Erma, 5, 25, 26, 77, 89, 96,
    99, 162, 267
Bond, Julia, 244
Boomer, 149
Booth, Mrs. Marion Clyde McCarroll,
    78
Booth News Service, 233
Borden's, 93
Borge, Victor, 94
Borgstedt, Doug and Jean, 214
Boston Evening Post, 37
Boston Globe, 54, 88, 99, 118, 197,
    203, 228, 244, 249
Boston Herald, 41, 257
Boston Herald American, 122
Boston Herald Traveler, 94, 189
Boston Times, 37
Bothwell, Angela and Ford, 151, 233
Bottel, Helen, 87, 88, 142, 144, 196
Bottel, Suzanne, 87
Bouchard, Lucille, 200
Bouvier, Jacqueline (Kennedy), 72
Bowing, Dave, 258
Bowles, Heloise, 10, 100, 144
Boychuk, Joseph M., 191
Boyd, L.M., 255

Boyd, Robert, 244
BP Singer Features, 199, 239
Brose, Irving A., 233
Braden, Tom, 158, 244
Bradford, Barbara, 25, 50, 158, 212
Bradford, Thomas A.,
Bradshaw, John, 223
Brady, James, 225
Brady, Dr. William, 41, 116, 122, 125
Brandstadt, Wayne, 127
Braque, Georges, 134
Brennan, John, 158, 237
Breslin, Jimmy, 3, 4, 25, 43, 45, 150,
    155, 226
Brett, Carl, 205
Brickfield, Cy, 257
Brickley, Terry, 226
Brickman, Arthur, 203
Bringham, June, 267
Brisbane, Arthur, 36, 72, 140, 141,
    142
Broder, David, 3, 21, 43, 48, 50, 62,
    63, 74, 175, 245
Broersme, Susan, 219
Brom-Hilda, 154
Brooks, Carroll Ann, 203
Brooks, Dorothea, 206
Brooks, Ellen, 233
Brooks Publ., 234
Brothers, Joyce, 23, 48, 71, 79, 126,
    127, 128, 143, 196, 237
Brothers, Milton J., 25, 129
Broun, Heywood, 27
Broun, Heywood Hale, 34, 67, 72,
    171, 175
Brown, Bob, 237
Brown, Gov. Jerry, 59
Brown, Jay, 216
Brown, Murray, 264
Brown, Vivian, 10, 48
Brown, William D., 267
Brown, 226
Brownstone, Cecily, 48, 92, 219
Bruss, Robert J., 49, 206
Bryan, William Jennings, 140, 189
Bryant, G., 265
Buch, Rabbi Arthur T., 15
Buchanan, Patrick J., 6, 45, 59, 62,
    74, 155, 245
Buchwald, Art, 4, 7, 26, 28, 29, 34,
    46, 48, 49, 62, 63, 157, 158, 159,
    175, 176, 187, 226, 245
Buck, Jerry, 261
Buckingham, Ross Roy, 166

275

Buckley, William F., Jr., 20, 25, 33, 34, 43, 46, 50, 60, 65, 66, 73, 142, 143, 245
Buffalo Courier Express, 100, 224
Buffalo News, 80
Bunderson, Dr. Herman, 119
Bundy, McGeorge, 58
Bunker, W.A., 39
Burg, Marcia, 149, 219
Burgin, Dave, 150
Burke, Wally, 216
Burmester, Bill, 233
Business Outlook, 162
Business Week, 176
Butcher, The, 188
Butler, Ron, 264
Butts, Harold, 261
Byrne, Dan, 157
Byrne, Robert, 233

Caen, Herb, 8, 28, 185, 188, 226
Cahill, Jerome, 206
Calgary Herald, 268
Callahan, Rosellen, 264
Callahan, Tom, 258
Campbell, Dave, 216
Campbell, Don G., 51, 149, 206
Canada Wide Feature Service, 223, 235
Can-Opener Cookbook, The, 93
Cannero, Richard, 200
Cannon, Poppy, 92, 93
Cannon, Jack and Tom, 5
Cannon, Jimmy, 5, 142, 179
Cannon, Thurlow, 226
Capital News Service, 198
Capp, Al, 153
Carlinski, Dan, 151, 226
Carlson, Harriet, 200
Carmichael, 157
Carnegie, Dale, 189
Carrell, Al, 145, 233
Carreno, Richard, 200
Carroll, Harrison, 142
Carter, Don, 42
Carter, Edith, 267
Carter, Jimmy, 59
Caruba, Alan, 203
Casey, 154
Casper, Billy, 42, 94
Cassels, Louis, 109
Cassill, Kay, 264
Cassini, Igor, 72, 155, 179, 216
Cassini, Oleg, 72

Castle Communications, 261
Cathcart, Henry, 142
Catledge, Turner, 19
Causey, Mike, 245
CB'ers News, 235
CBS, 150
CB Times, 234
Cerf, Bennet, 142
Chagall, Marc, 134
Chamberlain, John, 4, 8, 58, 65, 142, 145, 226
Channing, Carol, 94
Charleston Gazette, 157
Charlotte Observer, 226
Chase, Allen, 127
Chase, Lorlene, 126, 127
Chastain, Thomas, 176
Chattanooga Times, 99, 100
Chef Marcia, 149
Cheshire, Maxine, 25, 62, 155, 226
Chicago Daily News, 9, 41, 46, 158, 161, 162, 163
Chicago Express, 39
Chicago Herald, 41
Chicago Newspaper Union, 38
Chicago Sun-Times, 106, 109, 111, 117, 122, 126, 161, 162, 207, 228, 230, 238
Chicago Times, 162
Chicago Today, 118
Chicago Tribune, 32, 49, 75, 77, 90, 92, 94, 95, 117, 120, 121, 153, 155, 193, 208, 227, 238, 242, 258, 261
Chicago Tribune—New York News Syndicate, 2, 6, 26, 33, 45, 53, 79, 82, 86, 90, 91, 94, 96, 105, 108, 124, 126, 137, 153
Child, Julia, 158
Childs, Marquis, 20, 33, 61, 63, 67, 68, 149, 245
Cholly Knickerbocker, 68, 72, 143
Christensen, Bente, 261
Christian Science Monitor, 31, 49, 184, 251
Christianity Today, 112
Christophers, The, 190
Christy, Marian, 89, 149, 200
Chronicle Features, 115, 185, 188, 208, 237
Church, Frank, 59
Church, Ruth Ellen, 95, 219
Churchill, Bonnie, 85
Churchill, Reba, 85
Churchill, 170

278

279

Judge, Diane, 46, 216

Kahn, Steve, 166
Kaliff, Joseph A., 217, 242
Kandel, Myron (Mike), 151, 207
Kansas City Star, 99
Kansas City Times, 38
Kapel, Saul, 45, 155, 238
Karch, Randolph, 235
Karpin, Fred, 49, 154, 205
Karnow, Stanley, 49, 183, 247
Kassorla, Irene, 115
Katy, 46
Katz, Dolly, 238
Kaufman, Herbert, 139
Kaye, Danny, 94
Keane, Bil, 184
Keasler, John, 51, 149, 190, 228
Keller, Curtis B., 83
Kellner, Mark A., 235
Kelliher, Dick, 242
Kellogg, Ansel N., 37
Kellogg Newspaper Co., 38
Kelly, Sandra, 194, 201
Kelly, Tom, 66
Kempton, Murray, 33, 43
Kennedy, John F., 22, 58, 59, 70, 72,
    168, 171, 174, 177
Kennedy, Robert, 3, 175
Kennedy, Joyce Lain, 48, 196
Kenyon and Eckhardt, 91
Keogh, James, 70, 71
Kerr, Jean, 97
Kilgallen, Dorothy, 1, 14, 29, 68, 132,
    133, 143, 144
Kilgallen, James, 14
Killy, Jean-Claude, 42
Kilpatrick, James J., 7, 21, 22, 48, 50,
    59, 62, 65, 67, 247
King Features Syndicate, 2, 3, 6, 8,
    25, 29, 32, 33, 35, 53, 55, 80, 87,
    89, 91, 92, 96, 100, 118, 126, 128,
    132, 134, 139, 140, 141, 142, 143,
    144, 189, 196, 202, 203, 209, 221,
    225, 226, 231, 233, 234, 267
King, Llewellyn, 208
King, Martin Luther, 175
Kingdom, Dr. Frank, 68
Kinsolving, Rev. Lester, 190, 255
Kipling, Bogdan, 247
Kipling, Rudyard, 41
Kirk, Gov. Claude, 179
Kirk, Lisa, 16
Kirk, W.C., 140

Kirkland, Ellis, Hodson, Chaffetz and
    Misters, 54
Kirkpatrick, Clayton, 75
Kissinger, Henry A., 7, 43
Kitman, Marvin, 158, 262
Klein, Herb, 71
Kleinman, Bob, 238
Kleiner, Dick, 29, 150, 151, 262
Kline, Fred W., 198
Knapp, Ted, 248
Knauer, Virginia, 196, 208
Knickerbocker, H.R., 140
Knight-Ridder News Service, 2, 4, 51
Knight Wire, 153
Knoblock, John, 220
Knopf, Hans, 83
Knowledge News, 210, 230
Knox, Frances, 262
Koenigsberg, Moses, 139, 142
Kofoed, Jack, 51
Kohler, Saul, 6, 48
Kohlmeier, Louis, 248
Koltanowski, George, 235
Kornreich, Dave, 42
Kotulak, Ronald, 236
Kovel, Ralph and Terry, 183, 212
Kraft, Joseph, 20, 25, 33, 48, 49, 58,
    59, 62, 63, 64, 65, 66, 67, 70, 72,
    74, 162, 248
Kramer, Jack, 158
Krazy Kat, 140
Krebs, Albin, 29
Krock, Arthur, 4, 19, 20, 31, 61, 62,
    71, 167, 169, 172, 175
Krock, Martha Blair, 168
Kudlatz, Ed, 150
Kuhn, Mrs. Irene Corbally, 228
Kupcinet, Irv, 28, 29, 228
Kuran, John, 179
Kvallsposten, 90

Lada, Marina Tatiana, 170
Ladewig, Marion, 42
Ladies' Home Journal, 83, 93
Laffler, William D., 242
La Grenouille, 133
Lamb, Laurence E., Dr., 48, 116, 127,
    128, 150, 238
Lambert, Mrs. Eleanor, 89, 90, 91,
    92, 162, 201
Lambs Club, 15
Lamferty, Lillian, 140
Lamm, Michael, 198
Lance, Bert, 6

287

292

293

The text of *Syndicated Columnists* was phototypeset in Times Roman, the chapter headings in Times Roman Bold, and the listings of columnists in Helvetica Light. The book was designed and typeset by Corporate Graphics, 46-31 Skillman Avenue, Long Island City, N.Y. 11104, (212) 392-4422. It was printed on 50-lb. offset stock and bound by the Town House Press, 28 Midway Road, Spring Valley, N.Y. 10977, (914) 425-2232.